Applied Computer Keyboarding

4th Edition

Business Education lost a dedicated friend and teacher in 1997 with the passing of Dr. Jerry W. Robinson. Dr. Robinson had completed his manuscript for this book before his untimely death.

Jerry W. Robinson, Ed.D.
Former Keyboarding Instructor
Moeller High School
Cincinnati (OH)

Jack P. Hoggatt, Ed.D.
Professor, Department of
Business Communication
University of Wisconsin
Eau Claire (WI)

Jon A. Shank, Ed.D.
Professor of Education
Robert Morris College
Coraopolis (PA)

Lee R. Beaumont, Ed.D.
Professor of Business, Emeritus
Indiana University of Pennsylvania
Indiana (PA)

VISIT US ON THE INTERNET
www.swep.com

South-Western Educational Publishing
an International Thomson Publishing company I(T)P®
www.thomson.com

Cincinnati • Albany, NY • Belmont, CA • Bonn • Boston • Detroit • Johannesburg • London • Madrid
Melbourne • Mexico City • New York • Paris • Singapore • Tokyo • Toronto • Washington

Managing Editor:	Karen Schmohe
Production Coordinator:	Jane Congdon
Editor:	Martha Conway
Development:	Penworthy Learning Systems
Production:	CompuText Productions, Inc.
Design:	Grannan Graphic Design, Ltd.
Art/Design Coordinator:	Michelle Kunkler
Marketing Manager:	Tim Gleim
Marketing Coordinator:	Lisa Barto
Manufacturing Coordinator:	Carol Chase

Copyright® 1999
by South-Western Educational Publishing
Cincinnati, Ohio

I(T)P®

South-Western Educational Publishing is a division of International Thomson Publishing Inc. The ITP logo is a registered trademark used herein under license by South-Western Educational Publishing.

ISBN: 0-538-68760-6 (TM37DA)
0-538-68759-2 (TM37DB)

01 02 03 04 05 06 07 08 09 00 WC 03 02 01 00 99 98

Printed in the United States of America

Preface

Keyboarding has become a universal writing skill. Reporters, short story writers, poets, and novelists compose at computer keyboards. Many musicians use the computer keyboard to compose and arrange music, and artists use the keyboard for graphic design. In fact, a high percentage of people in all walks of life use a computer keyboard to simplify and speed up their work.

Keyboarding: A Universal Skill

Students, for example, from elementary school through college, use their keyboarding skill to prepare school assignments. Many former students say that, next to English, keyboarding is the most useful skill they learned in school.

Communication, the "central nervous system" of business and industry, starts in the brain and moves, quite often, through the fingers to a keyboard that converts ideas into memos, letters, reports, e-mail messages, and Internet home pages. Besides sending, you will often use a keyboard to *get* information from the Internet—information that, if available a generation ago, would have been found only in stacks of newspapers, magazines, and books. Whatever field you choose, communication—the sending and receiving of information—will be vital to it. And a computer keyboard is likely to be at the center of your communication.

Getting the Most out of Computers

To get maximum value from a computer's high-speed output, the user must be competent at the input end—the keyboard. A person who can type 50 words a minute produces in half the time the same amount of work as someone who can key only 25 words a minute. Furthermore, the person who can type only 25 words a minute often has to think about which key to tap. The person who can key 50 words a minute is free to think about "bigger things," such as the content of the message keyed. Some people say that accuracy of input makes no difference because errors can be corrected quickly and easily on a computer. The fact remains, though, that the quickest, easiest error to correct is the one that is not made.

Nothing Is as Constant as Change

Applied Computer Keyboarding represents South-Western's 75-plus years of teaching 75 million people to type. Time and experience have brought changes in keyboard equipment, publishing technology, business, society, education, and teaching and skill-building methods. Each new South-Western textbook met the unique needs of the students and teachers of its era.

Now, here we go again. With the same confidence as before, the publisher offers a textbook for the times. *Applied Computer Keyboarding* balances up-to-the-minute content with methods that experienced teachers know and trust.

The Book Is New; Method Is Tried and True

Regardless of changes in equipment and teaching methods over the years, instruction must center around *keying* (the manipulative skills), *formatting* (the arrangement, placement, and spacing of often-used documents), and *word processing* (transformation of text into meaningful, useful documents of quality). *Language skills* deserve and receive frequent emphasis, too. (Twelve 2-page sets of Language & Writing skills are included as optional material. Starting after Unit 1, these rule-based exercises appear intermittently throughout Part 2.)

Basic keying skills. Basic keying skill consists of fluent manipulation of letter, figure/symbol, and basic service keys by "touch." Part 1 is devoted to alphanumeric keying skill. In Part 2, emphasis is provided in Skill Builders placed between each pair of units. You will find the following "tried and true" attributes of keyboard learning and practice between the covers of this book.

- Presents two alphabet or figure keys in each new-key lesson to ensure mastery of keyboard operation. (Four symbol keys—to be learned to the acquaintance, rather than the mastery, level—are presented in each symbol-key lesson.)

- Delays keying skill on the top row until correct technique and an essential level of keying skill have been developed.

- Uses scientific, computer-controlled drills to develop maximum skill in minimum time.

- Employs paragraphs that are *triple-controlled* for copy difficulty. Easy copy gives way to *low-average* difficulty; then, average difficulty. This easy-to-average progression aids skill growth and ensures reliable measurement of speed and accuracy.

- Stresses keying technique **first** (*without* timing); **then,** speed of manipulation (*with* strategic timed writings); and accuracy of keyed copy **last** (using *restricted-speed* practice). This technique-first/accuracy-last plan is in harmony with skill-learning principles and research findings.

Formatting skills. Formatting includes arranging, placing, and spacing copy according to accepted conventions for specific documents, such as letters, memos, reports, and tables. It involves learning and applying basic word processing features, too! Look for these characteristics in Part 2 of *Applied Computer Keyboarding.*

- Shows simple formats (e.g., block letters, unbound reports, two-column tables) that are as easy to read as they are to prepare—and attractive, too.

- Integrates a read/learn/apply approach for current mastery of basic word processing features and document formats.

- Employs icons to indicate the many word processing features available in the publisher's all-in-one software, *Applied MicroType Pro* (see p. 120).

- Reviews and reinforces previous learning before presenting new or variant formats.

- Presents arranged documents, followed by semi-arranged and unarranged text, often in script or rough-draft form with standard proofreader's marks.

- Integrates language skills learning in formatting tasks.

- Offers a continuous project that requires students to go "above and beyond" simply applying what they have learned. The project culminates with students assembling portfolios (samples of their word processing work).

Check These Bonus Features

Large amounts of related learning round out this textbook:

- An overview of IBM PC/Compatible and Macintosh hardware, emphasizing keyboard arrangement.

- Useful information about *Windows.*

- Basic operations of word processing software, citing South-Western's *Applied MicroType Pro, Microsoft Word* and *Corel WordPerfect* as examples.

- Guidelines for maintaining and protecting hardware, software, disks, data—and users.

- Information for understanding repetitive stress injury and work out ideas for preventing it.

- Fifteen sets of Keyboard Mastery (Warmup) lines for those students and teachers who want to continue developing basic keying skill each day in Part 2.

- A "symbols supplement" introducing nine symbols associated with computer language and mathematics but rarely used in running copy.

- An introduction to the Internet, including activities for navigating *World Wide Web* using Uniform Resource Locaters (URL's), hyperlinks, and *keyword* searches.

- A handy chart of formatting guides for a memo, business and personal-business letter, unbound report, and table, plus a model of each document—all in one place for quick reference.

From the 1920s to the present, South-Western has led the way in keyboarding and computer instruction. *Applied Computer Keyboarding,* Fourth Edition—published at the close of the 20th century and Second millennium—leads the way to the future with a deft balance of innovation and convention.

The Publisher

Contents

PART 1 KEYBOARDING: PREPARATION FOR WORD PROCESSING

Contents

IBM PC or Compatible

The illustrations below show the major parts of an IBM PC and the keyboard arrangement. The following copy identifies each numbered part.

These parts are found on almost all computers, but their locations may vary. If you are using an IBM PC or compatible computer other than the model illustrated, see the manufacturer's user's guide for the exact location of each part.

Computer and Printer

1. **Keyboard:** an arrangement of letter, figure, symbol, control, function, and editing keys and a numeric keypad.
2. **CPU (Central Processing Unit):** the internal operating unit or "brain" of a computer.

3. **Disk drive:** a unit in or connected to a computer that reads stored data from and writes data to disks (magnetic or optical) for storage.
4. **Monitor:** a TV-like device used to display information on a screen.
5. **Mouse:** a device that is moved across a pad on the desk surface to control movements of a pointer on the screen.
6. **Printer:** a unit connected to a computer that prints copy on paper.

Keyboard Arrangement

7. **Function (F) keys:** perform particular software operations when used alone or in combination with other keys.

8. **Backspace:** deletes the character to the left of the insertion point.
9. **Enter:** causes the insertion point to move to the left margin and down to the next line.
10. **Delete:** deletes the character to the right of the insertion point.
11. **Insert:** switches between insert mode and typeover mode.
12. **Num Lock:** switches the numeric keypad on and off.
13. **Numeric keypad:** a calculator-type keyboard used to enter all-number copy and perform calculations.
14. **Arrow keys:** move the insertion point in the direction indicated by the arrow on each key.

15. **Control (CTRL):** performs a specific software operation when depressed as another key is struck.
16. **Shift key:** makes capital letters and certain symbols when used with those keys.
17. **Alternate (ALT):** performs a specific software command when depressed immediately before or as another key is struck.
18. **Space bar:** inserts space between words and sentences.
19. **Caps Lock:** capitalizes all letters when locked down.
20. **Tab:** moves the insertion point to a preset position.
21. **Escape (ESC):** "backs out" of commands.

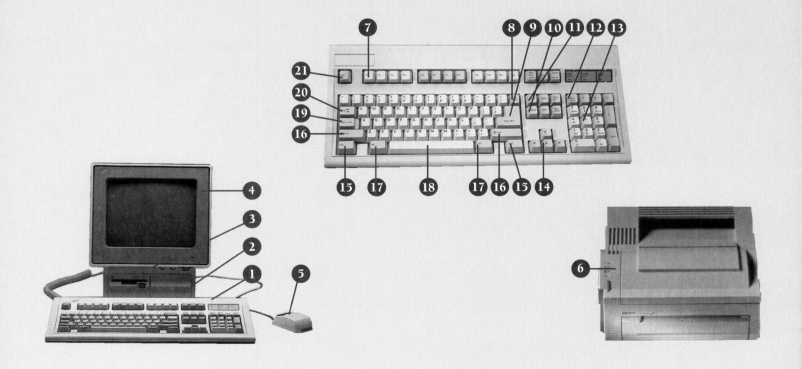

Macintosh

The illustrations below show the major parts of a Macintosh computer and the keyboard arrangement. The following copy identifies each numbered part.

These parts are found on almost all computers, but their location may vary. If you are using a Macintosh computer other than the model illustrated, see the manufacturer's user's guide for the exact location of each part.

Computer and Printer

1. **Keyboard:** an arrangement of letter, figure, symbol, control, function, and editing keys and a numeric keypad.
2. **CPU (Central Processing Unit):** the internal operating unit or "brain" of a computer.

3. **Disk drive:** a unit in or connected to a computer that reads stored data from and writes data to disks (magnetic or optical) for storage.
4. **Monitor:** a TV-like device used to display information on a screen.
5. **Mouse:** a device that is moved across a pad on the desk surface to control movements of an indicator on the screen.
6. **Printer:** a unit connected to a computer that prints information on paper.

Keyboard Arrangement

7. **Function (F) keys:** perform particular software operations

when used alone or in combination with other keys.
8. **Delete:** deletes the character to the left of the insertion point.
9. **Return:** causes the insertion point to move to the left margin and down to the next line.
10. **Del:** deletes the character at the insertion point.
11. **Num Lock:** switches the numeric keypad on and off.
12. **Numeric keypad:** a calculator-type keyboard used to enter all-number copy and perform calculations.
13. **Arrow keys:** move the insertion point in the direction indicated by the arrow on each key.

14. **Control:** performs a specific software operation when depressed while another key is struck.
15. **Shift key:** makes capital letters and certain symbols when used with those keys.
16. **⌘ (Command):** performs a specific software command when depressed with another key; menu alternative.
17. **Space bar:** inserts space between words and sentences.
18. **Caps Lock:** capitalizes all letters when locked down.
19. **Tab:** moves the insertion point to a preset position.
20. **Escape (ESC):** "backs out" of commands.

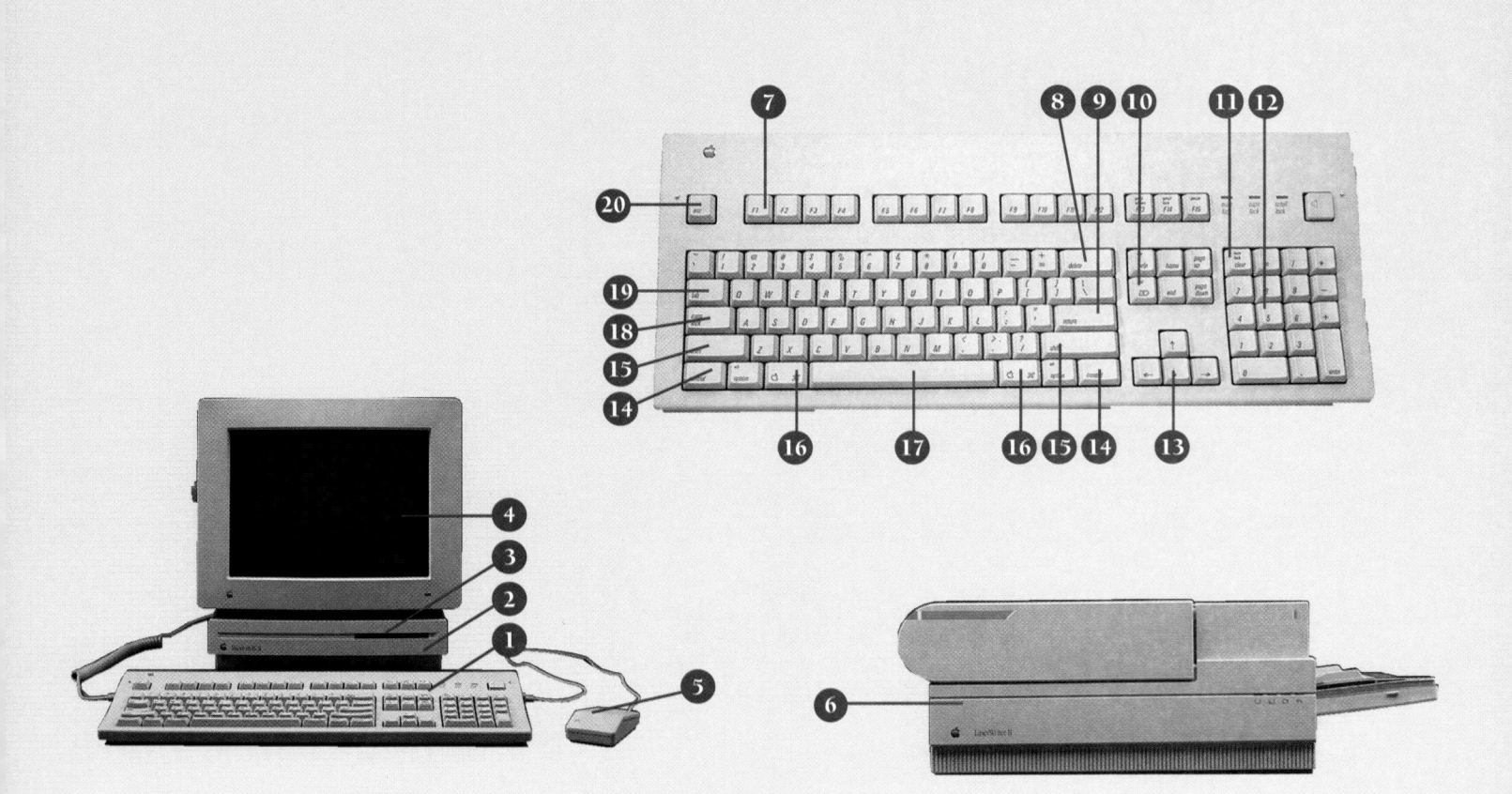

Know Your Desktop

Before you get ready to key, you need to know a few things about *Windows 95*, your computer's operating system software. *Windows 95* also controls the operation of peripherals, such as the mouse and printer hooked up to your computer. All programs that run under *Windows*—for example, South-Western's *Applied MicroType Pro*, keyboarding/word-processing software for this course, and *Microsoft Word* and *Corel WordPerfect*, much-used word processing programs—have features in common. (*Applied MicroType Pro*, *Word*, and *WordPerfect* are called "application" software. An application program enables you to do certain kinds of work, such as writing, editing, and printing a term paper or other report at the computer.) All *Windows* applications have similar buttons; and the menus are much alike, too. Once you learn the basics of *Windows*, you can use that knowledge in every *Windows* application.

Desktop

The opening screen of *Windows 95* simulates a desktop. The small symbols, called icons, on the screen represent items on a desk. Your screen may have other icons besides those listed below.

 My Computer displays the disk drives, CD-ROM drive, and printers that are attached to the computer.

 Network Neighborhood allows you to view the available resources if you are connected to a network environment.

 Recycle Bin stores files that have been deleted from the hard drive. Files deleted in error can be retrieved and put back into their folders. When the recycle bin is emptied, though, the files are gone.

 Start displays the Start menu. From the Start menu, you can open a program, open Help, change system settings, close and exit *Windows 95*, and more.

Mouse

Windows software requires the use of a mouse or other pointing device. The mouse is used to select items, to find and move files, and to carry out or cancel commands. The mouse pointer looks different depending on where it is on the screen and what it is doing.

I   The I-beam shows that the mouse is in the text area of an application. When you pause, it blinks. As you use your application, most of the time you will see the I-beam.

    The arrow selects items. It appears when the mouse is outside the text area.

    The hourglass shows that *Windows* is processing a command. You must wait until the hourglass disappears before keying text or entering another command.

Move the mouse on a flat, padded surface. If you run out of space, pick up the mouse and put it in another spot. The mouse is used to perform the following actions.

Point: Move the mouse so that the pointer touches a button or text (the words you key).

Click: Point to the desired menu item or button; then press and release the left mouse button once.

Double-click: Point to the desired item and quickly press and release the left mouse button twice.

Click with the right mouse button: Press and release the right mouse button once. A shortcut, or "pop-up," menu appears.

Drag: Point to the desired item; hold down the left mouse button; drag the item to a new location; then release the button.

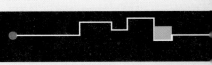
Taskbar

The strip across the bottom of the computer screen is called the *taskbar*. When *Windows 95* is running, the Start button shows on the taskbar (Figure 1). When you click Start, a menu displays with the commands for using *Windows 95* (Figure 2). The commands you will likely use most are Programs and Shut Down. Each time you open a program, a button with the name of that program appears on the taskbar, beside the Start button. The taskbar in Figure 1 shows that *Microsoft Word* is open.

Figure 1: *Windows 95* Opening Screen

Start

Taskbar

Figure 2: Start Menu

Programs

When you click the Programs command (Start menu), another menu displays. This menu shows the names of *Windows 95* applications installed on your computer (Figure 3). On this menu, the word *Accessories* stands for a group of applications built into *Windows 95* (Figure 4). (Other applications are installed separately, not built-in.) A *Windows accessory* that you may use with this book is the calculator (Figure 5).

Figure 3: Programs Menu

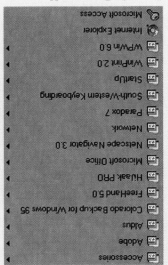

Figure 4: Accessories Menu

Figure 5: *Windows* Calculator Accessory

If *Applied MicroType Pro* has been installed, you will see it on the Programs menu. When you double-click the icon beside the name of this application, the software will open and an *Applied MicroType Pro* button will appear on the taskbar. (See Figure 6 for Open Screen).

If you will be using word processing software such as *Microsoft Word* or *WordPerfect* instead of *Applied MicroType Pro*, you should find the word processing application on the Programs menu. Clicking its icon will open it and add its button to the taskbar. Once the software opens, you can see features (Figure 7) that all *Windows 95* applications have in common.

Minimize, Restore, and Close buttons: Clicking the Minimize button reduces the application to an icon. Clicking the icon (on the taskbar) restores the application to full size. The Restore button makes a full-size application smaller and makes a small one full size. The Close button exits the application and removes its icon from the taskbar. Within the application, each document window (where you type) also has Minimize, Restore, and Close buttons.

Menu bar: Clicking any word on the Menu bar displays a drop-down menu. Arrows on the drop-down menu indicate sub-menus.

Scroll bars: Clicking an arrow on a scroll bar moves the window in the direction of the arrow—up or down and left or right.

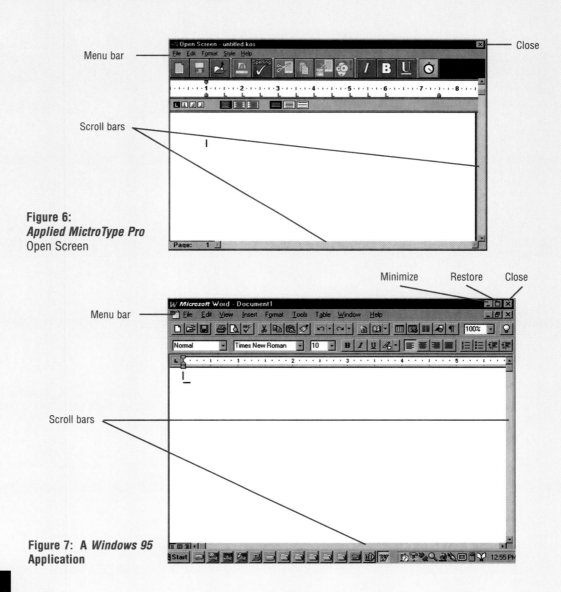

Figure 6:
Applied MictroType Pro
Open Screen

Figure 7: A *Windows 95*
Application

Turn on the Operating System (Start *Windows 95*)

Become familiar with the steps for turning on your computer equipment. Do the steps in the same order every time.

1. If a disk is in the disk drive, remove it.
2. If a printer will be used, turn on its power switch.
3. Turn on the power switch on the CPU (and monitor if it has a separate switch). The *Windows 95* screen will display.
4. If the *Windows 95* screen contains a tip, read the tip and click the Close button.

Open the Word Processing Program

Your word processing program, or application, may open automatically when *Windows 95* opens (if the program is in the Start-up group). If not, then you must open the word processing software.

1. Click the Start button on the taskbar (lower-left corner of screen).
2. On the Start menu, point to the Programs command.
3. On the drop-down menu, find the name of your word processing application, and click the icon beside the name. The word processing program opens and its button shows on the taskbar.

Do Basic Word Processing Operations

Using a word processing application involves creating, saving, closing, opening, and printing documents.

(Anything that you type in the text area is a *document*. Another word for a document is *file*.) These five operations are not all that you can do on word processing software—just the most basic operations. You need nothing more than the character keys (and space bar) on your keyboard to create a document. To save, close, open, or print, though, you need to access the function in one of three ways: (1) click a button on the Button bar, Power bar, or Toolbar; (2) use a keyboard command; or (3) select an option from a pull-down menu on the Menu bar.

Button bar/Power bar/Toolbar. A Button bar, or Power bar, or Toolbar is a series of buttons, or icons. See the illustrations at the top of this page. On all bars, the first, second, or third button stands for New document (a blank page), Open (an open folder), or Save (a disk). To use a function, click its button.

Keyboard commands. Many word processing operations, including save, close, open, and print, can be done with keyboard commands. The commands may be an F (unction) key (for example, F5) or a combination of Ctrl or Alt and another key (an F key or letter key). The keyboard commands are shown on the pull-down menus. On the *Applied MicroType Pro* menu, for example, you see that the keyboard command to start a new document is Ctrl+N. On the *WordPerfect* File menu, you see that the keyboard command to open a file is Ctrl+O; the command to close a file is Ctrl+F4. On the *Word* File menu, Ctrl+S is the keyboard command to save a file; Ctrl+P to print. The easiest commands to remember are the ones—like New (Ctrl+N), Open (Ctrl+O), and Save (Ctrl+S)—that combine Ctrl and the first letter of the function.

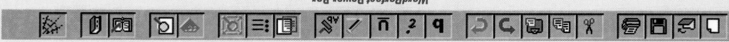

Microsoft Word Toolbar

WordPerfect Power Bar

Applied MicroType Pro Button Bar

Know Word Processing Software

Pull-down menus. A pull-down menu may be used to choose word processing operations. For the basic operations, pull down (click) the File menu on the Menu bar (upper-left corner). Then, click the option you want.

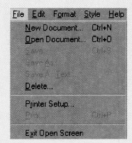

Applied MicroType Pro **File Menu**

WordPerfect **File Menu**

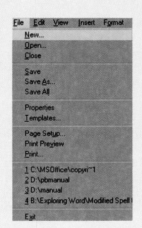

Microsoft Word **File Menu**

Create a Document (File)

The I-beam (mouse pointer) blinks in the text area. It is the *insertion point*. If you strike a character (letter, figure, or symbol) key, the character appears in that spot; and the insertion point moves to the right, ready for another character. The line spacing on the word processing application is preset for single spacing. The top, bottom, and side margins are preset at 1" in most cases. These settings are called *defaults*. Of course you may use the default line spacing and margins, but you also may choose to change these settings.

Set line spacing. With single spacing (1.0) being the default setting, one-and-a-half spacing (1.5) and double spacing (2.0) are common choices. Most word processing applications offer many more line spacing options (1.12, 1.75, 2.5, 4, etc.).

1. Place the insertion point (click the I-beam) where you want the line spacing to change. (In some software, line spacing will change for the entire paragraph in which the insertion point is placed.)

2. Select the option to change line spacing, using the proper Button bar/Power bar/Toolbar button, pull-down menu, or keyboard command.

3. Specify the line spacing you want.

4. Begin or continue keying.

Set margins. If you want to change the default margins, specify a different setting for the margin(s) you want changed.

1. Place the insertion point (click the I-beam) where the margin setting is to be changed (at the beginning or anywhere within a document).

2. Select the option that changes margins, using the proper Button bar/Power bar/Toolbar button, pull-down menu, or keyboard command.

3. Specify the new setting(s).

4. Begin or continue keying. To change margins back to the default settings, repeat these steps.

Save a Document (File)

When you save a file, you place a copy of it on a disk in one of the computer's disk drives, while leaving a copy of it on the screen. To save a document not saved before, you must give it a name (filename). A document may be saved before you key any text, while you are working, or when you are done working.

1. Select the Save option, using the proper Button bar/Power bar/Toolbar button, pull-down menu, or keyboard command. (The Save As box will display if the file has not been saved before.)

2. Choose where (which disk drive and/or directory or folder) you want to save the file.

3. Assign a filename that will help you find the file whenever you want to open it later. Check the software user's guide for how many letters you may use in a filename. **Note:** Newer software accepts filenames that have over two hundred characters, but some applications limit filenames to eight characters.

4. Begin or continue keying; or, if you are done working, close the file.

5. If you modify (change) this file and want to save the modified file, select the Save option, using the proper Button bar/Power bar/Toolbar button, pull-down menu, or keyboard command. To keep the original document and the modified document in separate files, select the Save As option, using the proper Button bar/Power bar/Toolbar button, pull-down menu, or keyboard command, and use a different filename.

Close a Document (File)

When you close a file, you remove it from the screen. If the copy on the screen has not been saved, or if it has been changed since it was last saved, you will be asked if you want to save the document before closing it.

1. Select the option that closes a file, using the proper Button bar/Power bar/Toolbar button, pull-down menu, or keyboard command. **Note:** If you are running *Windows 95*, click the X button at the far right on the Menu bar to close a file. Be careful: clicking the large X in the upper-right corner will close your word processing software.

2. If the *Save changes . . . ?* prompt comes on the screen, click Yes to save changes you have made in the original file. Click No to close the document without saving changes.

Open a Document (File)

When you open a file, you retrieve it from the disk drive and directory and/or folder in which you saved it. An open file appears in the text area.

1. Choose the correct disk drive, if necessary. **Note:** Disk drives are named with letters of the alphabet. In most cases, the main disk drive inside the computer is the c-drive (c:\). It is the default drive, which means that you do not have to choose a disk drive to open files saved on this drive. The drive that takes floppy (square plastic) disks is usually the a-drive (a:\). The drive that reads CD-ROM (round silver) disks may be the d-drive (d:\) or another letter.

2. Select the option that lets you see a list of items saved on the disk you chose. Use the proper Button bar/Power bar/Toolbar button, pull-down menu, or keyboard command.

3. If you saved the file in a subdirectory or folder, open (click) the subdirectory or folder; then select the file you want to open.

Print a Document (File)

When you print a document, you send a copy of it to a printer that can make a paper (hard) copy of the file.

1. If more than one printer is available, be sure that the printer you want to use is selected in the software. **Note:** The File menu may have an option just for selecting a printer. If not, select the printer in Step 2, after selecting the print option.

2. Select the print option, using the proper Button bar/Power bar/Toolbar button, pull-down menu, or keyboard command. **Note:** On some software, clicking the Button bar/Power bar/Toolbar Print button may print *all* pages of a document automatically. If you want to print only one page or selected pages, use Print on the pull-down menu or use the keyboard command. (The *current page* is the page that has the insertion point in it.) To print selected pages, type a range of pages (example: 2-5) or specific pages (example: 1,4,5).

3. Take your printed page(s) from the printer.

Turn off the Operating System (Shut Down)

The Shut Down command (Start menu) is used to close the *Windows 95* operating system. (Most computer users shut down after using the computer for the last time each day, not at the end of each session.)

1. Close the open files on your application software.
2. If a floppy disk is in the disk drive, remove it.
3. Click Shut Down on the Start menu.
4. Select (Click) Yes at the *Shut down computer?* prompt. Your word processing software will close.
5. Wait for this prompt: *It's now safe to turn off your computer.*
6. Turn off the power switch on the CPU (and monitor if it has a separate switch).

How to Maintain Your System & Media

Follow these guidelines when working with your computer to avoid a variety of problems and prevent harm to yourself, others, and the hardware, software, disks, and data.

Operating Electrical Equipment

A few safety rules apply to all **electrical equipment**, not just computers.

1. Do NOT unplug equipment by pulling on the cord. Instead, grasp the plug at the outlet.
2. Do NOT stretch an electrical cord across an aisle where someone might trip over it.
3. Do NOT overload extension cords.
4. Do NOT drop books or other objects on or near the equipment.
5. Do NOT take food or beverages near equipment; and do not use aerosol sprays, solvents, or abrasives to clean it.
6. Do NOT move equipment unaided. Avoid jostling or jolting equipment if you must move it.
7. Do NOT remove or insert computer cables without supervision or without turning off the equipment.
8. Replace (report to teacher) frayed electric cords immediately.

Maintaining Your Hardware

Here is a list of commonsense guidelines for using a **computer, monitor, and keyboard.**

1. Clean a computer, screen, and keyboard with a damp (not wet), lint-free cloth. A bit of mild soap may be used occasionally.
2. Keep air vents unobstructed to prevent overheating.
3. Place your keyboard where it won't get bumped off the desk.
4. Use correct keying techniques and hand and finger exercises (see p. A3) to prevent repetitive stress injury, though high school students are at low risk for it.
5. Adjust the angle, brightness, and focus of the monitor for comfortable viewing.
6. Avoid glare on the screen; use a glare guard if needed.
7. Keep the screen free of dust and fingerprints by dusting it often with a soft, lint-free cloth.
8. Do NOT put pencils or other implements into external disk drives.

Protecting Software and Data

Follow these precautions to avoid damage to **programs, data files, and storage media** such as floppy disks.

1. Handle floppy disks and compact disks (CD's) by their labels. Don't touch the shutter of a 3.5" disk.
2. Do NOT insert or remove a disk while the drive is active.
3. Keep disks away from extreme heat or cold and direct sunlight. Do not leave disks in a car.
4. Keep disks away from dust, including chalk dust; magnets; x-ray devices; and metal detectors.

These guidelines will help you **name files** that you create—and find them quickly.

1. Plan how you will name files (suggestions follow) and follow that plan throughout the course.
2. Store all files for the course in one place, such as a separate floppy disk with your name and the course title on the disk label.
3. If other files (not course-related) are stored on the same disk, create a separate folder/directory for course files.
4. Save each document (memo, letter, report, etc.) in a separate file.
5. Name files by the page number and/or lesson part number; then by document number if there is more than one document. If your operating system accepts filenames of 256 characters/spaces, more detailed filenames may be used. The following examples refer to pages 172, 181, and 184 in this book.

   Long filenames (256 characters/spaces) acceptable:
   Page 172 64D Table 3 Reading List
   Page 181 Document 3
   Lesson 70B Table 2

   Filenames limited to eight characters:
   p172-3
   p181-3
   l70b-2

6. Delete only those files you are SURE will not be needed later.
7. Before you recycle a disk (erase all contents by *formatting* it), view the list of files it contains. Do NOT rely on your memory or even the disk label to tell you exactly what is on the disk.

All computer users should be aware of potential problems caused by *pirates, hackers,* and *viruses.*

1. Do NOT copy a program you own to give to other computer users. Duplication is almost always illegal.

2. Do NOT install on your computer a program that another user copied for you. These days, software vendors "raid" schools/businesses in search of *pirates.*

3. Do NOT collaborate with a *hacker*—a person who tries to access a large computer database for the purpose of altering or destroying the data. Besides the serious, expensive damage such actions may cause, accessing a database without authorization is a federal offense under the Electronic Communications Privacy Act of 1986.

4. Avoid copying data files from other users if your computer is not equipped with up-to-date virus detection software. A *virus*—the work of a hacker or *cracker* (criminal hacker)—is a set of instructions that causes the computer to destroy data when given a certain signal. Whenever the program is copied, the virus is copied, too. Thus, a virus in one computer may spread to many others.

You probably cannot eliminate every "glitch" in your computer's **operating system**; in fact, you likely can't prevent an occasional "crash." But a few simple steps can help.

1. Only applications that are used frequently should be put in the *Windows* Start-up group. The more programs you have in the Start-up group (a) the longer it takes to get the computer "up and running," (b) the more things can go wrong, and (c) the slower the system will run.

2. When you see the hourglass (*Windows*) or other "wait" signal while using the computer, do NOT tap keys or click the mouse. Simply wait until the I-beam or pointer replaces the hourglass.

3. Unnecessary programs and data files (including word processing documents) should be removed from the hard disk periodically.

4. Do NOT remove any files from any computer that does not belong to you, such as computers at school.

5. Do NOT remove files from a home computer without knowing what effect removing the file will have on the computer's operation, or without the approval of all other users.

6. Now and then, computer users should run a special kind of software to "defrag" (defragment) the hard disk. Over time, a hard disk becomes fragmented (information stored on it is scattered about, instead of being neatly organized), which slows down the operating system. Running a defrag program reorganizes the disk and speeds up the system.

7. Following a system "crash" (an application quits, or closes, unexpectedly), reset the operating system and open the application you were using when the crash occurred.

8. Open any files that the application "recovers" following a crash. Save recovered file(s) with new filename(s); compare with the file saved before the crash (if any); save the file that contains the most updates and delete the other file.

9. Close all open files before shutting down the computer.

Here are some things to keep in mind when using the Internet.

the Internet.

1. Find out if your school has an *acceptable-use policy* (contract between a school; you, a student; and your parents/guardian); and, if so, read and follow it.

2. Learn and use proper *netiquette* (etiquette or manners). Some basic rules follow:
   a. Use caps and lowercase to write messages (for mailing lists, for example). ALL CAPS style, besides being hard to read, is interpreted as YELLING (rude).
   b. Make messages concise and clear.
   c. Show respect for others in your choice of language, expression of opinions, and so on.
   d. Before entering a chat room, seminar, or conference, find out what the rules are and follow them.

3. If you quote or paraphrase information from a web page, in a report, for example, give credit to the person or group who originated the site. Plagiarism is illegal.

Getting Help

Take advantage of **user's guides and online Help.**

1. Study the user's guides that come with your hardware and software to cut down on "experimenting" as you work at the computer.

2. All programs, including web browsers, give online Help. Make it the first place you turn to when you need assistance.

3. Spend a few minutes each day learning something new about your computer and how it works.

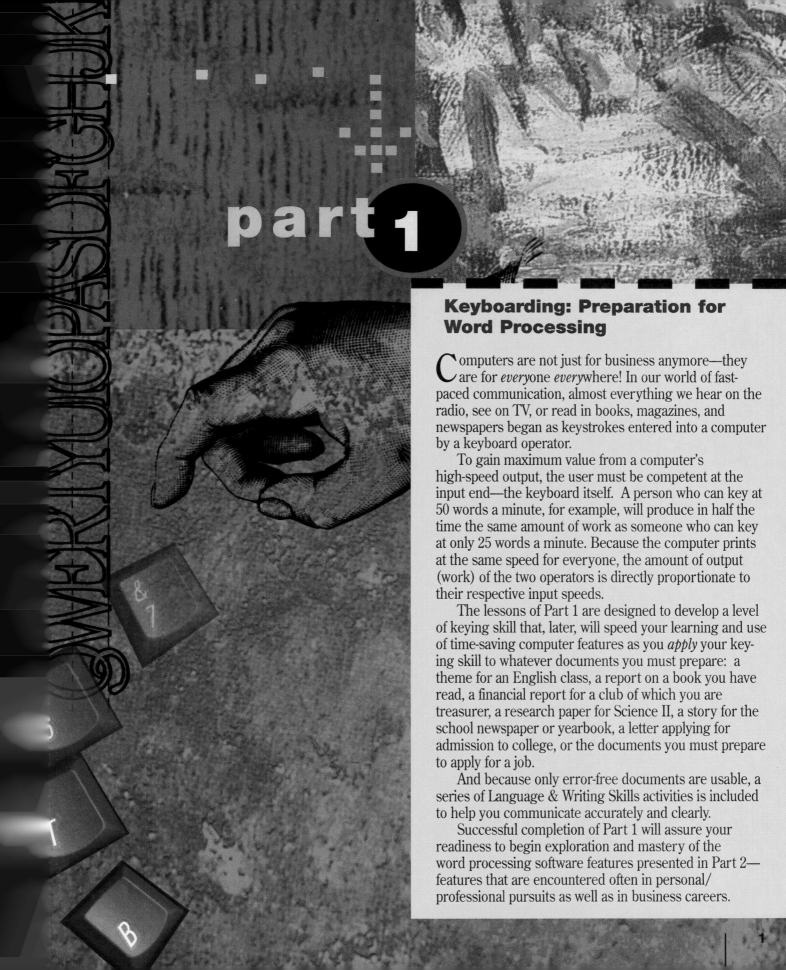

part 1

Keyboarding: Preparation for Word Processing

Computers are not just for business anymore—they are for *every*one *every*where! In our world of fast-paced communication, almost everything we hear on the radio, see on TV, or read in books, magazines, and newspapers began as keystrokes entered into a computer by a keyboard operator.

To gain maximum value from a computer's high-speed output, the user must be competent at the input end—the keyboard itself. A person who can key at 50 words a minute, for example, will produce in half the time the same amount of work as someone who can key at only 25 words a minute. Because the computer prints at the same speed for everyone, the amount of output (work) of the two operators is directly proportionate to their respective input speeds.

The lessons of Part 1 are designed to develop a level of keying skill that, later, will speed your learning and use of time-saving computer features as you *apply* your keying skill to whatever documents you must prepare: a theme for an English class, a report on a book you have read, a financial report for a club of which you are treasurer, a research paper for Science II, a story for the school newspaper or yearbook, a letter applying for admission to college, or the documents you must prepare to apply for a job.

And because only error-free documents are usable, a series of Language & Writing Skills activities is included to help you communicate accurately and clearly.

Successful completion of Part 1 will assure your readiness to begin exploration and mastery of the word processing software features presented in Part 2—features that are encountered often in personal/professional pursuits as well as in business careers.

Document 9
Letter to Judge of Dance Contest

From the desk of Ms. Winfrey

Format: Use block style, open punctuation.

Note: May need corrections. Use today's date. Put newspaper title in ital., not underlined.

Mr. Alexi Kosov │ Star Tribune │ 800 N. First St. │ Minneapolis, MN 55401-3627 │ Dear Mr. Kosov

How fortunate we are to have you join the panel of judges who will select the winners of the dance contest to be held at Falcon Heights High School at two p.m. on May 13th.

You will be joined on the panel by selected faculty members from Twin Cities University and local high schools. It is especially fitting, though, to have a professional critic on the panel.

Your insistence on serving without honorarium is most commendable, please know how grateful we are.

As the contest date nears, Ill send a friendly reminder.

Cordially yours │ Ms. Twyla Winfrey, Chair │ H.S. Teacher Committee

• •

Documents 10-12
Letters to Judges of Other Competitions

From the desk of Ms. Winfrey

Change the letter to Mr. Kosov (Document 9) for each addressee listed at the right. Change the salutation appropriately and change ¶ 1 as noted.

Ms. LuAnn Chang
Pioneer Press
345 Cedar St.
St. Paul, MN 55101-2266

¶ 1, line 2: *art contest;*
Roosevelt High School

Mr. Anton Navarro
Star Tribune
800 N. First St.
Minneapolis, MN 55401-3627

¶ 1, line 2: *music contest;*
Hiawatha High School

Mrs. Nadia Horowitz
Pioneer Press
345 Cedar St.
St. Paul, MN 55101-2266

¶ 1, line 2: *drama contest;*
Richfield High School
¶ 1, line 3: *May 20*

• •

Documents 13-14
Tables for Parents

From the desk of Ms. Winfrey

Some of the parents who come for the Final Event will arrive early Saturday and stay in the area overnight. I'd like to include two tables in the packets listing places to stay and places to eat.

Get information from the Internet (if you can). Use this address: **http://city.net**.

See my notes at right.

Notes:

I suggest that you start by creating the two tables (3 x 10) on the same page. Fill in only the title and column titles (*see titles below*); then print the tables. You can fill in the body with a pencil while you're online. After you disconnect, you can key from your pencil copy to complete the tables attractively.

Include *at least* four entries in each list. Choose places in Minneapolis *and* St. Paul, if possible. Select low to moderately priced hotels and restaurants. Be extra careful when copying the phone numbers. After you fill in your tables, delete any empty rows.

To use the web site: On the **city.net** home page, choose *North America.* From there, five more steps will each take you closer to the information you want: choose *United States;* then choose *States.* Next choose *M* (for Minnesota); then, *Minneapolis* or *St. Paul.* Finally, choose an option that promises information about hotels. Once you've gotten this information, you can go *back* and choose a *hyperlink* option that will give you information about restaurants.

WHERE TO STAY   WHERE TO EAT

Hotel Price Range Telephone   Restaurant Price Range Telephone

Learn Letter Keyboarding Technique
Lesson 1   Home Keys (FDSA JKL;)

O b j e c t i v e s :
1. **To learn control of home keys (FDSA JKL;).**
2. **To learn control of Space Bar and Return/Enter.**

1A◆
Work Area

Arrange work area as shown at right.

- alphanumeric (main) keyboard directly in front of chair; front edge of keyboard even with edge of table or desk
- monitor placed for easy viewing; disk drives placed for easy access
- the disk(s) you will need within easy reach
- book behind or at right of keyboard, resting on easel for easy reading

Properly arranged work area

1B◆
Keying Position

The essential features of proper position are shown at right and listed below:

- fingers curved and upright over home keys
- wrists low, but not touching frame of keyboard
- forearms parallel to slant of keyboard
- body erect, sitting back in chair
- feet on floor for balance

Proper position at computer

Proper position at computer

Lesson 1

Document 6
Letter to Parents

From the desk of Ms. Winfrey

Format: Use block style, open punctuation.

Date: Please insert *Date Code* (if available).

Address: Key > on first address line. Leave three lines blank to fill in later.

Salutation: Key **Dear.** Fill in the rest of it when you get addresses.

Body: Bold the place, time, and date in ¶ 1.

Complimentary closing: Cordially

Signature: Miss Adele Chiodi, Chair/Invitation Committee

Purpose: To invite parents of camp participants to final event.

Document 7
Final Event Program

From the desk of Ms. Winfrey

Format: 2-column table

Purpose: To include with letter inviting parents to final event.

Note: Attach to the letter (Document 6).

Document 8
Revisions to Summary

From the desk of Ms. Winfrey

Open the report you keyed recently and make the changes indicated at the right. Print it after making changes.

You are invited to attend the Final Event of the Twin Cities Youth Camp for Fine & Performing Arts.   This exciting event, "Voices of Harmony," will be held in Nokomis Auditorium on the TCU campus at 730 P.m., July 22.   Admission for parents is free.

A copy of the preliminary program is enclosed.   You will note the multi-cultural focus of the program, which reflects the theme of the 2-week camp in which the student participants will be engaged.   The youth campers are highlighted, but some TCU faculty and students are included when necessary to supplement the cast.

In addition to the variety of music, drama, and dance that comprise the program, you will enjoy viewing the artwork of the "Art Campers" that will be exhibited in the foyer of the auditorium.

The Final Event is designed to delight you, to surprise you, and to expand your perspective.   Please come and bring other members of your family (if any to support these happy campers.

VOICES OF HARMONY
Youth Camp ~~Main~~ *Final* Event   ) *bold*

Theme	Focus
Voices of Freedom	Gospel ⊂ music/drama
Voices of Expression	Hispanic music/~~drama~~ *dance*
Voices of the Spirit	Native American poetry/~~cadence~~ *rhythm*
Voices of Jazz	African-American jazz/dance
Voices of Movement	Oriental music/~~drama~~ *dance*
Voices of Tradition	Classical/folk music
Voices of the American Stage	Tribute to American musicals
Voices of ~~Youth~~ *Hope*	Youth look toward the future

1. In the Art Camp section, the high school is **Roosevelt,** not *Roseville.*
2. Same section: In the second sentence, change *from TCU* to **from Twin Cities University (TCU)**. Also in the second sentence, insert these words after *local high school,:* **a docent at Walker Art Center,**.
3. In the Theater Camp section, after TCU, change *two music teachers* to **two class play directors;** then change the end of the same sentence to read: "one drama/theater critic **each from the** *Star Tribune* **and the** *Pioneer Press*."

1C ◆

Home-Key Position

1. Find the home keys on the chart: **F D S A** for left hand and **J K L ;** for right hand.
2. Locate the home keys on your keyboard. Place left-hand fingers on **F D S A** and right-hand fingers on **J K L ;** *with your fingers well curved and upright (not slanting).*
3. Remove your fingers from the keyboard; then place them in home-key position again, curving and holding them *lightly* on the keys.

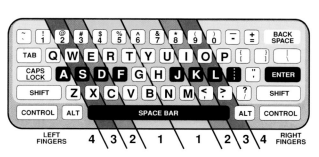

1D ◆

Technique: Home Keys and Space Bar

1. Read the statements and study the illustrations at right.
2. Place your fingers in home-key position as directed in 1C above.
3. Strike each letter key for the first group of letters in the line of type below the technique illustrations.
4. After striking **;** (semicolon), strike the **Space Bar** once.
5. Continue to key the line; strike the **Space Bar** once at the point of each arrow.

TECHNIQUE CUES:

Keystroking: Strike each key with a light tap with the tip of the finger, snapping the fingertip toward the palm of the hand.

Spacing: Strike the Space Bar with the right thumb; use a quick down-and-in motion (toward the palm). Avoid pauses before or after spacing.

Light tap with fingertip

Snap fingertip toward palm

Strike Space Bar with right thumb

Quick down-and-in spacing motion

Space once.

fdsajkl; f d s a j k l ; ff jj dd kk ss ll aa ;;

Music Camp

As many as ten music students will be chosen on the basis of their performance at competitive auditions to be held at Hiawatha High School on Saturday May 13. The judges will include two professors of music from TCU, two music teachers from local high schools, and two music critics (one from the Star Tribune, the other from the Pioneer Press). Both vocalists and instrumentalists may enter the competition. For the first time, a computerized synthesizer may be used for accompaniment.

Theater Camp

Eight to ten theater students will be chosen on the basis of there performance at competitive auditions to be held at Richfield High School on Saturday, May 20. Judges will include two professors of drama and theater from TCU, two music teachers from local high schools, and one drama/theater critic from each of our local newspapers. Musical theater students may enter as actors, vocalists, or both.

Dance Camp

Up to ten dance students will be selected on the basis of their performance at a dance competition to be held at Falcon Heights High School on Saturday, May 13. Judges will be specialists in ballet and modern dance from TCU, a dance theater critic from the Star Tribune, and the director of Twin Cities Dance Company. Entrants may dance solo in pairs, or in groups.

Living Accommodations

All students will live in campus dormitories. Each group will be mentored by a TCU faculty member and a high school teacher. Meals will be provided for all youth campers in the Student Center cafeteria. Student living costs are covered by the grants.

. . . .

Document 5
Table of Art Museum Tour Highlights

From the desk of Ms. Winfrey

Format: 3 x 11 table; join each pair of the following cells in column A to make four deep cells: A4 and A5, A6 and A7, A8 and A9, A10 and A11.

Purpose: To include in promotion packet for students/parents.

HIGHLIGHTS OF ART MUSEUM TOUR

New Perspectives

Gallery	Artist	Subject
African-American Gallery	A Collection	Prints
	Robert Scott	Murals
Hispanic Gallery	Julio Larraz	Sketches
	Rafael Ortiz	Abstracts
Main Gallery	Thomas Sierak	Sketches
	Camille Pissaro	Landscapes
Oriental Gallery	Tat Shinno	Florals
	Sherrie McGraw	Still Life

1E ◆

Technique: Hard Return at Line Endings

To return the insertion point to left margin and move it down to next line, strike **Return/Enter** key (hard return).

Study illustration at right; then return 4 times (quadruple-space) below the line you completed in 1D, p. 3.

Hard Return

Striking the **Enter** (IBM or compatible) or **Return** (Macintosh)

key is called a *hard return.* You will use a hard return at the end of all drill lines in this lesson and those that follow in this unit. Reach the little finger of the right hand to the **Enter** or **Return** key, tap the key, and return the finger quickly to home-key position.

1F ◆

Home-Key and Space Bar Practice

1. Place your hands in home-key position (left-hand fingers on **F D S A** and right-hand fingers on **J K L ;**).
2. Key the lines once: single-spaced (SS) with a double space (DS) between 2-line groups. Do not key line numbers.

Fingers curved and upright

Down- and-in spacing motion

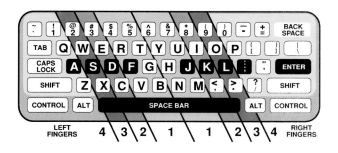

Strike Space Bar once to space.

```
1 j  jj  f  ff  k  kk  d  dd  l  ll  s  ss  ;  ;;  a  aa  jkl;  fdsa
2 j  jj  f  ff  k  kk  d  dd  l  ll  s  ss  ;  ;;  a  aa  jkl;  fdsa
```
Strike the Return/Enter key twice to double-space (DS).

```
3 a  aa  ;  ;;  s  ss  l  ll  d  dd  k  kk  f  ff  j  jj  fdsa  jkl;
4 a  aa  ;  ;;  s  ss  l  ll  d  dd  k  kk  f  ff  j  jj  fdsa  jkl;
                                                                 DS
```

```
5 jf  jf  kd  kd  ls  ls  ;a  ;a  fj  fj  dk  dk  sl  sl  a;  a;  f
6 jf  jf  kd  kd  ls  ls  ;a  ;a  fj  fj  dk  dk  sl  sl  a;  a;  f
                                                                 DS
```

```
7 a;fj  a;sldkfj  a;sldkfj  a;sldkfj  a;sldkfj  a;sldkfj
8 a;fj  a;sldkfj  a;sldkfj  a;sldkfj  a;sldkfj  a;sldkfj
```
Strike the Return/Enter key 4 times to quadruple-space (QS).

1G ◆

Technique: Return

each line twice single-spaced (SS); double-space (DS) between 2-line groups

SPACING CUE:

When in SS mode, strike **Return/Enter** twice to insert a DS between 2-line groups.

Reach out with right little finger; tap **Return/Enter** key quickly; return finger to home key.

```
1 a;sldkfj  a;sldkfj
                    DS
2 ff  jj  dd  kk  ss  ll  aa  ;;
                               DS
3 fj  fj  dk  dk  sl  sl  a;  a;  asdf  ;lkj
                                           DS
4 fj  dk  sl  a;  jf  kd  ls  ;a  fdsa  jkl;  a;sldkfj
                                                    QS
```

From the desk of
Ms. Winfrey

Format: 3 x 19 table; can you show (print) cell borders between the departmental groups—but nowhere else?

YOUTH CAMP FOR FINE & PERFORMING ARTS — *center & bold*

Participating TCU *Faculty & Staff*

Name	Function	Department
Dr. John M. Lenz	Coordinator	Art
Ms. Lucia del Rio	Instructor	Art
Mr. Frederick Marx	Instructor	Art
Miss Bella Spear	Coach	Art
Mr. Paul Mehta	coach	Dance
Miss Ana de Avila	Coordinator	Dance
Mr. Ari Baccus	Instructor	Dance
Ms. Tamera Bryant	Instructor	Dance
Mr. Danuis Brown	Cordinator	Music
Mr. Felix Ardelli	Instructor	Music
Ms. Anita Fry Carr	Instructor	"
Miss Susan Parish	Coach	"
Dr. Olivia Habjan	Coordinator	Theater
Ms. Serena Conte	Instructor	"
Mr. Henri DeLong	Instructor	"
Mr. Cyril Pierce	Coach	"

Document 4
Summary in
Unbound Report Format

From the desk of
Ms. Winfrey

Format: Check the *Formatting Manual* to set up this summary.

Body: Italicize newspaper titles; attach report to the memo (Document 2).

Note: Wait to print this until after I get feedback.

Purpose: To promote summer youth camp.

TWIN CITIES YOUTH CAMP FOR FINE & PERFORMING ARTS

July 9 - 22, ----

The Twin Cities Youth Camp for Fine & Performing Arts on the Twin Cities University campus is scheduled for two weeks, from Sunday afternoon, July 9, to Saturday night, July 22. Made possible by grants from the Carnegie Foundation and the National Endowment for the Arts, the camp will give approximately forty students a rare opportunity to study and work with outstanding specialists in the fields of art, music, theater and dance. The camp can accomodate up to ten students in each of these fields.

Art Camp

Up to ten art students will be chosen on the basis of their entries in a competitive art exhibit to be held at Roseville high school on Saturday, May 13. Entries will be judged by an art professor from TCU, an art teacher from a local high school, and an art critic from the Minneapolis Institute of Art. Each student must enter at least three but not more than five pieces--at least one in oils, one in watercolor, and one in charcoal. Other categories include sculpture and computer graphics.

1H◆
Home-Key Mastery

1. Key the lines once (without the numbers); strike the **Return/Enter** key twice to double-space (DS).
2. Rekey the drill at a faster pace.

Correct finger alignment

1 aa ;; ss ll dd kk ff jj a; sl dk fj jf kd ls ;a jf
DS

2 a a as as ad ad ask ask lad lad fad fad jak jak la
DS

3 all all fad fad jak jak add add ask ask ads ads as
DS

4 a lad; a jak; a lass; all ads; add all; ask a lass
DS

5 as a lad; a fall fad; ask all dads; as a fall fad;

1I◆
End-of-Lesson Routine

1. Exit the software.
2. Remove from disk drive any disk you have inserted.
3. Store materials.

Disk removal

Most computer manufacturers recommend turning a computer off at the end of the day, rather than immediately after each use.

Enrichment

1. Key drill once as shown to improve control of home keys.
2. Key the drill again to quicken your keystrokes.

1 ja js jd jf f; fl fk fj ka ks kd kf d; dl dk dj a;
DS

2 la ls ld lf s; sl sk sj ;a ;s ;d ;f a; al ak aj fj
DS

3 jj aa kk ss ll dd ;; ff fj dk sl a; jf kd ls ;a a;
DS

4 as as ask ask ad ad lad lad all all fall fall lass
DS

5 as a fad; as a dad; ask a lad; as a lass; all lads
DS

6 a sad dad; all lads fall; ask a lass; a jak salad;
DS

7 add a jak; a fall ad; all fall ads; ask a sad lass

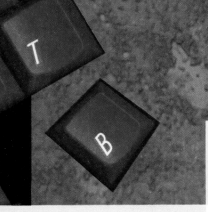

Objectives:

| Approx. time: 3.5 hrs. |

1. **To apply keying and word processing skills in a work setting.**
2. **To work with general, rather than specific, directions.**

71A-75A
Keyboard Mastery

Use Skill Builder 6, p. 186, lines 1, 2, and 9, or L on p. A7.

71B-75B
Simulation

Document 1
Announcement

From the desk of Ms. Winfrey

Format: Center each line; bold the title; insert heavy (2 pt.) horizontal line or double arrowhead above "Courtesy of" line.

Purpose: To be posted on H.S. bulletin boards.

TWIN CITIES UNIVERSITY *AND* MINNEAPOLIS/ST. PAUL

n
anounce*s*

Font: Arial Black Twin Cities Youth ~~Cared~~ *Camp* for Fine & Performing Arts

TCU Campus, *July 9-22*

Student for

High School Artists, Musicians, Actors, and Dancers

Participants Determined by Competitive Auditions *Exhibits/*

Admission g # ~~Attendance:~~ Free

of

Courtesy Carnegie Foundation & National Endowment for the Arts

Further Information to be Available Soon!

. . . .

Document 2
Memo

From the desk of Ms. Winfrey

TO: Members of Youth Camp Planning Committee

FROM: Twyla Winfrey, Chair, H.S. Teacher Committee

DATE: [Today's date]

SUBJECT: Youth Camp Participant Selection Process

Here is a first-draft summary of the selection process to be used in choosing students for the Twin City Youth Camp for Fine & Performing Arts to be held at Twin Cities University this summer.

I believe the decisions reached at are last joint meeting are reflected accurately in the summary. To be sure, please read the attachment carefully and note any changes you think should be made.

After I get your feedback; I'll prepare a revised summary to be included in the information packet sent to prospective participants and their parents.

Objectives:

1. **To improve control of the home keys (FDSA JKL;).**
2. **To improve control of Space Bar and Return/Enter.**

RA◆
Get Ready to Key

1. Arrange your work area (see p. 2).
2. Get to know your hardware and software (see pp. vii-xvi).
3. Use default margins and spacing. The word **default** refers to margins and spacing that the software chooses, rather than choices you indicate.
4. Take keying position as shown at right.

RB◆
Home-Key Position

1. Locate the home keys on the chart: **F D S A** for left hand and **J K L ;** for right hand.
2. Locate the home keys on your keyboard. Place left-hand fingers on **F D S A** and right-hand fingers on **J K L ;** *with fingers well curved and upright (not slanting).*
3. Remove fingers from the keyboard; then place them in home-key position again.

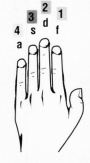

RC◆
Technique Review

Remember to use a hard return at the end of all drill lines. To double-space (DS), use two hard returns.

Keystroke
Curve fingers over home keys. Strike each key with a quick-snap stroke; release key quickly.

Space
Strike the **Space Bar** with a quick down-and-in motion of the right thumb. Do not pause before or after spacing stroke.

Hard Return
Reach the right little finger to the **Return/Enter** key; strike the key and return the finger quickly to home key.

unit 16

Twin Cities Youth Camp:
A Word Processing Simulation
Lessons 71-75

Setting and Organization

This coming summer Twin Cities University (TCU) will sponsor a Twin Cities Youth Camp for Fine & Performing Arts. The camp is made possible by grants from the Carnegie Foundation and the National Endowment for the Arts. A committee of local high school teachers will assist in planning and coordinating the camp.

The purpose of the camp is to give approximately forty qualified high school seniors in the Minneapolis-St. Paul area an opportunity to study and work with outstanding performers in the fields of art, music, theater, and dance. The camp will be limited to eight to ten students in each category.

The study program will include formal classes, demonstrations, individualized coaching, and workshop-style performances of both students and teachers. Campers will also visit art galleries and museums and attend evening events in which professionals perform in recital or concert.

You have been chosen to work as a part-time office assistant to Ms. Twyla Winfrey of Lake Como High School, who chairs the high school teacher committee. She works directly with Dr. Jorgi Franco of TCU, who chairs the university planning committee.

In addition to running the fax machine and copier, you will process memos, letters, reports, and other documents. Even though your teacher has verified that you know how to process documents in standard formats, Ms. Winfrey gives you the following excerpts from the *Formatting Manual* used by the Twin Cities Youth Camp office personnel. You are to consult this manual for format questions.

Excerpts from *Formatting Manual*

Announcements
- Center page vertically.
- DS throughout.

Memos
- Use 2" top margin.
- Use default side margins.
- DS between all parts; SS ¶s, DS between them.

Letters
- Center page vertically.
- Use default side margins.
- QS between date and letter address and between complimentary close and writer's name; DS between all other parts.

Reports
- Use 2" top margin, first page and reference page if separate; otherwise, 1".
- Leave at least 1" bottom margin.
- QS between title and body; DS all other lines.
- Page numbers: Do *not* number page 1; number all other pages at top right.
- Title(s) and side headings in bold Arial.

Tables
- Use 2" top margin.
- Center table horizontally.
- Alignment: Vertically center all cells; left- or center-align words horizontally; right-align numbers.
- Column width: adjust to length of data entries in column.
- Center and bold main, secondary, and column titles.

The first time you report for work, Ms. Winfrey explains some details of your job; and you take the notes shown at left.

Notes:

1. Use current date on memos & letters unless noted otherwise.
2. If document mentions attachment/enclosure, key notation automatically.
3. Key MY reference initials on all memos & letters.
4. Copy that I key from may contain errors! CORRECT them.
5. Use Spelling and/or Grammar; PROOFREAD, too!
6. Look for ways to save time w/o losing quality. Ex: Block Text, Copy & Paste, Date Text, etc.

RD◆

Home Keys and Space Bar

Key the lines once (without numbers), single-spaced (SS) with a double space between 2-line groups.

Technique goals
- curved, upright fingers
- quick-snap keystrokes
- down-and-in spacing
- quick return without spacing at line endings

Correct finger curvature

Correct finger alignment

Strike Space Bar once to space.

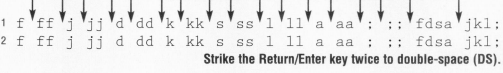

```
1 f ff j jj d dd k kk s ss l ll a aa ; ;; fdsa jkl;
2 f ff j jj d dd k kk s ss l ll a aa ; ;; fdsa jkl;
```

Strike the Return/Enter key twice to double-space (DS).

```
3 j jj f ff k kk d dd l ll s ss ; ;; a aa asdf ;lkj
4 j jj f ff k kk d dd l ll s ss ; ;; a aa asdf ;lkj
```
                                                                    DS

```
5 a;a sls dkd fjf ;a; lsl kdk jfj a;sldkfj a;sldkfj
6 a;a sls dkd fjf ;a; lsl kdk jfj a;sldkfj a;sldkfj
```

Strike the Return/Enter key 4 times to quadruple-space (QS).

RE◆

Home-Key Stroking

Key the lines once single-spaced (SS) with a double space (DS) between 2-line groups. Do not key the line numbers.

Goal
To improve keying and spacing techniques.

```
1 f f ff j j jj d d dd k k kk s s ss l l ll a a aa;;
2 f f ff j j jj d d dd k k kk s s ss l l ll a a aa;;

3 fj dk sl a; jf kd ls ;a ds kl df kj sd lk sa ;l ja
4 fj dk sl a; jf kd ls ;a ds kl df kj sd lk sa ;l ja

5 sa as ld dl af fa ls sl fl lf al la ja aj sk ks ja
6 sa as ld dl af fa ls sl fl lf al la ja aj sk ks ja
```

RF◆

Technique: Return

each line twice single-spaced (SS); double-space (DS) between 2-line groups

Technique goals
- curved, upright fingers
- quick-snap keystrokes
- down-and-in spacing
- quick return without spacing at line endings

> ### TECHNIQUE CUE:
> Reach out with the little finger, not the hand; tap **Return/Enter** quickly; return finger to home key.

```
1 a;sldkfj a;sldkfj
                    DS
2 a ad ad a as as ask ask
                          DS
3 as as jak jak ads ads all all
                                DS
4 a jak; a lass; all fall; ask all dads
                                        DS
5 as a fad; add a jak; all fall ads; a sad lass
                                                QS
```

Skill Builder 6

1. Key lines 1-9 once at an easy, steady pace.
2. Key the lines again at a quicker pace.
3. Key a 1' writing on each of lines 7-9; find *gwam* on each writing.

alphabet	1	Jacki had won first place by solving my tax quiz in only an hour.
top row	2	The 1999 net profit was $2,183,764 (up 30% from 5 years earlier).
keypad	3	207.461.1851 304.671.5020 316.821.2854 817.941.2364 907.7411.3647
apostrophe	4	Don't say you can't unless you're certain you've tried your best.
quote marks	5	Cristina said, "Use 'whose' instead of 'who's' in that sentence."
diagonal	6	Add the following fractions: 1/4, 1/3, 3/5, 2/3, 3/10, and 5/16.
one-hand	7	My union drew upon abstracted data in a gas tax case as you read.
combination	8	Dave may serve on a union panel to set up pay rates for the work.
balanced-hand	9	Six of the antique firms may lend us a hand with the city social.

| 1 | 2 | 3 | 4 | 5 | 6 | 7 | 8 | 9 | 10 | 11 | 12 | 13 |

---

1. Key a 1' writing on ¶ 1; find *gwam*.
2. Add 4 *gwam* for a new goal rate. (See checkpoint chart below.)
3. Key two 1' *guided* writings on the ¶ to reach the checkpoint each 1/4'.
4. Key ¶ 2 and ¶ 3 in the same manner.
5. Key two 3' writings on ¶s 1-3 combined; find *gwam* and count errors on each.

Quarter-Minute Checkpoints

gwam	1/4'	1/2'	3/4'	Time
20	5	10	15	20
24	6	12	18	24
28	7	14	21	28
32	8	16	24	32
36	9	18	27	36
40	10	20	30	40
44	11	22	33	44
48	12	24	36	48
52	13	26	39	52
56	14	28	42	56

a all letters used

	3'	5'
Everyone has to make choices, and every decision has its own	4	2	33
consequences. You are no exception. You select all your friends;	9	5	35
you decide which of many careers you want to pursue; and you deter-	13	8	38
mine how you will act or behave in every situation.	16	10	40
If you acquire friends who aspire to follow a high standard	20	12	42
of decorum, you will probably do similarly. Since your friends	25	15	45
can have a major impact on how you behave, you should no doubt	29	17	48
select all friends carefully and prize every exemplary choice.	33	20	50
People tend to be drawn to others who appear to be similar to	37	22	53
themselves, but you should not exclude everyone who has a different	42	25	55
interest or point of view. To expand your perspective, you should	46	28	58
look for companions who come from other backgrounds and cultures.	50	30	61

| 1 | 2 | 3 | 4 |
| 1 | 2 | 3 |

RG◆
Home-Key Mastery

each line twice single-spaced
(SS); double-space (DS) between
2-line groups

Technique goals
- curved, upright fingers
- eyes on copy in book or on screen
- quick-snap keystrokes
- down-and-in spacing
- steady pace

Correct
finger
curvature

Correct
finger
alignment

Down-
and-in
spacing
motion

```
1 a jak; a jak; ask dad; ask dad; as all; as all ads
                                          Return twice to DS.
2 a fad; a fad; as a lad; as a lad; all ads; all ads
                                                        DS
3 as a fad; as a fad; a sad lass; a sad lass; a fall
                                                        DS
4 ask a lad; ask a lad; all jaks fall; all jaks fall
                                                        DS
5 a sad fall; a sad fall; all fall ads; all fall ads
                                                        DS
6 add a jak; a lad asks a lass; as a jak ad all fall
```

RH◆
End-of-Lesson Routine

1. Exit the software.
2. Remove from disk drive any disk you have inserted.
3. Store materials.

Disk removal

Most computer manufacturers
recommend turning a computer
off at the end of the day, rather
than immediately after each
use.

Enrichment

1. Key each line twice SS; DS between 2-line groups.
2. Key each line again to quicken your keystrokes if time permits.

PRACTICE CUE:
Key slowly the first time you key
a line to master the required
motions. As you key a line a
second time, try to make each
motion a bit faster.

```
1 ff jj dd kk ss ll aa ;; fj dk sl a; jf kd ls ;a a;
2 aa ;; ss ll dd kk ff jj ja js jd jf fj fk fl f; fj
3 fjf dkd sls a;a jfj kdk lsl ;a;a a;sldkfj a;sldkfj
4 fdsa jkl; asdf ;lkj all all ask ask jak jak ad add
5 a a as as ask ask ad ad lad lad add add fall falls
6 a jak ad; a sad dad; a lad asks; a lad asks a lass
7 a sad fall; all fall ads; as a lass asks a sad lad
8 as a fall fad; add a jak salad; as a sad lad falls
```

Above & Beyond
PROJECT

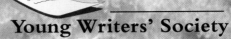

Young Writers' Society

On the bulletin board at school (see below), you see a job announcement. You decide to volunteer for the position as Ms. Winfrey's office assistant. First, you will prepare samples of your work from the Career Day and Job Explo documents; then, compose a memo applying for the job.

Your *portfolio* (samples of your work) should include the following four items: the bulletin announcing Career Day (p. 125, Task 3), one of the letters to Career Day speakers (p. 150), the process report for the Job Explo web site (p. 165), and the six-column table of follow-up information (p. 176). You should proofread, correct errors, and improve the overall appearance of your documents before placing them in your portfolio.

Your memo to Ms. Winfrey should have four to six paragraphs. The first and last two paragraphs are shown below. Suggestions for other paragraphs are listed at the left.

Suggestions for memo ¶s:

¶ 2 Name specific job skills that you would bring to this job, such as your speed (*gwam*) and accuracy (number of errors) on 3' or 5' writings, and the word processing software that you use. Also mention job-related skills, such as: excellent language and writing skills, good proofreading skills resulting in error-free documents, ability to follow both spoken and written directions, ability to finish assigned tasks without being reminded of due dates.

¶ 3 (*optional*) Mention other qualities that make you "right" for the job, such as: . . . a team player as a result of participating in Young Writers' Society and [insert name of student organization you participate in]; . . . a dependable, mature attitude; . . . average grades of B or better; . . . good attendance record [state number of days absent and number of times tardy this school year].

¶ 4 (*optional*) Tell about hobbies or interests that add to your general skills. For example: . . . . use the Internet about [insert number] hours a week; . . . work on weekends at [insert name of employer], where duties include [insert main job duties].

HELP WANTED

Student Volunteer for

PART-TIME OFFICE ASSISTANT

Working for

MS. TWYLA WINFREY

Lake Como High School

Chair of High School Teacher Committee

Twin Cities Youth Camp for Fine & Performing Arts

Requirements: Keyboarding, word processing, and language and writing skills.

Duties: Process memos, letters, reports, etc.; run fax machine and copier.

Applications: Send memo with name of a faculty reference and samples of your work to Ms. Winfrey, Room 215.

¶ 1 My teacher, **[insert teacher's name]**, encouraged me to apply for your part-time office assistant job. I know from my experience on the Career Day program committee that I like the kind of work it involves.

¶ 5 The enclosed portfolio shows the quality of work I did on the Career Day committee. Besides processing these documents, I wrote some of them. The report, **[insert process report title]**, in particular, shows my writing skills.

¶ 6 I would like to talk with you about the job and my qualifications for it. I am in Room **[insert room number and the days and time your class meets there]**.

Lesson 2 New Keys: H and E

O b j e c t i v e s :
1. **To learn reach technique for H and E.**
2. **To combine smoothly H and E with home keys.**

2A◆
Get Ready to Key

At the beginning of each practice session, follow the *Standard Plan* given at the right to get ready to key the lesson.

Standard Plan for Getting Ready to Key

1. Arrange work area as shown on p. 2.
2. Check to see that the computer, monitor, and printer (if any) are plugged in.
3. Turn on the computer and monitor.
4. Open your program (Start menu) if it is not open. (Your teacher will give you the program's name. When the program is open, you will see a button with the name of the program at the bottom of the computer screen.) Choose the Open Screen in *Applied MicroType Pro.*
5. Align the front of the keyboard with the front edge of the desk or table.
6. Position the monitor and this book for easy reading.

2B◆
Plan for Learning New Keys

All keys except the home keys (**FDSA JKL;**) require the fingers to reach in order to strike them. Follow the *Standard Plan* given at the right in learning the proper reach for each new key.

Standard Plan for Learning New Keys

1. Find the new key on the keyboard chart given on the page where the new key is introduced.
2. Look at your own keyboard and find the new key on it.
3. Study the reach-technique picture at the left of the practice lines for the new key. (See p. 10 for illustrations.) Read the statement below the illustration.
4. Identify the finger to be used to strike the new key.
5. Curve your fingers; place them in home-key position (over **FDSA JKL;**).
6. Watch your finger as you reach it to the new key and back to home position a few times (keep it curved).
7. Refer to the set of 3 drill lines at the right of the reach-technique illustration. Key each line twice SS (single-spaced):
   - once slowly, to learn new reach;
   - then faster, for a quick-snap stroke. DS (double-space) between 2-line groups.

2C◆
Home-Key Review

each line twice single-spaced (SS): once slowly; again, at a faster pace; double-space (DS) between 2-line groups

All keystrokes learned

1 a;sldkfj a; sl dk fj ff jj dd kk ss ll aa ;; fj a;

2 as as ad ad all all jak jak fad fad fall fall lass

3 a jak; a fad; as a lad; ask dad; a lass; a fall ad

Return 4 times to quadruple-space (QS) between lesson parts.

Lesson 70 Table Assessment

Objectives:

1. **To assess knowledge of formatting simple tables.**
2. **To assess table formatting skill.**

Approx. time: 45'

70A◆
Keyboard Mastery

Use Skill Builder 5, p. 179, lines 1, 8, and 9, or I on p. A7.

70B◆
Assess Table Skills

Tables 1-3:
Top margin: 2"
Row height: default
Vertical alignment: Center all.
Tables: Center horizontally.

Table 1

Column width: A, 2.25"; B, 1"
Horizontal alignment: Center rows 1 and 2 and column B.

Table 2

Column widths: student's choice
Horizontal alignment: Center rows 1, 2, and 3; right-align column B (body).

Table 3

Column widths: Adjust A and B to 1.7"; adjust C to appropriate width. Join (merge) cells A9 and B9.
Horizontal alignment: Center rows 1and 2 and cell A9, and columns B and C (body). Bold copy in rows 1-3.

Table 4

If time permits, copy/paste Table 1; then substitute your favorite novels and authors in the cells.

		words
MY ALL-TIME FAVORITE NOVELS		6
Title	Author	8
East of Eden	Steinbeck	13
Grapes of Wrath	Steinbeck	18
The Old Man and the Sea	Hemingway	25
The Red Badge of Courage	Crane	31
The Yearling	Rawlings	36

		words
MOST-VISITED CIVIL WAR SITES		6
(1.0 = 1,000,000)		9
Site	Visitors	13
Gettysburg, PA	1.4	16
Chickamauga-Chatanooga, GA-TN	1.0	23
Vicksburg, VA MS	1.9 0	27
Kennesaw, GA	0.9	30
Manasas, VA	0.6	34
Source: U.S. News & Word Report, April 10, 1955		41

			words
ALL-TIME BEST-SELLING MUSIC ALBUMS			7
Sales Stated in Millions of Units			14
Title	Artist	Sold	18
Thriller	Michael Jackson	24	24
Rumours	Fleetwood Mac	17	29
Boston	Boston	15	32
Eagles Greatest Hits	Eagles	14	39
Born in the U.S.A.	Bruce Springsteen	14	47
Total Sales		84	50
Source: USA Today, May 5, 1995.			57

2D◆
New Keys: H and E

Use the *Standard Plan for Learning New Keys* (p. 9) for each key to be learned. Study the plan now.

Relate each step of the plan to the illustrations below and copy at right. Then key each line twice SS; leave a DS between 2-line groups.

h *Right index* finger

e *Left middle* finger

Do not attempt to key the headings (Learn h), line numbers, or vertical lines separating word groups.

Learn h

1 j j hj hj ah ah ha ha had had has has ash ash hash

2 hj hj ha ha ah ah hah hah had had ash ash has hash

3 ah ha; had ash; has had; a hall; has a hall; ah ha
Return twice to double-space (DS) after you complete the set of lines.

Learn e

4 d d ed ed el el led led eel eel eke eke ed fed fed

5 ed ed el el lee lee fed fed eke eke led led ale ed

6 a lake; a leek; a jade; a desk; a jade eel; a deed

Combine h and e

7 he he he | she she she | shed shed | heed heed | held held

8 a lash; a shed; he held; she has jade; held a sash

9 has fled; he has ash; she had jade; she had a sale
Return 4 times to quadruple-space (QS) between lesson parts.

2E◆
New-Key Mastery

1. Key the lines once SS; DS between 2-line groups.
2. Key the lines again with quick, sharp strokes at a faster pace.

SPACING CUE:
Space once after ; used as punctuation.

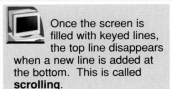
Once the screen is filled with keyed lines, the top line disappears when a new line is added at the bottom. This is called **scrolling**.

Fingers curved

Fingers upright

home row
1 ask ask|has has|lad lad|all all|jak jak|fall falls
2 a jak; a lad; a sash; had all; has a jak; all fall

h/e
3 he he|she she|led led|held held|jell jell|she shed
4 he led; she had; she fell; a jade ad; a desk shelf

all keys learned
5 elf elf|all all|ask ask|led led|jak jak|hall halls
6 ask dad; he has jell; she has jade; he sells leeks

all keys learned
7 he led; she has; a jak ad; a jade eel; a sled fell
8 she asked a lad; he led all fall; she has all jade

69B (continued)

<u>Revise the Copy</u>   370

To *revise*, read and study **what** you wrote.   379
Try to read the text as the reader will--   388
without knowing what you meant to say.   396
Ask again and again: Does it do what I set   404
out to do--to get the message from my mind   413
into the reader's mind in a favorable way?   422
If not, why not? Check for and eliminate   430
clichés, faulty logic, irrelevant facts or ideas,   440
lack of examples, or vague statements.   448
Revise the message until it cannot be *mis-*   457
understood.   460

<u>Edit the Text</u>   463

To *edit*, study the revised draft and   470
analyze **how** you said what you wrote, looking   479
at each word, phrase, and sentence. Put   487
yourself in the reader's place again. Ask these   497
questions: Is the text interesting? Did I   506
use active verbs? Do sentences vary in length   515
and structure? Do the ideas flow evenly   524
and smoothly and support the core idea or   532
theme? Free the text of common defects: 540
excess words, impressive-sounding words and   548
technical jargon, passive verbs, indefinite   558
words, long words, short choppy sentences   566
or complicated ones, and ill-chosen words   575
or lack of transitional words or phrases.   583
For a "proof of the pudding" check, have the   592
text read by **another set of eyes** and revise   601
the text again if any part of the message   610
is unclear or confusing. Excellent reports   619
result from multiple revisions. (Harcourt, and   628
others, 1996, 76)   632

<u>Format the Report</u>   636

To *format* or present the report, leave   644
blank space around the text and between   652

parts. Use a standard report format for   660
placement and spacing. Use emphasis devices   669
for items you want to stress: bold, italic,   678
underline, and bullets. Use such devices judi-   687
ciously because if you emphasize everything,   696
you emphasize nothing.   701

You may choose a distinctive typeface   709
of larger size for the report title. Generally,   719
though, use 10- or 12-point type for the body   728
copy and one or two emphasis devices to   736
highlight different levels of internal headings   745
(ALL CAPS, bold, italic, and underline). Such   755
final touches make the report appear inviting,   764
well organized, and easy to read.   771

Finally, support your report with a list   779
of references from which you paraphrased   788
or directly quoted. Quoting or paraphrasing   796
without giving credit is illegal; further,   805
supporting your report with relevant refer-   814
ences helps to authenticate what you have   822
said.   823

REFERENCES   825

Bemidji State University Writing Resource   834
    Center. "How to Proofread and Edit Your   842
    Writing." [Online] Available: http://   850
    cal.bemidji.msus.edu/WRC/Handouts/   859
    ProofAndEdit.html [1997].   862

Clippinger, Dorinda A. "Write This Way." *The*   872
    Small Business Journal, March 1995.   879

Gibaldi, Joseph. *MLA Handbook for Writers of*   889
    Research Papers. New York: Modern   896
    Language Association, 1995.   902

Harcourt, Jules, and others. *Business Com-*   910
    munication. Cincinnati: South-Western   918
    Publishing Co., 1996.   923

Lesson 3 New Keys: I and R

Objectives:

1. To learn reach technique for I and R.
2. To combine smoothly I and R with all other learned keys.

3A◆ 3
Get Ready to Key
Follow the steps on p. 9.

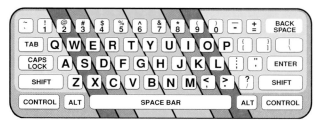

3B◆ 5
Conditioning Practice
each line twice SS; DS between 2-line groups

Practice goals
■ Key each line first at a slow, steady pace, striking and releasing each key quickly.
■ Key each line again at a faster pace; move from key to key quickly–keep insertion point moving steadily.

home keys 1 a;sldkfj a;sldkfj as jak ask fad all dad lads fall
Return twice to DS.

h/e 2 hj hah has had sash hash ed led fed fled sled fell
DS

all keys learned 3 as he fled; ask a lass; she had jade; sell all jak
Return 4 times to quadruple-space (QS) between lesson parts.

3C◆ 5
Speed Building
each line once DS

> **SPACING CUE:**
> To DS when in SS mode, strike **Return/Enter** twice at the end of each line.

> **SPEED CUE:**
> In lines 1-3, quicken the keying pace as you key each letter combination or word when it is repeated within the line.

1 hj hj|ah ah|ha ha|had had|ash ash|has has|had hash
2 ed ed|el el|ed ed|led|eke eke|lee lee|ale kale
3 he he|she she|led led|has has|held held|sled sleds
4 he fled; she led; she had jade; he had a jell sale
5 a jak fell; she held a leek; he has had a sad fall
6 he has ash; she sells jade; as he fell; has a lake
7 she had a fall jade sale; he leads all fall sales;
8 he held a fall kale sale; she sells leeks as a fad

Lesson 69 Unbound Report Assessment

Objectives:

Approx. time: 45'

1. **To assess knowledge of unbound report format.**
2. **To assess unbound report formatting skill.**

69A◆
Keyboard Mastery

Use Skill Builder 5, p. 179, lines 1, 7, and 9, or G on p. A6.

69B◆

Assess Report Skills

Format/key the text shown at right and on p. 183 as a three-page unbound report, errors corrected. Place the reference list on a separate sheet, page 4.

words

ENHANCE YOUR REPORT IMAGE · · · · · · · · · · · · 5

Whether in school or on the job, you must prepare and present 18
reports. Written reports create an image of you--on paper. To achieve the 33
most positive image, written reports must be prepared carefully and pre- 47
sented forcefully. 51

To prepare an excellent report, Clippinger (1995) suggests five 64
equally vital steps that must be taken in the order listed: (1) plan, 78
(2) draft, (3) revise, (4) edit, (5) format. 88

Plan the Report 91

To *plan*, ask: What is **my purpose** for writing, and what is the 104
reader's purpose for reading what I write? The answers become the <u>core</u> 119
of the message. Compose and key the core idea. Then as they come to 133
mind through listening, reading, and thinking, jot (on the computer 146
screen) ideas and facts that are related to the core idea. Next, check the 162
list for missing items (and add them), unneeded items (and delete them), 176
and redundant items (and combine them). Put the items in psychological 191
order (main point followed by details, usually) and arrange them logically 206
(in chronological, geographical, or importance order, for example). 219
Finally, check the list to see that the items are tied together and related 235
to the core idea. When appropriate, use tables, charts, or graphs to 249
condense data; then list only summaries of what the visuals reveal in 263
greater detail. 266

Draft the Message 270

To *draft* or compose the message, pretend that the reader is sitting 284
before you. Write (at the keyboard) as you would talk with that person 298
(level of vocabulary, degree of formality, and so on). Focus on the core of 313
your message as you follow your listed items. Ignore for now such things 328
as grammar, spelling, and style. Complete the entire report in one work 343
session, if possible. If that is not possible, finish at least a major section 359
without stopping (to gain continuity). 367

3D◆ 18

New Keys: I and R

each line twice SS (slowly, then faster); DS between 2-line groups; if time permits, key lines 7-9 again

Technique goals
- curved, upright fingers
- finger-action keystrokes
- eyes on copy

i *Right middle* finger

r *Left index* finger

Follow the *Standard Plan for Learning New Keys* outlined on p. 9.

Learn i

1 k k ik ik is is if if did did aid aid kid kid hail

2 ik ik if if is is kid kid his his lie lie aid aide

3 a kid; a lie; if he; he did; his aide; if a kid is
                                                        DS

Learn r

4 f f rf rf jar jar her her are are ark ark jar jars

5 rf rf re re fr fr jar jar red red her her far fare

6 a jar; a rake; a lark; red jar; hear her; are dark
                                                        DS

Combine i and r

7 fir fir|rid rid|sir sir|ire ire|fire fire|air airs

8 a fir; if her; a fire; is fair; his ire; if she is

9 he is; if her; is far; red jar; his heir; her aide

Quadruple-space (QS) between lesson parts.

3E◆ 19

New-Key Mastery

1. Key the lines once SS with a DS between 2-line groups.
2. Key the lines again at a faster pace.

Technique goals
- fingers deeply curved
- wrists low, but not resting
- hands/arms steady
- eyes on copy as you key

reach review

1 hj ed ik rf hj de ik fr hj ed ik rf jh de ki fr hj

2 he he|if if|all all|fir fir|jar jar|rid rid|as ask
                                                        DS

h/e

3 she she|elf elf|her her|hah hah|eel eel|shed shelf

4 he has; had jak; her jar; had a shed; she has fled
                                                        DS

i/r

5 fir fir|rid rid|sir sir|kid kid|ire ire|fire fired

6 a fir; is rid; is red; his ire; her kid; has a fir
                                                        DS

all keys learned

7 if if|is is|he he|did did|fir fir|jak jak|all fall

8 a jak; he did; ask her; red jar; she fell; he fled
                                                        DS

all keys learned

9 if she is; he did ask; he led her; he has her jar;

10 she has had a jak sale; she said he had a red fir;

68B◆

Assessment: Memo and Letters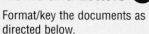

Format/key the documents as directed below.

Document 1
Memo

Top margin: centered vertically
Side margins: default
Date: current year with the date given (- - - -) OR Today's date
Errors: all corrected

TO: Members of Lakeview Chorale	FROM: Cecilia Valdez, Choral	13

TO: Members of Lakeview Chorale │ FROM: Cecilia Valdez, Choral   13
Director │ DATE: November 26, ---- │ SUBJECT: REHEARSALS FOR   24
SOUNDS OF LAKEVIEW   28

Next Monday, formal rehearsals will begin for our holiday program,   42
Sounds of Lakeview.   46

These rehearsals will be held in the auditorium at **2:30** on **Monday,**   60
Wednesday, and Friday afternoons. Each rehearsal is scheduled for two   74
hours. Make plans now for transportation home. If someone is to pick you   89
up, be sure he or she is here **no later than 4:45**.   100

We have an exciting program planned, so arrive on Monday in good voice   114
and with your usual enthusiasm. │ xx   121

. . . .

Document 2
Business Letter

Top margin: centered vertically
Side margins: default
Date: current year with the date given (----) OR Today's date
Errors: all corrected

November 26,---- │ Mrs. Evelyn M. McNeil │ 4582 Campus Dr. │ Fort   12
Worth, TX 76119-1835 │ Dear Mrs. McNeil   19

We invite you to visit our exciting Gallery of Gifts. Gift-giving can be a   34
snap any time of year because of our vast array of gifts "for kids of all   49
ages."   51

What's more, many of our gifts are prewrapped for presentation. All can   65
be packaged and shipped from right here in the store--to anywhere in the   80
world.   82

A catalog of our hottest gift items and a schedule of hours for preferred   96
charge-card customers are enclosed. Please stop in and let us help you   111
select that special gift, or visit our home page (**www.gallerygift.com**)   125
and shop without leaving your home.   132

Cordially yours │ Ms. Carol J. Suess, Manager │ xx │ Enclosures   144

. . . .

Document 3
Personal-Business Letter

Top margin: 2"
Side margins: default
Date: current year with the date given (- - - -) OR Today's date
Errors: all corrected

2299 Riverside Dr. │ Tulsa, OK 74105-3896 │ November 26, ---- │   11
Miss Melissa Monaco │ Fallsington Hall for Women │ 500 Ash St. │   23
Houston, TX 77044-2145 │ Dear Melissa   30

Won't it be wonderful to "close the books" for a few days during term   44
break.   I look forward to seeing you soon after I get home on the 20th.   59

Naturally I remember how much we both liked working on those fantastic   73
musicals during our senior year.   I bought two tickets for the production   88
of *Grease* on the 23d at 8. I hope you can go as my guest.   99

I'm sure many other former Drama Club members will be there, too.   113
Imagine the stories about "college life" that will be shared! Please say   128
you'll go.   130

Cordially │ Adrian Forbes   135

Lesson 4

Objectives:

1. **To improve reach-stroke control and keying speed.**
2. **To improve technique on Space Bar and Return/Enter.**

4A ◆ 3
Get Ready to Key

1. Review the steps for arranging your work area (see p. 2).
2. Review the steps required to ready your equipment.
3. Take good keying position.

■ fingers curved and upright
■ wrists low, but not touching frame of keyboard
■ forearms parallel to slant of keyboard
■ body erect, sitting back in chair
■ feet on floor for balance

4B ◆ 5
Conditioning Practice

each line twice SS; DS between 2-line groups

```
1 a;sldkfj fj dk sl a; jh de ki fr hj ed ik rf fj a;
2 a if is el he la as re led fir did she has jak jar
3 he has fir; she had a jak; a jade jar; a leek sale
                                                   QS
```

4C ◆ 10
Technique: Space Bar

1. Key lines 1-6 once SS; DS between 3-line groups. Space *immediately* after each word.
2. Key the lines again at a faster pace.

Use down-and-in motion

Short, easy words
```
1 if is ha la ah el as re id did sir fir die rid lie
2 as lad lei rah jak had ask lid her led his kid has
3 hah all ire add iris hall fire keel sell jeer fall
                                                   DS
```

Short-word phrases
```
4 if he|he is|if he is|if she|she is|if she is|as is
5 as he is|if he led|if she has|if she did|had a jak
6 as if|a jar lid|all her ads|as he said|a jade fish
                                                   QS
```

4D ◆ 10
Technique: Return

each line twice SS; DS between 2-line groups

```
1 if he is;
2 as if she is;
3 he had a fir desk;
4 she has a red jell jar;
5 he has had a lead all fall;
6 she asked if he reads fall ads;
7 she said she reads all ads she sees;
8 his dad has had a sales lead as he said;
                                         QS
```

Reach out and tap Return/Enter

PRACTICE CUE:

Keep up your pace to the end of the line, return quickly, and begin the new line without a pause or stop.

unit 15

Assessing Word Processing Applications
Lesson 67   Prepare for Assessment

O b j e c t i v e s : | Approx. time: 60' |

1. **To review format features of memos, block letters, and unbound reports.**
2. **To review word processing features learned.**

67A◆
Keyboard Mastery

Use Skill Builder 5, p. 179, lines 1, 2, and 9, or B on p. A6.

67B◆

Review 🖳

1. Key each line at right as shown (omit line numbers); DS. SS lines 8 and 9.
2. Change line 6 to ALL CAPS.
3. Use the Spelling feature; proofread and correct errors.
4. Center text vertically; then view it.

1 *center* GIVE EMPLOYERS A DATA SHEET THEY CAN SCAN
2 Send a *laser* copy printed on **one side <u>only</u>**.
3 Use standard fonts like Times New Roman and Arial.
4 Use **bold**, *italics*, and <u>underline</u> in headings ONLY.
5 *right-align* Use white or light colored paper.
6 List each telephone number on a separate line.
7 These rules compiled by [Your name] on [Today's date].
8 Resumix, Inc. Preparing the Ideal Scannable Resume.
9 [Online] Available: http://www.resumix.com/resume.
hanging indent

67C◆

Assessment Preparation

To prepare for assessment, key selected documents from those listed at the right. Make a list of page numbers to avoid having to return to this page as you work.

Review the placement and spacing of document parts. Also recall how to use any of the following word processing features available on your software: Center (line, page); Bold, Italic, Underline; Change Case; Font;

Date Text; Hyphenation; Spelling; View, Zoom; Alignment: Right, Full; Indent: Hanging, Paragraph.

Memo, p. 130
Business letter, p. 142
Personal-business letter, p. 148 (57G)
Unbound report, pp. 156-157

Lesson 68   Memo and Letter Assessment

O b j e c t i v e s : | Approx. time: 45' |

1. **To assess knowledge of memo and block letter formats.**
2. **To assess memo and letter processing skills.**

68A◆
Keyboard Mastery

Use Skill Builder 5, p. 179, lines 1, 5, and 9, or D on p. A6.

Lesson 68

4E◆ 10
Speed Building: Words

1. Key each line once SS; DS below line 3.
2. Key each line again at a faster pace; QS (4 hard returns) at end of drill.

Fingers curved

Goal: to speed up the combining of letters

```
1 is is|if if|ah ah|he he|el el|irk irk|aid aid|aide
2 as as|ask ask|ad ad|had had|re re|ire ire|are hare
3 if if|fir fir|id id|did did|el el|eel eel|jak jaks
```
                                                          QS

4F◆ 12
Speed Building: Phrases

1. Key each line once SS.
2. Key the lines once more to improve your speed.

Space with right thumb

Use down-and-in motion

Goal: to speed up spacing between words

```
1 ah ha|ah ha|if he|if he|as if|as if|as he|as he is
2 if a|if a|a firla firla jarla jarlirk herlirks her
3 he did|he did|if all|if all|if she led|if she fled
4 a lad|a lad|if her|if her|as his aide|as his aides
```

Enrichment

1. Key the drill once SS at an easy pace to gain control of all your reach-stroke motions. DS between 2-line groups.
2. Key the drill again to speed up your motions and build continuity (keeping the insertion point moving steadily across the screen).

reach review

```
1 hj ed ik rf jh de ki fr jhj ded kik frf hj ed ik ;
2 he if fir sir she jar rid ask led kid his did risk
```

h/e

```
3 he el she elf her led had held desk dash jade fled
4 her dad led; a lad fled; he has jade; she had eel;
```

i/r

```
5 is his kid ski fir rid ire die slid kids fife dike
6 a kid led; she is fair; as her aide; he is a risk;
```

all keys learned

```
7 if a jail; as he fled; risk a lead; has a red sled
8 a jade fish; ask if she slid; she has irked a kid;
```

all keys learned

```
9 as if he did; he asked a lad; his dad has red jars
10 he has a sled; if she has a jar; ask if he is here
```

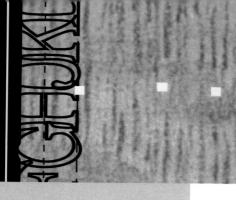

Skill Builder 5

1. Key lines 1-9 once at an easy, steady pace.
2. Key the lines again at a quicker pace.
3. Key a 1' writing on each of lines 7-9; find *gwam* on each writing.
4. Key 1 or 2 more 1' writings on the 2 slower lines.

alphabet	1	Val did enjoy the amazing water tricks of six quaint polar bears.
top row	2	She entered #12-93-45 and #10-87-36 on the computer repair cards.
keypad	3	.. 651.30 829.45 407.62 935.91 258.63 471.58 392.46 174.65 529.46
space bar	4	Fran asks if we wish to go to the lake to fish and dig for clams.
shift keys	5	Jason McNally and Sophia Spurr spoke at the Salt Lake conference.
CAPS LOCK	6	TIME reported highlights of both the AMA and the ADA conventions.
double letters	7	Jeff will give a full account of his success at the fall meeting.
combination	8	You see, only a few men of their town are to join the auto union.
balanced-hand	9	They paid for the six maps of the ancient city with their profit.

| 1 | 2 | 3 | 4 | 5 | 6 | 7 | 8 | 9 | 10 | 11 | 12 | 13 |

1. Key a 1' writing on ¶ 1; find *gwam*.
2. Add 4 *gwam* for a new goal rate. (See checkpoint chart below.)
3. Key two 1' *guided* writings on the ¶ to reach the checkpoint each 1/4'.
4. Key ¶ 2 in the same manner.
5. Key two 3' writings on ¶s 1-2 combined; find *gwam* and count errors on each.

Quarter-Minute Checkpoints				
gwam	1/4'	1/2'	3/4'	Time
20	5	10	15	20
24	6	12	18	24
28	7	14	21	28
32	8	16	24	32
36	9	18	27	36
40	10	20	30	40
44	11	22	33	44
48	12	24	36	48
52	13	26	39	52
56	14	28	42	56

a — all letters used

		3'	5'
If you plan to purchase a computer, determine what you will		4	2	30
use it for before you actually buy it. Will you use it to key		8	5	33
copy, create graphics or spreadsheets, scan photos, or send e-mail?		13	8	36
Are there other requirements?		15	9	37
Next, consider what software programs you need to download		19	11	39
and determine how much hard drive space and random access memory		23	14	42
will be necessary to run them. It is better to buy extra memory		27	16	44
now than to have it installed later.		30	28	46
Finally, choose a backup system. There are several on the		34	21	49
market. Tape, zip, jazz, and optical drives are some that are		38	23	51
available. How often you will use the system and the amount of		43	26	54
data you will back up are the determining factors.		46	28	56

| 1 | 2 | 3 | 4 |
| 1 | 2 | 3 |

Lesson 5 New Keys: O and T

Objectives:
1. **To learn reach technique for O and T.**
2. **To combine smoothly O and T with all other learned keys.**

5A◆ 8
Conditioning Practice

each line twice SS (slowly, then faster); DS between 2-line groups

In Lessons 5-10, the time for the *Conditioning Practice* is changed to 8'. During this time, you are to arrange your work area, prepare your equipment for keying, and practice the lines of the *Conditioning Practice* as directed.

Fingers curved

Fingers upright

home row 1 a sad fall; ask a lass; a jak falls; as a fall ad;

3d row 2 if her aid; all he sees; he irks her; a jade fish;

all keys learned 3 as he fell; he sells fir desks; she had half a jar

5B◆ 20
New Keys: O and T

each line twice SS (slowly, then faster); DS between 2-line groups; if time permits, key lines 7-9 again

o *Right ring* finger

t *Left index* finger

Follow the *Standard Plan for Learning New Keys* outlined on p. 9.

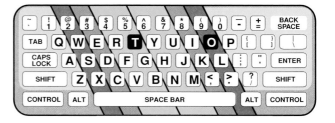

Learn o

1 l l ol ol do do of of so so lo lo old old for fore

2 ol ol of of or or for for oak oak off off sol sole

3 do so; a doe; of old; of oak; old foe; of old oak;

DS

Learn t

4 f f tf tf it it at at tie tie the the fit fit lift

5 tf tf ft ft it it sit sit fit fit hit hit kit kite

6 if it; a fit; it fit; tie it; the fit; at the site

DS

Combine o and t

7 to to|too too|toe toe|dot dot|lot lot|hot hot|tort

8 a lot; to jot; too hot; odd lot; a fort; for a lot

9 of the; to rot; dot it; the lot; for the; for this

QS

L&W

Activity 4:

1. Read at the right the case of the "extra change" error.
2. After considering the comments and suggestions of your friends, what would you do in this situation?
3. Compose/key a paragraph to indicate your choice, how you made it, and why.
4. As a group, discuss the decision(s) reached by various members of the class in terms of *honesty*, *fair play*, and *caring about others*.

Compose (think) as you key

You are looking forward to this weekend because you and your friends have arranged to go to dinner together before separating for other activities: a ball game, a movie, a "mixer." To pay for the dinner, you have collected money from each friend.

The restaurant is upscale, the food very good, and the service excellent. Your server has been friendly and has quickly met all your needs. Your server has not rushed you to finish, so you and your friends have enjoyed conversation and laughter long after the meal ended. It is great that all of you get along so well.

When it is time to go, you ask your server for the check and pay it. When you receive your change and are leaving a tip, you notice that your change is ten dollars more than you should have received.

A discussion takes place among the six of you regarding this error. Various comments and suggestions are made:

1. Keep the money; the server will never know to whom she gave the extra change.

2. Are you lucky! This never happens to me.

3. You have to return the money. If you don't, the server will have to make up the loss of money at the end of the evening.

Several thoughts go through your mind as you listen to the comments of your friends. You know it would be great to have ten extra dollars to share with your friends. What will my friends think if I return the money, or if I keep it? The server has been very pleasant and has worked hard this evening. If I keep the money, is it right to make the server pay for the error? How would I want to be treated if I made the same mistake at my job?

5C◆ 22

New-Key Mastery

1. Key the lines once SS; DS between 2-line groups.
2. Key the lines again at a faster pace.

Technique goals
- curved, upright fingers
- wrists low, but not resting
- down-and-in spacing
- eyes on copy as you key

PRACTICE CUE:

In lines of repeated words (lines 3, 5, and 7), speed up the second keying of each word.

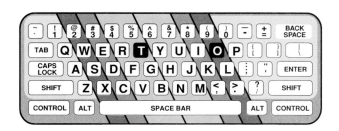

reach review
1 hj ed ik rf ol tf jh de ki fr lo ft hj ed ol rf tf
2 is led fro hit old fit let kit rod kid dot jak sit

h/e
3 he he|she she|led led|had had|see see|has has|seek
4 he led|ask her|she held|has fled|had jade|he leads

i/t
5 it it|fit fit|tie tie|sit sit|kit kit|its its|fits
6 a kit|a fit|a tie|lit it|it fits|it sits|it is fit

o/r
7 or or|for for|ore ore|fro fro|ar oar|roe roe|rode
8 a rod|a door|a rose|or for|her or|he rode|or a rod

space bar
9 of he or it is to if do el odd off too for she the
10 it is|if it|do so|if he|to do|or the|she is|of all

all keys learned
11 if she is; ask a lad; to the lake; for the old jet
12 he or she; for a fit; if she left the; a jak salad

Enrichment

1. Key the drill once SS at an easy pace to gain control of all your reach-stroke motions. DS between 2-line groups.
2. Key the drill again to speed up your motions and build continuity (keeping the insertion point moving steadily across the screen).

reach review
1 hj ed ik rf jhj ded kik frf a;sldkfj a;sldkfj fja;
2 if led ski fir she ire sir jak has did jar kid rid

o/t
3 ol ol|old old|for for|oak oak|ode ode|doe doe|does
4 tf tf|it it|to to|kit kit|the the|fit fit|sit sits

i/r
5 ik ik|if if|it it|fir fir|ski ski|did did|kid kids
6 rf rf|or or|for for|her her|fir fir|rod rod|or for

h/e
7 hj hj|he he|ah ah|ha ha|he he|she she|ash ash|hash
8 ed ed|el el|he he|her her|elk elk|jet jet|she shed

all keys learned
9 of hot kit old sit for jet she oak jar ore lid lot
10 a ski; old oak; too hot; odd jar; for the; old jet

all keys learned
11 she is to ski; is for the lad; ask if she has jade
12 he sold skis for her; she sells jade at their lake

Language & Writing Skills 12

Activity 1:

1. Study the spelling/definitions of the words in the color block at the right.
2. Key the *Learn* line in the first set of sentences.
3. Key the *Apply* lines, choosing the right words to complete each sentence correctly.
4. Key the second set of lines in the same way.
5. Check work; rekey lines containing word-choice errors.

Choose the right word

> **sew** *(vb)* to fasten by stitches
> **so** *(adj/conj)* in the same manner or way; in order that; with the result that
> **sow** *(vb)* to plant seed; scatter; disperse
>
> **raise** *(vb/n)* to lift up; to collect; an increase in amount, as of wages
> **rays** *(n)* beams of energy or light; lines of light from a bright object
> **raze** *(vb)* to tear down; to demolish

Learn 1 He can sew the bags so that we can use them to sow the grass seed.
Apply 2 I can have them (sew, so, sow) the oats if you say (sew, so, sow).
Apply 3 The design is intricate, (sew, so, sow) I can't (sew, so, sow) it now.
Apply 4 She is to (sew, so, sow) in the words "(Sew, So, Sow) seeds of kindness."

Learn 5 The sun's rays caused the flowers to raise their heads.
Learn 6 If we raise the price, will they raze the old building this month?
Apply 7 The (raise, rays, raze) of the sun will (raise, rays, raze) the fog.
Apply 8 After they (raise, rays, raze) the gym, work on a new arena can begin.

Activity 2:

As you key the lines shown at the right, select and key the proper verb shown in parentheses.

Proofread & correct   Subject/Predicate agreement

1 (Wasn't, Weren't) you aware that the matinee began at 2:30 p.m.?
2 Our senior debate team (has, have) won the city championship.
3 A number of our workers (are, is) to receive proficiency awards.
4 Either the coach or an assistant (are, is) to speak at the assembly.
5 Maria (doesn't, don't) know whether she can attend the beach party.
6 Ms. Yamamoto and her mother (are, is) now American citizens.
7 (Was, Were) the director as well as his assistants at the meeting?
8 The number of applicants for admission (are, is) greater this year.
9 The logic behind their main arguments (elude, eludes) me.
10 It (doesn't, don't) matter to me which of the two is elected.

Activity 3:

As you key the lines shown at the right, supply appropriate capitalization and express numbers properly (as words or figures).

Proofread and correct   Capitalization/Number expression

1 "the jury," said the judge, "must reach a unanimous decision."
2 for what percentage of total sales is mrs. rhodes responsible?
3 i need a copy of *the dictionary of composers and their music.*
4 miss valdez told us to go to room eight of corbett hall.
5 the institute of art is at fifth avenue and irving place.
6 "don't you agree," he asked, "that honesty is the best policy?"
7 is the tony award show to be shown on tv on april seventeen?
8 dr. robin j. sousa is to address fbla members in orlando.
9 see page 473 of volume one of *encyclopedia americana.*
10 here is pbc's check #2749 for $83 (less ten percent discount).

Lesson 6 New Keys: N and G

6A◆ 8
Conditioning Practice

each line twice SS (slowly, then faster); DS between 2-line groups

home row 1 has a jak; ask a lad; a fall fad; had a jak salad;

o/t 2 to do it; as a tot; do a lot; it is hot; to dot it

e/i/r 3 is a kid; it is far; a red jar; her skis; her aide

6B◆ 20
New Keys: N and G

each line twice SS (slowly, then faster); DS between 2-line groups; if time permits, key lines 7-9 again

n *Right index* finger

g *Left index* finger

Follow the *Standard Plan for Learning New Keys* outlined on p. 9.

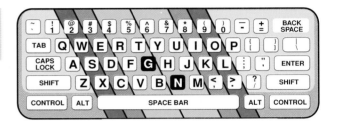

Learn n

1 j j nj nj an an and and end end ant ant land lands

2 nj nj an an en en in in on on end end and and hand

3 an en; an end; an ant; no end; on land; a fine end

Learn g

4 f f gf gf go go fog fog got got fig figs jogs jogs

5 gf gf go go got got dig dig jog jog logs logs golf

6 to go; he got; to jog; to jig; the fog; is to golf

Combine n and g

7 go go|no no|nag nag|ago ago|gin gin|gone gone|long

8 go on; a nag; sign in; no gain; long ago; into fog

9 a fine gig; log in soon; a good sign; lend a hand;

6C◆ 5
Technique: Return

each line twice SS; DS between 2-line groups

PRACTICE CUE:

Keep up your pace to end of line; return quickly and start new line without pause.

Reach out
and tap
Return/Enter

1 she is gone;

2 she got an old dog;

3 she jogs in a dense fog;

4 she and he go to golf at nine;

5 he is a hand on a rig in the north;

Above & Beyond
P R O J E C T

Young Writers' Society

Read the information at right, then do Tasks 10 and 11 as directed below.

Task 10

1. Create a 6 x 9 table with these column titles: **Name, Organization, Topic, Attendance, Rating,** and **Next Year**.
2. Insert the main title: **STANDINGS OF 30TH ANNUAL CAREER DAY SPEAKERS**.
3. Fill in the *Name, Organization,* and *Topic* columns from the information on the notepad at right.
4. Fill in the *Attendance* column (the total number of students addressed by each speaker) and the *Rating* column (derived from students' rating forms) from the notes on the index card.
5. Determine the data for the *Next Year* column on the basis of three criteria:
   a. If attendance was 15 or more *and* the rating was Average to Excellent, fill in YES.
   b. If attendance was 10 or fewer *and* the rating was Fair or Poor, fill in NO.
   c. For all others, fill in MAYBE.

Task 11

Prepare a memo to the teacher who will chair next year's Career Day program committee. Use the copy at right and the information below.

1. Insert a 2 x 2 table (no titles). Fill in the name and organization for each YES from your 6 x 9 table.
2. Insert a table to show the name and organization for each MAYBE from your 6 x 9 table.

Career Day is over, but follow-up remains to be done. One important follow-up task is giving next year's chairperson some data about this year's speakers. That way, the planning committee can ask students' favorite speakers to return for the 31st Annual Career Day.

Young Writers' Society   Notes

1. Mr. Jack L. Day—Weinberg & Associates—"Job Interviews: What to Say After Hello"
2. Mrs. M. Kathryn Lawler—MKL Meeting Management—"Say It with Slides"
3. Miss Mie-Yun Lee—Word Tailor—"Step Write Up!"
4. Mr. Lyle Schaber—CSR Consultants—"Talking to Your Computer: Voice Recognition and Writing"
5. Mr. Domonique A. Smith—Towne Properties, Inc.—"Turn Your Career Path into a Two-Lane Highway"
6. Ms. Victoria Veneziano—Sharp Shot Photography—"Resumes with Winning Ways"
7. Ms. Sabrina Wells—Biz-Write Services—"E-Mail Etiquette"

Attendance / Rating		
Day	19	Fair
Lawler	10	Poor
Lee	23	Fair
Schaber	17	Excellent
Smith	28	Fair
Veneziano	9	Poor
Wells	15	Average

TO: Ms. Monica Iberra-Burke, Teacher | FROM: **[Your Name]**, Young Writers' Society | DATE: **[Today]** | SUBJECT: 31ST ANNUAL CAREER DAY PROGRAM

(¶) On the basis of students' ratings of Career Day speakers this year, the following individuals are recommended to conduct sessions again next year:

Insert table described in Step 1 at left.

(¶) Your committee may want to invite the following persons back next year as members of a panel or presentation team:

Insert table described in Step 2 at left.

(¶) For your information, the student attendance sheets and evaluation forms are attached.

(¶) No. 31 is sure to be a success with you in charge!

6D ◆ 17

New-Key Mastery

1. Key the lines once SS; DS between 2-line groups.
2. Key the lines again at a faster pace.

Technique goals

- curved, upright fingers
- wrists low, but not resting
- quick-snap keystrokes
- down-and-in spacing
- eyes on copy as you key

reach review
1 a;sldkfj ed ol rf hj tf nj gf lo de jh ft nj fr a;
2 he jogs; an old ski; do a log for; she left a jar;

n/g
3 an an|go go|in in|dig dig|and and|got got|end ends
4 go to; is an; log on; sign it; and golf; fine figs

space bar
5 if if|an an|go go|of of|or or|he he|it it|is is|do
6 if it is|is to go|he or she|to do this|of the sign

all keys learned
7 she had an old oak desk; a jell jar is at the side
8 he has left for the lake; she goes there at eight;

all keys learned
9 she said he did it for her; he is to take the oars
10 sign the list on the desk; go right to the old jet

Enrichment

each line twice SS; DS between 2-line groups; QS after each grouping

Lines 1-3
curved, upright fingers; steady, easy pace

Lines 4-7
space immediately after each word; down-and-in motion of thumb

Lines 8-12
maintain pace to end of line; return quickly and start new line immediately

Lines 13-16
speed up the second keying of each repeated word or phrase; think words

Reach review

1 nj nj gf gf ol ol tf tf ik ik rf rf hj hj ed ed fj
2 go fog an and got end jog ant dog ken fig fin find
3 go an on and lag jog flag land glad lend sign hand

Spacing

4 if an it go is of do or to as in so no off too gin
5 ah ha he or if an too for and she jog got hen then
6 he is to go|if it is so|is to do it|if he is to go
7 she is to ski on the lake; he is also at the lake;

Returning

8 he is to go;
9 she is at an inn;
10 he goes to ski at one;
11 he is also to sign the log;
12 she left the log on the old desk

Keying short words and phrases

13 do do|it it|an an|is is|of of|to to|if if|or or or
14 he he|go go|in in|so so|at at|no no|as as|ha ha ha
15 to do|to do|it is|it is|of it|of it|is to|is to do
16 she is to do so; he did the sign; ski at the lake;

Lesson 66 Tables: Mastery and Assessment

Objectives:

1. **To format tables with multiple features.**
2. **To build skill in processing tables.**

66A◆
Keyboard Mastery

Use Skill Builder 4, p. 166, lines 1, 8, and 9, or P on p. A7.

66B◆

Table Mastery

Tab technique goals
- Reach quickly with the little finger.
- Keep other fingers near the home keys.
- Keep eyes on copy.
- Do not pause before or after tapping the Tab key.

1. Take a 3' writing on Model 2, p. 168. Before timing starts, create the table but do not fill it in.
2. When time is up, use the Spelling feature; then proofread and correct all errors.
3. Select the *entire* table and copy it; then paste it on a new page.
4. In the copy, format the cells to look like the model.
5. In your original table, select the *entire* table; delete all text from the cells.
6. In your second table, select and *delete the entire table*.
7. Take another 3' writing on Model 2, filling in the table that remains on the screen.

66C◆

Table Assessment

Table 1

Number type: General (default)
1. Create and fill in a table.
2. Center table horizontally; center copy vertically in all cells; center copy horizontally in rows 1-2 and column A.
3. Change column widths: A, 0.75"; B, 2.0"; and C, 1.25".
4. Proofread and correct all errors.

words

PULITZER PRIZES IN POETRY			5
Mid-1990s			7
Year	Poem or Collection	Author	14
1993	The Wild Iris	Gluck	19
1994	Neon Vernacular	Komunyakaa	25
1995	Simple Truth	Levine	30
1996	Dream of the Unified Field	Graham	38
1997	Alive Together	Mueller	44
Source: *The New York Times Almanac*, 1998.			52

Table 2

Number type: General (default)
1. Create and fill in a table.
2. Center table horizontally; center copy vertically in all cells; center copy horizontally in rows 1-2 and column B.
3. Change column widths: A, 1.5"; B, 0.5"; and C, 1". Change the height of row 1 to 0.75".
4. Proofread and correct all errors.

TOP FIVE CONCERT ~~S~~ *TOURS*			5
< # OF ALL TIMES			7
Performe ~~R~~	Year	Gross Revenue △	14
Rolling Stones	1994	$121,200,000	20
Pink Floyd	1994	103,500,000	26
Rolling Stones	1989	98,000,000	32
Eagle △s	1994	79,400,00 ∧	37
New Kids ~~in~~ the Block	1 990	74,100,000	44
Source: *The Wall Street Journal Almanac* ∧ 1998.			52

Lesson 7 New Keys: Left Shift and . (Period)

Objectives:

1. **To learn reach technique for Left Shift and . (period).**
2. **To combine smoothly Left Shift and . (period) with all other learned keys.**

Finger-action keystrokes

Down-and-in spacing

Quick out-and-tap return

7A◆ 8
Conditioning Practice
each line twice SS (slowly, then faster); DS between 2-line groups

reach review 1 ed ik rf ol gf hj tf nj de ki fr lo fg jh ft jn a;

space bar 2 or is to if an of el so it go id he do as in at on

all keys learned 3 he is; if an; or do; to go; a jak; an oak; of all;

7B◆ 20
New Keys: Left Shift and . (Period)
each line twice SS (slowly, then faster); DS between 2-line groups; if time permits, rekey lines 7-9

Left Shift *Left little* finger

. (period) *Right ring* finger

SHIFTING CUE:
Shift, strike key, and release both in a quick 1-2-3 count.

SPACING CUE:
Space once after . following abbreviations and initials. Do not space after . within abbreviations. Space twice after . at end of a sentence except at line endings. There, return without spacing.

Learn Left Shift key

1 a a Ja Ja Ka Ka La La Hal Hal Kal Kal Jae Jae Lana

2 Kal rode; Kae did it; Hans has jade; Jan ate a fig

3 I see that Jake is to aid Ki at the Oak Lake sale.

Learn . (period)

4 l l .l .l fl. fl. ed. ed. ft. ft. rd. rd. hr. hrs.

5 .l .l fl. fl. hr. hr. e.g. e.g. i.e. i.e. in. ins.

6 fl. ft. hr. ed. rd. rt. off. fed. ord. alt. asstd.

Combine Left Shift and . (period)

7 I do. Ian is. Ola did. Jan does. Kent is gone.

8 Hal did it. I shall do it. Kate left on a train.

9 J. L. Han skis on Oak Lake; Lt. Haig also does so.

65D
Three-Column
Tables with Amounts

Top margin: 2" for Tables 1-3

Table 1

Number type: Text

1. Create and fill in a 3 by 9 table.
2. Right-align the body of columns B and C; center copy in rows 1-3 and cell A9.
3. Adjust cell height and width for appearance; center the table horizontally.

Underline column titles and last amounts if gridlines do not print. (This note applies to all tables.)

Table 2

Number type: Currency (may insert $ as first character in each amount)

1. Create and fill in a table. If available, use the Number Type feature instead of keying the $'s, commas, decimal points, and 00's.
2. Center and bold titles.
3. Adjust column widths. If the title wraps, put only the date on the second line.

Table 3

Number type: Amount (arrangement of $'s may differ from copy at right)

1. Create a table for the data shown at right. If available, use the Number Type feature: Key decimal points; but do not key $'s, commas, or 00's.
2. Right-align the body of all columns; full-align the source note.
3. Vertically, use center alignment in rows 1-3.
4. Adjust height and width. Create two-line column titles (insert hard returns) if you wish.

words

UNITED WAY CONTRIBUTIONS
In Thousands

Department	Goal	Final
Accounting/Credit	$ 4.5	$ 5.0
Human Resources	3.8	3.9
Manufacturing/Shipping	5.6	7.1
Marketing/Sales	9.4	10.2
Purchasing	2.0	2.7
Total	$ 25.3	$ 28.9

5
8
13
19
23
30
36
41
45

Operating Statement for Period Ending January 31, ----

	Budget	Actual
Income	$ 27,170.00	$ 28,735.00
Expenses	22,391.00	19,998.00
Net Profit or Loss	$ 4,779.00	$ 8,737.00

11
14
20
26
28
34

GROWTH IN SAVINGS
Interest Compounded Quarterly at Six Percent (6%)

Monthly Savings	End of 5 Years	End of 10 Years
$5.00	$350.32	$822.16
$10.00	$700.47	$1,644.32
$25.00	$1,751.62	$4,110.79
$35.00	$2,452.26	$5,755.11
$50.00	$3,503.24	$8,221.59

3
13
23
27
32
38
43
49

Source: Anne Scott Daugherty and others, *Introduction to Business* (Cincinnati: South-Western Publishing Co., 1992), p. 452.

60
76

7C◆ 17
New-Key Mastery

1. Key the lines once SS; DS between 2-line groups.
2. Key the lines again at a faster pace.

Technique goals
- curved, upright fingers
- finger-action keystrokes
- quiet hands/arms
- out-and-down shifting

TECHNIQUE CUE:
Eyes on copy except when you lose your place.

abbrev./ initials	1 He said ft. for feet; rd. for road; fl. for floor.
	2 Lt. Hahn let L. K. take the old gong to Lake Neil.
3d row emphasis	3 Lars is to ask at the old store for a kite for Jo.
	4 Ike said he is to take the old road to Lake Heidi.
key words	5 a an or he to if do it of so is go for got old led
	6 go the off aid dot end jar she fit oak and had rod
key phrases	7 if so|it is|to do|if it|do so|to go|he is|to do it
	8 to the|and do|is the|got it|if the|for the|ask for
all letters learned	9 Ned asked her to send the log to an old ski lodge.
	10 O. J. lost one of the sleds he took off the train.

7D◆ 5
Technique: Space Bar and Return

1. Key each line once SS; DS at end of line 7.
2. Key the drill again at a faster pace if time permits.

SPACING CUE:
Quickly strike **Space Bar** *immediately* after last letter in the word.

1 Jan is to sing.

2 Karl is at the lake.

3 Lena is to send the disk.

4 Lars is to jog to the old inn.

5 Hanna took the girls to a ski lake.

6 Hal is to take the old list to his desk.

7 Lana is to take the jar to the store at nine.

Return and start each new line quickly.

Enrichment

1. Key each line once SS; DS between groups.
2. Rekey the drill at a faster pace if time permits.

PRACTICE CUE:
In lines 4-7, keep insertion point moving steadily—no stops or pauses within the line.

Spacing/Shifting
1 K. L. Jakes is to see Lt. Hahn at Oak Lake at one.
2 Janet Harkins sent the sales sheet to Jack Hansen.
3 Karla Kent is to go to London to see Laska Jolson.

Keying easy sentences
4 Kae is to go to the lake to fish off an old skiff.
5 Joel is to ask his good friend to go to the shore.
6 Lara and her dad took eight girls for a long hike.
7 Kent said his dad is to sell the oak and ash logs.

Lesson 65 Tables with Amounts and Totals

Objectives:

1. To process tables with column titles and totals.
2. To improve skill in processing simple tables.
3. To process 3-column tables.

65A◆
Keyboard Mastery

Use Skill Builder 4, p. 166, lines 1, 7, and 9, or O on p. A7.

65B◆
Tables with Multiple Features

Table 1

Top margin: 2"

1. Create and fill in a 3 by 9 table.
2. Vertically center all cells.
3. Center-align row 1, columns A and C, and cell B2; full-align row 9.
4. Bold rows 1 and 2.
5. Adjust cell width and height attractively; center the table horizontally.

Table 2

Top margin: 2"

1. Create a table and fill in the data shown at the right.
2. Center-align and bold copy in rows 1-3 and cell A11; right-align the body of column B. Center all cells vertically.
3. Adjust width and height of cells; make the main title and the longest entry wrap to 2 lines. Center table horizontally.

If your software does not print gridlines, underline the last entry in column B. The line should be as long as the six characters in the total.

			words
HEISMANN TROPHY WINNERS			5
Year	Player	College	9
1992	Gino Toretta	Miami (FL)	15
1993	Charlie Ward	Florida State	21
1994	Rashaan Salaam	Colorado	27
1995	Eddie George	Ohio State	33
1996	Danny Wuerffel	Florida	39
1997	Charles Woodson	Michigan	45

Sources: *New York Times Almanac*, 1998. CBS Sportswire at http://www.sportsline.com, 6 February, 1998. 53 / 62 / 65

		words
HOW FAMILIES SPEND THEIR INCOME		6
Showing Percent of Total		11
Item	Percent	15
Housing	31.3%	17
Transportation	22.2	22
Food	15.8	24
Insurance and Retirement Plans	9.4	31
Apparel, Services	6.1	36
Savings	4.3	38
Other	10.9	41
Total	100.0%	43

65C◆ ⬥FEATURE
Number Types

Read the copy at right. Determine if your software has this feature; if so, learn how to use it.

Your word processing software may permit you to specify how numbers are to be displayed in a table. Not all packages do this. In some programs, though, you can specify percents, dollars, and negative numbers, for example. When used, this feature causes appropriate symbols, such as % and $ and parentheses around negative numbers, to appear automatically. The feature also eliminates the need to key commas in large amounts, key zeros after a decimal point, or align decimal points in decimal numbers. **Note:** For the tables that follow, directions indicate the number type.

Lesson 8

Objectives:
1. **To improve use of Space Bar, Left Shift key, and Return/Enter.**
2. **To improve keying speed on words, phrases, and sentences.**

8A ◆ 8
Conditioning Practice

each line twice SS (slowly, then faster); DS between 2-line groups; if time permits, practice each line again

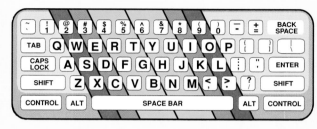

Space once.

reach review 1 ik rf ol ed nj gf hj tf .1 ft. i.e. e.g. rt. J. L.
spacing   2 a an go is or to if he and got the for led kit lot
left shift   3 I got it. Hal has it. Jan led Nan. Kae is gone.

8B ◆ 8
Keyboard Mastery

each line once SS; DS between 2-line groups; QS at end of drill

Technique goals
- curved, upright fingers
- wrists low, but not resting
- quick-snap keystrokes
- finger reaches; hands and arms steady

h/e   1 hj ed jhj ded ha el he she led had eke hal ale die
      2 Heidi had a good lead at the end of the first set.
                                                        DS
i/r   3 ik rf kik frf is or sir ire ore his risk fire ride
      4 Kier is taking a high risk if he rides that horse.
                                                        DS
o/t   5 ol tf lol ftf so it of too oft hot toe lot the old
      6 Ola has lost the list she took to that food store.
                                                        DS
n/g   7 nj gf jnj fgf go an got and nag gin hang gone sign
      8 Lang and she are going to sing nine songs at noon.
                                                        DS
left   9 Oak Lake; N. J. Karis; Lt. L. J. Oates; Lara Nador
shift/. 10 J. K. Larkin is going to Idaho to see Linda Jakes.

8C ◆ 4
Technique: Return

each line once SS; DS between 2-line groups

> **RETURN CUE:**
> Keep up your pace to the end of the line; return immediately; start the new line without pausing.

1 Nan has gone to ski;
2 she took a train at nine.

3 Janet asked for the disk;
4 she is to take it to the lake.

5 Karl said he left at the lake
6 a file that has the data she needs.

7 Nadia said she felt ill as the ski
8 lift left to take the girls to the hill.

Keep eyes on copy as you return.

Tables with Secondary Titles

Top margin: 2" for Tables 1-3

Table 1

1. Create a table and fill in the data shown at the right.
2. Center the text in rows 1 and 2 and in column B.
3. Change column widths to fit the entries (about 2.5" and 0.75").
4. Make row height about 0.5" (36 points) for rows 1 and 2; about 0.33" (24 points) for rows 3-7.
5. Center table horizontally.
6. Proofread and correct errors.

Table 2

1. Create a 2 by 11 table; join the cells in rows 1, 2, and 11.
2. Fill in the data shown at the right.
3. Adjust column widths and row heights to fit the entries. DS two-line titles; SS the source note.
4. Center-align the titles and column B; use full alignment for the source note.
5. Proofread and correct all errors.

Table 3

1. Create a table and fill in the data at right.
2. Center copy in rows 1, 2, and cells A3 and B3 and change the font to Arial Black or another choice.
3. Center the table vertically and horizontally.

Note: If your software does not print gridlines, underline the column titles.

words

FEDERAL SERVICE ACADEMIES	5
By Year Founded	9
U.S. Military Academy, 1802	14
U.S. Naval Academy 1845	19
U.S. Coast Guard Academy 1876	25
U.S. Merchant Marine Academy 1943	32
U.S. Air Force Academy 1954	37

TOP ALL-TIME GRAMMY WINNERS		6
With Total Awards Won		10
Sir George Solti	30	14
Quincy jones	26	17
Vladimir Horowitz	(52)	22
Henry Mancinni	20	25
Steve Wonder	17	28
Leonard Bernstein	16	33
Paul Simon	16	35
John Williams	16	39
Source: USA Today, March 3, 1995. *ital.*		46

summer reading list		4
Read at Least ③ sp.		8
Author	Title	12
Dante Alighieri	The Divine Comedy	20
Charles Baudelaire	Les Fleurs du mal	26
Robert Frost	The Road Not Taken	33
Victor Hugo	Les Miserables	38
Niccolo Machiavelli	The Prince	44
William Shakespeare	Measure for Measure	52

8D◆ 10
Technique: Space Bar and Left Shift

each line twice SS; DS between 2-line groups

Goals
- to reduce the pause between words
- to reduce the time taken to shift/strike key/release when making capital letters

Down-and-in spacing

Out-and-down shifting

Upright fingers

Space Bar (Space *immediately* after each word.)

1 if is an he go is or ah to of so it do el id la ti

2 an el| go to| if he| of it| is to| do the| for it| and so

3 if she is| it is the| all of it| go to the| for an oak

Left Shift key (Shift; strike key; release both quickly.)

4 Lt. Ho said he left the skiff at Ord Lake for her.

5 Jane or Hal is to go to Lake Heed to see Kate Orr.

6 O. J. Halak is to ask for her at Jahn Hall at one.

8E◆ 20
Speed Building

each line twice SS (slowly, then faster); DS between 2-line groups

Correct finger curvature

Correct finger alignment

Key words (*Think, say,* and *key* the words.)

1 an the did oak she for off tie got and led jar all

2 go end air her dog his aid rid sit and fir ask jet

3 talk side jell gold fled sign stir fork high shall

Key phrases (*Think, say,* and *key* the phrases.)

4 to do| it is| of an| if he| is to| or do| to it| if he is

5 to aid| if she| he did| of the| to all| is for| is a tie

6 is to ask| is to aid| he or she| to rig it| if she did

Key sentences (Strike keys at a brisk, steady pace.)

7 Joan is to go to the lake to get her old red skis.

8 Les asked for a list of all the old gold she sold.

9 Laska said she left the old disk list on his desk.

O b j e c t i v e s :

> **Approx. time: 75'**

1. **To review parts and formatting of simple tables.**
2. **To format tables with secondary titles and source notes.**
3. **To change width of table columns and height of table rows.**

64A◆

Keyboard Mastery

Use Skill Builder 4, p. 166, lines 1, 5, and 9, or N on p. A7.

64B◆

Table with Secondary Title

Top margin: 2"

1. Create a table and fill in the data at the right. (Center the secondary title in a separate row.)
2. Center the data in column B.
3. Proofread and correct all errors.
4. Keep the table open for use in **64C**.

words

OLDEST AMERICAN UNIVERSITIES		5
Founded Before 1750		10
Harvard	1636	13
Yale	1701	15
Pennsylvania	1740	18
Denver	1743	21
Princeton	1746	24
Washington and Lee	1749	29

64C◆ **FEATURE**

Width and Height

1. Read the copy at right.
2. Learn how to change column width and row height using your software.
3. Follow the directions at the right to revise two of your tables.

All columns are the same width in a newly created table. Some software allows you to set column width at the same time you create the table. Otherwise, the Table feature can be used to change the width of one or more columns, or you can change column width simply by dragging (with the mouse) gridlines to the left or right.

The Table feature also allows you to set a precise depth, or height, for rows. Inserting hard returns is another way to make a row deeper.

1. In the table above (**64B**), change the column widths so that each column is only slightly wider than the longest entry in the column.
2. Center the revised table horizontally.
3. Open the table you formatted in **63D**.
4. Change both columns to a width of 1.75".
5. Change the title cell to a height of 0.5" (36 points).
6. Change rows 2-7 to a height of about 0.33" (24 points).
7. In all cells, center entries vertically; center the table horizontally on the page.

Select cell height and width

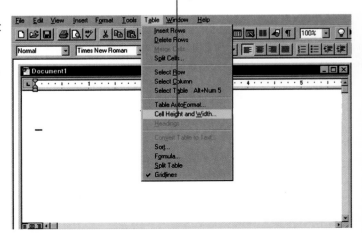

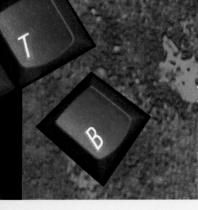

Lesson 9 New Keys: U and C

9A◆   8
Conditioning Practice

each line twice SS (slowly, then faster); DS between 2-line groups

reach review
1 nj gf ol rf ik ed .l tf hj fr ki ft jn de lo fg l.

space bar
2 an do in so to go fan hen log gin tan son not sign

left shift
3 Olga has the first slot; Jena is to skate for her.

9B◆   20
New Keys: U and C

each line twice SS (slowly, then faster); DS between 2-line groups; if time permits, repeat lines 7-9

u *Right index* finger

c *Left middle* finger

Follow the *Standard Plan for Learning New Keys* outlined on p. 9.

Learn u

1 j j uj uj us us us jug jug jut jut due due fur fur

2 uj uj jug jug sue sue lug lug use use lug lug dues

3 a jug; due us; the fur; use it; a fur rug; is just

Learn c

4 d d cd cd cod cod cog cog tic tic cot cot can cans

5 cd cd cod cod ice ice can can code code dock docks

6 a cod; a cog; the ice; she can; the dock; the code

Combine u and c

7 cud cud cut cuts cur curs cue cues duck ducks clue

8 a cud; a cur; to cut; the cue; the cure; for luck;

9 use a clue; a fur coat; take the cue; cut the cake

63D ◆ FEATURE

Format Cells

1. Read the copy at right.
2. Learn how to format a cell, column, row, and table using your software.
3. Follow the directions at right below to revise the table (63C).

Note: The columns of your table are the original width. Leave them this way for now.

*Remember, *justification* is another word for horizontal alignment.

Within cells, data can be left-aligned (default), centered, or right-aligned.★ Vertically, data can be aligned at the top, center, or bottom of cells if the cells contain more than one line space. You can set alignment for each cell or set it once for a column, row, or an entire table.

You can also choose the appearance (bold, italic) and font of text for a cell, column, row, or table.

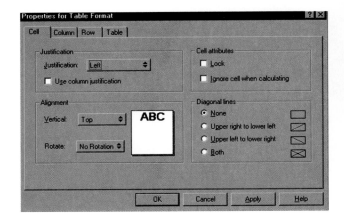

1. Center the table title.
2. In column B, center data horizontally.

3. Save the table to use later.

63E ◆

Two-Column Tables

Table 1

Top margin: 2"

1. Create a 2 by 8 table and fill in the data shown at the right.
2. Join cells A1 and B1.
3. Center and bold the title.
4. Proofread and correct errors.

Note: To move from right to left or bottom to top in a table, use the arrow keys.

Table 2

Top margin: 2"

1. Count the number of rows needed for the data shown at the right.
2. Create a 2-column table and fill in the data.
3. Center the title and change its font to Arial, bold.
4. Proofread and correct errors.

Table 3

1. Copy Table 2; paste it to a new page.
2. Center the table vertically.

words

SPELLING DEMONS		3
adequate	customer	7
appropriate	electrical	11
categories	eligible	15
compliance	employees	20
compliment	implemented	24
correspondence	installation	30
corporate	monitoring	34

MORE SPELLING DEMONS		4
opportunity	prior	8
permanent	pursuant	12
personnel	received	15
participants	reference	20
patient	similar	23
possibility	successful	28
previously	sufficient	32

9C ◆ 17
New-Key Mastery

1. Key the lines once SS; DS between 2-line groups.
2. Key the lines again at a faster pace.

Technique goals
- reach up without moving hands away from you
- reach down without moving hands toward your body
- use quick-snap keystrokes

3d/1st rows	1	in cut nut ran cue can cot fun hen car urn den cog
	2	Nan is cute; he is curt; turn a cog; he can use it
left shift and .	3	Kae had taken a lead. Jack then cut ahead of her.
	4	I said to use Kan. for Kansas and Ore. for Oregon.
key words	5	and cue for jut end kit led old fit just golf coed
	6	an due cut such fuss rich lack turn dock turf curl
key phrases	7	an urn|is due|to cut|for us|to use|cut off|such as
	8	just in|code it|turn on|cure it|as such|is in luck
all keys learned	9	Nida is to get the ice; Jacki is to call for cola.
	10	Ira is sure that he can go there in an hour or so.

9D ◆ 5
Technique: Space Bar and Left Shift

Key the lines once SS; DS between 3-line groups. Keep hand movement to a minimum.

	1	Ken said he is to sign the list and take the disk.
space bar	2	It is right for her to take the lei if it is hers.
	3	Jae has gone to see an old oaken desk at the sale.
	4	He said to enter Oh. for Ohio and Kan. for Kansas.
left shift	5	It is said that Lt. Li has an old jet at Lake Ida.
	6	L. N. is at the King Hotel; Harl is at the Leland.

Enrichment

1. Key each line once SS; DS between 2-line groups.
2. If time permits, key the lines again at a faster pace.

PRACTICE CUE:
Try to reduce hand movement and the tendency of unused fingers to fly out or follow reaching finger.

u/c	1	uj cd uc juj dcd cud cut use cog cue urn curl luck
	2	Huck can use the urn for the social at the church.
n/g	3	nj gf nj gin can jog nick sign nigh snug rung clog
	4	Nan can jog to the large sign at the old lake gin.
all keys learned	5	nj gf uj cd ol tf ik rf hj ed an go or is to he .l
	6	Leona has gone to ski; Jack had left here at nine.
all keys learned	7	an or is to he go cue for and jak she all use curt
	8	Nick sells jade rings; Jahn got one for good luck.

Lesson 63 Two-Column Tables

Objectives:

Approx. time: 75'

1. **To learn the parts and format of simple tables.**
2. **To format tables using word processing features.**

63A◆
Keyboard Mastery

Use Skill Builder 4, p. 166, lines 1, 2, and 9, or M on p. A7.

63B◆ 🔲 FEATURE

Create and Fill a Table

1. Read the copy at right.
2. Learn how to create and fill in a table on your software.
3. With a 2" top margin, create a "2 by 7" table (2 columns, 7 rows). Keep the table open for use in **63C**.

The **Table** feature displays a grid for arranging copy in columns and rows. Tables consist of vertical columns (named A, B, C, etc.) and horizontal rows (named 1, 2, 3, etc.). The crossing of columns and rows makes "windows" called *cells* (named A1, B2, C3, etc.). **Note:** Cell names do not appear on screen in some software.

When text is keyed into a cell, it wraps around in that cell—instead of wrapping around to the next row. A line space is added to the cell each time the text wraps around.

When filling in cells, use the Tab key or right arrow key to move from cell to cell in a row and from one row to the next. (Striking Return/Enter simply inserts a blank line space in the cell.) To move around in a filled-in table, use the arrow keys, Tab, or the mouse (click the desired cell).

Insert or create a table

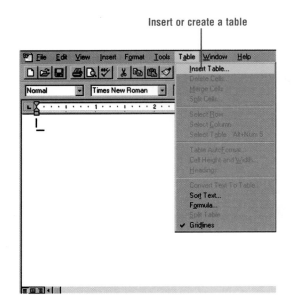

63C◆ 🔲 FEATURE

Join (Merge)

1. Read the copy at right.
2. Learn to join table cells using your software.
3. In the table on your screen (**63B**), join cells A1 and B1.
4. Fill in the data shown in the table on p. 168 (top). (Data in every cell will be left-aligned.) Keep the table open for use in **63D**.

Use the **Join** or **Merge** feature to merge two or more cells into one cell. This feature is useful whenever information in a table spans more than one row or column. The title, for example, spans all columns.

Join or merge cells

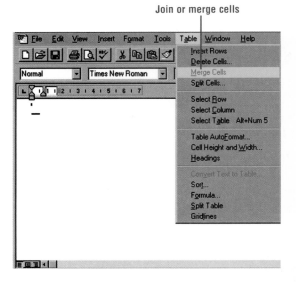

Lesson 10 New Keys: W and Right Shift

O b j e c t i v e s :
1. **To learn reach technique for W and Right Shift.**
2. **To combine smoothly W and Right Shift with other learned keys.**

10A◆ 8
Conditioning Practice

each line twice SS (slowly, then faster); DS between 2-line groups

reach review 1 a;sldkfj a;sldkfj uj cd ik rf nj ed hj tf ol gf .1

u/c 2 us cod use cut sue cot jut cog nut cue con lug ice

all letters learned 3 Hugh has just taken a lead in a race for a record.

10B◆ 20
New Keys: W and Right Shift

each line twice SS (slowly, then faster); DS between 2-line groups; if time permits, rekey lines 7-9

w *Left ring* finger

Right Shift *Right little* finger

SHIFTING CUE:
Shift, strike key, and release both in a quick 1-2-3 count.

Follow the *Standard Plan for Learning New Keys* outlined on p. 9.

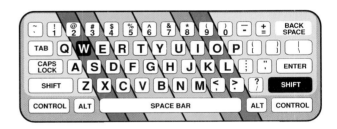

Learn w

1 s s ws ws sow sow wow wow low low how how cow cows

2 sw sw ws ws ow ow now now row row own own tow tows

3 to sow; is how; so low; to own; too low; is to row

Learn Right Shift key

4 A; A; Al Al; Cal Cal; Ali or Flo; Di and Sol left.

5 Ali lost to Ron; Cal lost to Elsa; Di lost to Del.

6 Tina has left for Tucson; Dori can find her there.

Combine w and Right Shift

7 Dodi will ask if Willa went to Town Center at two.

8 Wilf left the show for which he won a Gower Award.

9 Walt will go to Rio on a golf tour with Wolf Towe.

2" top margin or center table vertically

Title

NEW *PERISCOPE* STAFF

Editor	Kristi Stojko
Associate Editor	Brian Poole
Business Manager	Anita Solena
Photography/Layout	Malik Fredericks
Advertising/Sales	Xen Chueng
Advisor	Marcella Proust

Body

Shown in 12-point Times New Roman, photoreduced.

Two-Column Table Centered Horizontally

In some word processing software, gridlines appear between columns and rows as a default condition.

PULITZER PRIZES IN DRAMA		
Since 1990		
Year	Play	Playwright
1990	The Piano Lesson	August Wilson
1991	Lost in Yonkers	Neil Simon
1992	The Kentucky Cycle	Robert Schenkkan
1993	Angels in America: Millenium Approaches	Tony Kushner
1994	Three Tall Women	Edward Albee
1995	The Young Man from Atlanta	Horton Foote
1996	Rent	Jonathan Larson
1997	No Award	
1998	How I Learned to Drive	Paula Vogel
Sources: *New York Times Almanac*, 1998. The Internet: http//www.pulitzer.org/year/1998.		

Title
Secondary Title
Column Titles
Body
Gridlines
Source Note

Three-Column Table with Multiple Features   **Shown in 12-point Times New Roman, photoreduced.**

10C◆ 17

New-Key Mastery

1. Key the lines once SS; DS between 2-line groups.
2. Key the lines again at a faster pace.

PRACTICE CUE:

Key at a steady pace; space quickly after each word; keep the insertion point moving steadily.

Goal: finger-action reaches; quiet hands and arms

w and right shift	1 Dr. Rowe is in Tulsa now; Dr. Cowan will see Rolf.
	2 Gwinn took the gown to Golda Swit on Downs Circle.
n/g	3 to go|go on|no go|an urn|dug in|and got|and a sign
	4 He is to sign for the urn to go on the high chest.
key words	5 if ow us or go he an it of own did oak the cut jug
	6 do all and for cog odd ant fig rug low cue row end
key phrases	7 we did|for a jar|she is due|cut the oak|he owns it
	8 all of us|to own the|she is to go|when he has gone
all keys learned	9 Jan and Chris are gone; Di and Nick get here soon.
	10 Doug will work for her at the new store in Newton.

10D◆ 5

Technique: Spacing with Punctuation

each line once DS

SPACING CUE:

Do not space after an internal period in an abbreviation; space once after each period following initials.

No space   Space once.

1 Use i.e. for that is; cs. for case; ck. for check.
2 Dr. Wong said to use wt. for weight; in. for inch.
3 R. D. Roth has used ed. for editor; Rt. for Route.
4 Wes said Ed Rowan got an Ed.D. degree last winter.

Enrichment

1. Key each pair of lines once SS.
2. Key each even-numbered line again to increase speed.

Technique goals

- steady hands/arms
- finger-action keystrokes
- unused fingers curved, upright over home keys
- eyes on copy as you key

u/c	1 uj cd uc cut cut cue cue use use cod cod dock dock
	2 Jud is to cut the corn near the dock for his aunt.
w and right shift	3 Don and Willa|Dot or Wilda|R. W. Gowan|Dr. Wilford
	4 Dr. Wold will set the wrist of Sgt. Wills at noon.
left shift and .	5 Jane or Harl|Jae and Nan|L. N. Hagel|Lt. J. O. Hao
	6 Lt. Hawser said that he will see us in New London.
n/g	7 nj gf ng gun gun nag nag got got nor nor sign sign
	8 Angie hung a huge sign in front of the union hall.
o/t	9 ol tf to too dot dot not not toe toe got goat goat
	10 Todd took the tool chest to the dock for a worker.
i/r	11 ik rf or ore fir fir sir sir ire ire ice ice irons
	12 Risa fired the fir log to heat rice for the girls.
h/e	13 hj ed he the the hen hen when when then then their
	14 He was with her when she chose her new snow shoes.

Formatting Tables
Lessons 63-66

Format Guides: Tables

Although you will use a word processing feature to create tables, you will need these guidelines for making your tables easy to read and attractive.

Parts of a Simple Table

A table is an arrangement of data (words and/or numbers) in rows and columns. Tables range in complexity from those with only two columns and a title to those with several columns and special features. The tables in this unit are limited to those with the following parts:

1. Main title usually in ALL CAPS (centered).
2. Secondary title in Capital and lower-case letters (C/lc).
3. Column titles (centered).
4. Body (data entries).
5. Source note (bottom-left).
6. Gridlines (may be hidden).★

Study Models 1 and 2 on p. 168. The first tables in this unit consist of only a title and two columns of data, like Model 1.

★Some software prints the gridlines between columns and rows (as shown in Model 2, p. 168) or allows you to hide all or some of the lines before printing. **Note:** If your software prints gridlines by default, leave the lines in all your tables unless your teacher directs you to hide them. If gridlines do not print, column titles should be underlined. Also, the last entry in an amount column with a total should be underlined.

Later tables include three columns and several of the listed parts, similar to Model 2.

Vertical placement. A table may be centered vertically, or it may begin 2" from the top edge of the page.

Horizontal placement. Tables are most appealing when centered horizontally (side to side) on the page.

Column width. Generally, each column should be only slightly wider than the longest data entry in the column. Table columns should be identical widths or markedly different widths. Columns that are only slightly different widths should be avoided.

Row height (depth). All rows, including title rows, may be the same height. To enhance appearance, the main title row may be slightly higher (deeper) than the secondary title row, which may be deeper than the column title row. The column title row may be deeper than the data entry rows.

Vertical alignment. Within rows, data entries can be aligned at the top, center, or bottom. Most often you will center entries vertically.

Horizontal alignment. Within columns, words may be left-aligned or center-aligned. Whole numbers are right-aligned if a column total is shown; decimal numbers are decimal-aligned. Other figures may be center-aligned.

Lesson 11 New Keys: B and Y

O b j e c t i v e s :
1. **To learn reach technique for B and Y.**
2. **To combine smoothly B and Y with all other learned keys.**

Fingers curved

Fingers upright

11A◆ 7
Conditioning Practice
each line twice SS (slowly, then faster); DS between 2-line groups

reach review **1** uj ws ik rf ol cd nj ed hj tf .l gf sw ju de lo fr

c/n **2** an can and cut end cue hen cog torn dock then sick

all letters learned **3** A kid had a jar of fruit on his cart in New Delhi.

11B◆ 5
Technique: Space Bar
each line once

Technique goal
Space with a down-and-in motion *immediately* after each word.

1 He will take an old urn to an art sale at the inn.

2 Ann has an old car she wants to sell at this sale.

3 Len is to work for us for a week at the lake dock.

4 Gwen is to sign for the auto we set aside for her.

5 Jan is in town for just one week to look for work.

6 Juan said he was in the auto when it hit the tree.

11C◆ 4
Technique: Return
1. Key each line once SS: return and start each new line quickly.
2. On line 4, see how many words you can key in 30 seconds (30").

1 Dot is to go at two.

2 He saw that it was a good law.

3 Rilla is to take the auto into the town.

4 Wilt has an old gold jug he can enter in the show.

| 1 | 2 | 3 | 4 | 5 | 6 | 7 | 8 | 9 | 10 |

A **standard word** in keyboarding is 5 characters or any combination of 5 characters and spaces, as indicated by the number scale under line 4 above. The number of standard words keyed in 1' is called gross words a minute (*gwam*).

To find 1-minute (1') *gwam*:
1. Note on the scale the figure beneath the last word you keyed. That is your 1' *gwam* if you keyed the line partially or only once in 1'.

2. If you completed the line once and started over, add the figure determined in Step 1 to the figure 10. The resulting figure is your 1' *gwam*.

To find 30-second (30") *gwam*:
1. Find 1' *gwam* (total words keyed in 1').
2. Multiply 1' *gwam* by 2. The resulting figure is your 30" *gwam*.

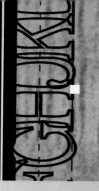

1. Key lines 1-9 once at an easy, steady pace.
2. Key the lines again at a quicker pace.
3. Key a 1' writing on each of lines 7-9; find *gwam* on each writing.
4. Key 1 or 2 more 1' writings on the 2 slower lines.

alphabet	1	Jevon was quick to fix my prized watch and the big clock for you.
top row	2	My taxes (1999) were $2,386 on a $214,570 home on Eastwood Drive.
keypad	3	741852 936215 475869 142536 172829 465798132 564897211 4174286394
CAPS LOCK	4	We saw a superb review of EXECUTIVE ORDERS in the NEW YORK TIMES.
hyphen	5	He bought state-of-the-art software for this up-to-date computer.
parentheses	6	Is the spacing after a : for stating time (a) 0, (b) 1, or (c) 2?
one-hand	7	Edward was up at my mill after you saw him free up my union case.
combination	8	Teresa's goal was to work for them after she got a degree in art.
balanced-hand	9	Jane may make an authentic map of the ancient city for the firms.

| 1 | 2 | 3 | 4 | 5 | 6 | 7 | 8 | 9 | 10 | 11 | 12 | 13 |

1. Key a 1' writing on ¶ 1; find *gwam*.
2. Add 4 *gwam* for a new goal rate. (See checkpoint chart below.)
3. Key two 1' *guided* writings on the ¶ to reach the checkpoint each 1/4'.
4. Key ¶ 2 in the same manner.
5. Key two 3' writings on ¶s 1-2 combined; find *gwam* and count errors on each.

Quarter-Minute Checkpoints

gwam	1/4'	1/2'	3/4'	Time
20	5	10	15	20
24	6	12	18	24
28	7	14	21	28
32	8	16	24	32
36	9	18	27	36
40	10	20	30	40
44	11	22	33	44
48	12	24	36	48
52	13	26	39	52
56	14	28	42	56

a all letters used

	3'	5'
A firm concerned with improving both the quality and quantity	4	2	33
of the documents produced by its office staff may want to examine	9	5	36
the latest word processing equipment on the market. Equipment that	13	8	39
was once too expensive is now affordable for even the smallest of-	17	10	41
fice. To a great extent this is due to amazing strides that have	22	13	44
been made in recent years in the field of computer technology.	26	16	47
New word processing programs can turn a computer into a word	30	18	49
processor that has many of the features of highly advanced informa-	34	21	52
tion processing equipment. It is now a simple job to review and	39	23	54
edit letters, reports, and tables on a computer. Copy, search and	43	26	57
replace, and undo are common features of current programs. As a	48	29	60
result, an office worker's job is much easier today.	52	31	62

| 1 | 2 | 3 | 4 |
| 1 | 2 | 3 |

11D◆ 19

New Keys: B and Y

each line twice SS (slowly, then faster): DS between 2-line groups; QS between groupings; if time permits, rekey lines 7-9

b *Left index* finger

y *Right index* finger

Follow the *Standard Plan for Learning New Keys* outlined on p. 9.

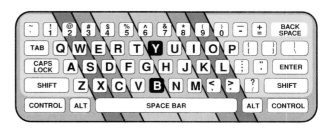

Learn b

1 f f bf bf fib fib rob rob but but big big fib fibs

2 bf bf rob rob lob lob orb orb bid bid bud bud ribs

3 a rib; to fib; rub it; an orb; or rob; but she bid

Learn y

4 j j yj yj jay jay lay lay hay hay day day say says

5 yj yj jay jay eye eye dye dye yes yes yet yet jays

6 a jay; to say; an eye; he says; dye it; has an eye

Combine b and y

7 by by buy buy boy boy bye bye byte byte buoy buoys

8 by it; to buy; by you; a byte; the buoy; by and by

9 Jaye went by bus to the store to buy the big buoy.

11E◆ 15

New-Key Mastery

1. Key the lines once SS; DS between 2-line groups.
2. Key the lines again at a faster pace.

PRACTICE CUES:

■ reach *up* without moving hands away from you
■ reach *down* without moving hands toward your body
■ use quick-snap keystrokes

reach
review

1 a;sldkfj bf ol ed yj ws ik rf hj cd nj tf .l gf uj

2 a kit low for jut led sow fob ask sun cud jet grow

3d/1st
rows

3 no in bow any tub yen cut sub coy ran bin cow deck

4 Cody wants to buy this baby cub for the young boy.

key
words

5 by and for the got all did but cut now say jut ask

6 work just such hand this goal boys held furl eight

key
phrases

7 to do|can go|to bow|for all|did jet|ask her|to buy

8 if she|to work|and such|the goal|for this|held the

all letters
learned

9 Becky has auburn hair and wide eyes of light jade.

10 Juan left Bobby at the dog show near our ice rink.

| 1 | 2 | 3 | 4 | 5 | 6 | 7 | 8 | 9 | 10 |

Lesson 11

Above & Beyond
P R O J E C T

Young Writers' Society

Read the information at right. Complete Task 9 below it.

The 30th Annual Career Day is history. As a result of careful planning and coordination, the event went off with only a few minor problems.

The panel discussion arranged by Young Writers' Society was a sure success. In YWS, students have done creative writing, often sharing their essays, poems, and play scripts with one another and offering each other feedback. The panel talked about another kind of writing: process writing.

Process writing tells readers how to do something, one step at a time. The writer leads readers through the process, detailing how to do each step. Therefore, such writing often has numbered paragraphs—the steps of a process in 1-2-3 order. Unlike a book report, a process report is written in second person. The writer talks directly to readers, using the pronoun *you*. An example of process writing is the "Effective Study" report (pp. 163 and 164).

You may recall an announcement about Job Explo Forum (p. 125), a web site that business people planned to help students prepare for careers. Because process writing is important to many careers, Job Explo is to include a library of examples written by high school students. You have been asked to prepare a process report to help furnish the library.

- -

Task 9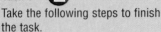

Take the following steps to finish the task.

1. Proofread and revise/rewrite as needed to make the steps clear and easy to follow.
2. Use Grammar and Spelling if available on your word processing software and make suggested changes that you think will improve your writing.
3. If the same word occurs over and over, use Thesaurus (if available) to find synonyms.
4. Apply the unbound report format. (Remember to number pages.)
5. If available, apply some of these word processing features to enhance your document: Bold, Case, Center, Font, Italic, Drawing Lines, Underline.
6. Proofread the report several times; check references and textual citations extra carefully. Correct all errors.
7. Staple pages in the upper-left corner if you print your report.

Write a process report on one of the following topics (or a topic your teacher suggests).

- making tacos
- mowing a lawn
- writing an F paper
- using a skateboard
- talking with animals
- taking a driver's test

- getting along with family
- equipping for a backpacking trip
- using the Heimlich maneuver to save a choking victim
- getting up after falling down while wearing rollerblades or skis

To prepare your report, consult at least two sources (references). A source may be a book or newspaper that you read; a web site that you visit; or a person—including another student—who gives a group presentation or grants you an interview.

For book and newspaper references, follow the examples on p. 164. For a web site reference or other unprinted source—presentation, interview, video, movie— follow the examples below.

Morgan, M. C. *Things You Might Want to Unlearn to Help You Edit.* [Online] Available: cal.bemidji.msus.edu/WRC/ Handouts/ ProofAndEdit.html [September, 1997].

Hocutt, Jerry. "Cold Calling on the Telephone." Cold Calling for Cowards Workshops. Cincinnati Marriott, Sharonville, OH. June 9, 1998.

A textual citation for a web reference shows the author's last name and the year the web page was posted or updated: (Morgan, 1997). If a year is not shown, give the month and year that you visited the site.

A textual citation for an unprinted source shows the originator's last name and the year the event took place: (Hocutt, 1998).

See the list of steps at left.

Objectives:

1. **To improve spacing, shifting, and returning.**
2. **To increase keying control and speed.**

Before you begin each practice session:

- Position your body directly in front of the keyboard; sit erect, with feet on the floor for balance.
- Curve your fingers deeply and place them in an upright position over the home keys.
- Rest the book on the easel.

Body properly positioned

Fingers properly curved

Fingers properly upright

12A◆   7

Conditioning Practice

each line twice SS (slowly, then faster); DS between 2-line groups; if time permits, practice each line again

reach review 1 we ok at in be on by re no us if la do ah go C. J.

b/y 2 by rub jay fib lay rob hay big say buy boy yet but

all letters learned 3 Fran knew it was her job to guide your gold truck.

12B◆   13

Technique: Space Bar and Shift Keys

1. Key the lines once SS; DS between 2-line groups.
2. Key lines again at a faster pace.

Down-and-in spacing

Out-and-down shifting

Space Bar (Space *immediately* after each word.)

1 an by win buy den sly won they than flay when clay
2 in a way|on a day|buy a hen|a fine day|if they win

3 Jay can bid on the old clay urn he saw at the inn.
4 I know she is to be here soon to talk to the club.

Shift keys (Shift; strike key; release both quickly.)

5 Lt. Su; Nan and Dodi; Karl and Sol; Dr. O. C. Goya
6 Kara and Rod are in Italy; Jane and Bo go in June.

7 Sig and Bodie went to the lake with Cory and Lana.
8 Aida Rios and Jana Hardy work for us in Los Gatos.

62C◆

Unbound Report Assessment

1. DS the report on p. 163 and at right as an unbound report, all errors corrected.
2. Place the reference list on a separate page; number pages after page 1.

2. As you read the material, convert the headings into questions; then seek answers to those questions as you read.

3. If you own the book, use color markers to highlight important ideas: headings, topic sentences, special terms, definitions, and supporting facts. Otherwise, make notes of these ideas.

4. After reading the material, review the highlighted items (or your notes that contain them).

5. Using the headings stated as questions, see if you can answer those questions based on your reading.

6. Test yourself to see if you recall definitions of important terms and lists of supporting facts or ideas.

A high correlation exists between good study habits and good grades for courses taken in high school.

REFERENCES

Dansereau, D. F. "Learning Strategy Research." *Thinking and Learning Skills.* Vol. 1. Hillsdale, NJ: Lawrence Erlbaum, 1985.

Huber, Rose. "Teaching Students How to Study." *Eastside Weekend.* September 1-7, 1994.

Silver, Theodore. *Study Smart.* New York: Villard Books, 1992.

	words
2. As you read the material, convert the headings	342
into questions; then seek answers to those ques-	351
tions as you read.	355
3. If you own the book, use color markers to	364
highlight important ideas: headings, topic sen-	374
tences, special terms, definitions, and supporting	384
facts. Otherwise, make notes of these ideas.	394
4. After reading the material, review the high-	403
lighted items (or your notes that contain	412
them).	413
5. Using the headings stated as questions, see	423
if you can answer those questions based on	431
your reading.	434
6. Test yourself to see if you recall definitions	445
of important terms and lists of supporting	453
facts or ideas.	457
A high correlation exists between good study	465
habits and good grades for courses taken in high	475
school.	477
REFERENCES	479
Dansereau, D. F. "Learning Strategy Research."	489
Thinking and Learning Skills. Vol. 1. Hillsdale,	499
NJ: Lawrence Erlbaum, 1985.	505
Huber, Rose. "Teaching Students How to Study."	515
Eastside Weekend. September 1-7, 1994.	523
Silver, Theodore. Study Smart. New York:	532
Villard Books, 1992.	536

12C◆ 15
Speed Building

1. Key the lines once SS; DS between 2-line groups.
2. Key the lines again at a faster pace.

Technique goals
- curved, upright fingers
- quiet hands/arms
- quick spacing—no pause between words
- finger-reach action to shift keys

Finger-action keystrokes

Down-and-in thumb motion

Key words and phrases (*Think*, *say*, and *key* words and phrases.)

1 by dig row off but and jet oak the cub all got rid
2 ah she own dug irk buy cog job for yet ask led urn

3 of us|if the|all of|and do|cut it|he got|to do the
4 is to be|as it is|if we do|in all the|if we own it

All letters learned (Strike keys at a brisk, steady pace.)

5 Judy had gone for that big ice show at Lake Tahoe.
6 Jack said that all of you will find the right job.

7 Cindy has just left for work at the big ski lodge.
8 Rudy can take a good job at the lake if he wishes.

| 1 | 2 | 3 | 4 | 5 | 6 | 7 | 8 | 9 | 10 |

12D◆ 15
Speed Check

1. Key each line once DS. To DS when in SS mode, strike **Return/Enter** twice at line ends.
2. Key a 20-second (20") writing on each line.
3. Key another 20" writing on each line. Try to increase your keying speed.

Goal
At least 15 *gwam*.

Your rate in gross words a minute (*gwam*) is shown on this scale.

20"   3| 6| 9| 12| 15| 18| 21| 24| 27| 30

1 Al is to do it.
2 Di has gone to work.
3 Jan is to go to the sale.
4 Rog is to row us to your dock.
5 Harl has an old kayak and two oars.
6 She told us to set a goal and go for it.
7 It is our job to see just how high we can go.
8 Jake will go to the city to work on the big signs.

Enrichment

1. Key each line twice SS (slowly, then faster); DS between 2-line groups.
2. Rekey the drill for better control of reach-strokes.

1 Rob saw the bird on the lake by the big boat dock.
2 June had left for the club just as the news ended.
3 Bro led a task force whose goal was to lower cost.
4 Lyn knew the surf was too rough for kids to enjoy.
5 Ceil hikes each day on the side roads near school.

| 1 | 2 | 3 | 4 | 5 | 6 | 7 | 8 | 9 | 10 |

Objectives:

Approx. time: 75'

1. To process an unbound report with listed items.
2. To format a separate reference page.
3. To demonstrate mastery of unbound report formatting.

62A◆
Keyboard Mastery

Use Skill Builder 3, p. 153, lines 1, 7, and 9, or L on p. A7.

62B◆
Unbound Report Mastery

1. Take three 1' writings on the copy at right, in unbound report format, DS. Begin each writing at the top of a new page. Try to add 2 *gwam* (10 keystrokes) on the second and third writings.
2. On a new page, format/key the report title **A PLAN FOR STUDY**.
   a. Beginning with the fourth paragraph in the text at right, key to the end of the body on p. 164. Omit the textual citation.
   b. Key this heading below the body:
      REFERENCE
   c. Key the first reference only.
   d. Full-align the numbered items.
   e. Proofread and correct all errors.

SPACING CUE:

SS numbered items and references; but DS above, below, and between them.

words

EFFECTIVE STUDY — 3

Effective learning depends upon good study skills, but "Many students--both traditional and nontraditional--entering college have few, if any, practical study skills." (Huber, 1994, 29) Good study skills do not simply occur; they must first be learned and then applied consistently. Efficient study strategies include a preset time, a desirable place, and a well-designed plan for study. — 15 / 30 / 46 / 60 / 75 / 82

A Time for Study — 85

Many of us think we have more to do than we have time to do, and studying gets shortchanged. It is important to prepare a schedule of daily activities that includes time slots for doing the studying you have to do. Within each study slot, write in the specific study activity; for example, "Read Unit 6 in *Modern Writing*, answer Questions 1-10." Keep the schedule flexible so that it can be modified if you meet your study goals early-- or late. — 98 / 113 / 128 / 143 / 158 / 173 / 175

A Place to Study — 179

Choose the best place to study and use the same time each day. Doing so will help to put you in a study mood when you enter that place. Choose a place that has the fewest distractions: people traffic, conversation, telephone, TV, and outside noises. Usually study is best done alone in the absence of sights and sounds that distract the eye and ear. Force the mind to focus intently on the study task. (Silver, 1992, 26) — 192 / 207 / 222 / 237 / 252 / 265

A Plan for Study — 268

Research on the effects of specific study skills on student performance suggests that the following study tactics help to improve academic performance. (Dansereau, 1985, 39) — 282 / 296 / 304

1. Skim a unit or a chapter, noting headings, topic sentences, key words, and definitions to clue you to what you are going to study. — 318 / 331

Lesson 13 New Keys: M and X

Objectives:
1. To learn reach technique for M and X.
2. To combine smoothly M and X with all other learned keys.

13A◆   7
Conditioning Practice

each line twice SS (slowly, then faster); DS between 2-line groups

reach review   1 bf ol rf yj ed nj ws ik tf hj cd uj gf by us if ow
b/y   2 by bye boy buy yes fib dye bit yet but try bet you
all letters learned 3 Robby can win the gold if he just keys a new high.

13B◆   20
New Keys: M and X

each line twice SS (slowly, then faster); DS between 2-line groups; if time permits, rekey lines 7-9

m *Right index* finger

x *Left ring* finger

Follow the *Standard Plan for Learning New Keys* outlined on p. 9.

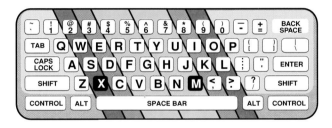

Learn m
1 j j mj mj am am am me me ma ma jam jam ham ham yam
2 mj mj me me me may may yam yam dam dam men men jam
3 am to; if me; a man; a yam; a ham; he may; the hem

Learn x
4 s s xs xs ox ox ax ax six six fix fix fox fox axis
5 xs xs sx sx ox ox six six nix nix fix fix lax flax
6 a fox; an ox; fix it; by six; is lax; to fix an ax

Combine m and x
7 me ox am ax ma jam six ham mix fox men lax hem lox
8 to fix; am lax; mix it; may fix; six men; hex them
9 Mala can mix a ham salad for six; Max can fix tea.

Page Break

1. Read the copy at right.
2. Learn how to insert and delete a page break on your software.
3. Open the report in **61D** if you closed it.
4. Do Steps 1-4 at the right.

Word processing software has two types of page breaks: soft and hard. Both a **soft** and **hard page break** signal the end of a page and the beginning of a new page. The software inserts a soft page break automatically when the current page is full. You insert hard page breaks manually when you want a new page to begin before the current one is full. When a hard page break is inserted, the software adjusts any following soft page breaks so that those pages will be full before a new one is started. Hard page breaks do not move unless you move them. If you want to change the location of a hard page break, you can either delete it and let the software insert soft page breaks at appropriate places, or insert a new page break where you want.

1. In the report, insert a hard page break at the end of each section of the report (end of second ¶, end of third ¶, end of fourth *numbered* ¶).
2. Use View to verify that you have four pages.
3. Delete the page number at the top of page 2.
4. Keep the four-page document open for use in **61F**.

Page Numbering

1. Read the copy at right.
2. Learn how to number pages and suppress, or hide, page numbers with your software.
3. With the four-page document in **61E** (above) on the screen, do Steps 1-5 at right (below).

Use the **Page Numbering** feature to select the type of page numbers you want and to place them in specific locations on the pages. Most word processing software allows you to number pages with Arabic numbers (1, 2, 3, etc.), lowercase Roman numerals (i, ii, iii, etc.), uppercase Roman numerals (I, II, III, etc.), uppercase letters (A, B, C, etc.), and lowercase letters (a, b, c, etc.). Some software permits the use of text with the number (such as *Page 2*). You can usually place numbers at the top or bottom of the page, aligned at the left margin, center, or right margin. Often you will need to keep a number from printing on a page, such as page 1 of an unbound report. On some software a separate feature called Suppress or Hide keeps a page number from appearing or printing on a designated page or pages.

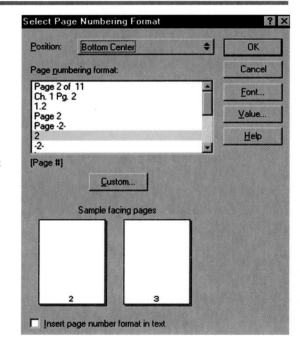

1. Using the Page Numbering feature, number all pages *at the bottom center*. (No text should appear beside the number.)
2. Use the View feature to verify that the page numbers have been added.
3. Change the page numbers on all pages to bottom-right corner; use View to verify.
4. Finally, change the numbers on pages 2-4 to upper-right corner; hide (suppress) the page number on page 1.
5. Use the View feature to verify that a page number does not appear on the first page.

Unbound Report with Numbered Pages

1. Open the report in **59F**.
2. On page 2, delete the page number.
3. Insert a hard page break after the last paragraph.
4. Use the feature to number pages, except page 1.

13C ◆ 17
New-Key Mastery

1. Key each line once SS; DS between 2-line groups.
2. Key the lines again at a faster pace.

Technique goals
- reach *up* without moving hands away from you
- reach *down* without moving hands toward your body
- use quick-snap keystrokes

Goal: finger-action keystrokes; quiet hands and arms

3d/1st rows
1 by am end fix men box hem but six now cut gem ribs
2 me ox buy den cub ran own form went oxen fine club

space bar
3 an of me do am if us or is by go ma so ah ox it ow
4 by man buy fan jam can any tan may rob ham fun guy

key words
5 if us me do an sow the cut big jam rub oak lax boy
6 curl work form born name flex just done many right

key phrases
7 or jam|if she|for me|is big|an end|or buy|is to be
8 to fix|and cut|for work|and such|big firm|the call

all letters learned
9 Jacki is now at the gym; Lex is due there by four.
10 Joni saw that she could fix my old bike for Gilda.

13D ◆ 6
Technique: Spacing with Punctuation

each line once DS

> ### SPACING CUE:
> Do not space after an internal period in an abbreviation, such as Ed.D.

1 Mrs. Dixon may take her Ed.D. exam early in March.
2 Lex may send a box c.o.d. to Ms. Fox in St. Croix.
3 J. D. and Max will go by boat to St. Louis in May.
4 Owen keyed ect. for etc. and lost the match to me.

Enrichment

1. Key each line twice SS (slowly, then faster); DS between 2-line groups.
2. Key each line once more at a faster pace.

> ### PRACTICE CUE:
> Keep the insertion point moving steadily across each line (no pauses).

m/x 1 Max told them that he will next fix the main axle.
b/y 2 Byron said the boy went by bus to a bayou to hunt.
w/right shift 3 Will and Rona work in Tucson with Rowena and Drew.
u/c 4 Lucy cut a huge cake for just the four lucky boys.
./left shift 5 Mr. and Mrs. J. L. Nance set sail for Long Island.
n/g 6 Bing may bring a young trio to sing songs at noon.
o/t 7 Lottie will tell the two little boys a good story.
i/r 8 Ria said she will first build a large fire of fir.
h/e 9 Chet was here when the eight hikers hit the trail.

61D (cont.)

Reminder: SS listed items even within a DS report body.

words

get jobs that have some relationship to your career plans. If, for example, 273
you want a career involving frequent contact with people--as in sales--seek 289
part-time and summer work that give you experience in dealing with peo- 303
ple. (Hamel, 1989, 10) 309

How to Handle Yourself on the Job 315

Whatever the job you are able to get, the following 326
pointers will help you succeed in getting a good recom- 337
mendation for the next job you seek. 345

1. Be punctual. Get to work on time and return from 356
lunch and other breaks promptly. 363

2. Get along well with others. Do your job well and 373
offer to assist others who may need help. Take direction 385
with a smile instead of a frown. 392

3. Speak proper English. Teenage jargon is 401
often lost on adults who are likely to be your 411
supervisors. 413

4. Dress the part. Observe the unwritten dress code; 424
dress as others on the job do. Always be neat and clean. 436

REFERENCES 438

Giesking, Hal, and Paul Plawin. 30 Days to a Good Job. 450
New York: Simon & Schuster, 1994. 457

Hamel, Ruth. "Making Summer Earnings Work for You." 468
USA Weekend, 2-4 June 1989, 20-21. 475

Lesson 14 New Keys: P and V

O b j e c t i v e s :
1. **To learn reach technique for P and V.**
2. **To combine smoothly P and V with all other learned keys.**

14A◆ 7
Conditioning Practice

each line twice SS (slowly, then faster); DS between 2-line groups

**Fingers
curved**

**Fingers
upright**

one-hand
words   1   in we no ax my be on ad on re hi at ho cad him bet

phrases   2   is just|of work|to sign|of lace|to flex|got a form

all letters
learned   3   Jo Buck won a gold medal for her sixth show entry.

14B◆ 20
New Keys: P and V

each line twice SS; DS between 2-line groups; if time permits, rekey lines 7-9

p *Right little* finger

v *Left index* finger

Follow the *Standard Plan for Learning New Keys* outlined on p. 9.

Learn p

1   ;   ; p; p; pa pa up up apt apt pen pen lap lap kept

2   p; p; pa pa pa pan pan nap nap paw paw gap gap rap

3   a pen; a cap; apt to pay; pick it up; plan to keep

Learn v

4   f f vf vf via via vie vie have have five five live

5   vf vf vie vie vie van van view view dive dive jive

6   go via; vie for; has vim; a view; to live; or have

Combine p and v

7   up cup vie pen van cap vim rap have keep live plan

8   to vie; give up; pave it; very apt; vie for a cup;

9   Vic has a plan to have the van pick us up at five.

61C FEATURE

Paragraph Indent

Line spacing: SS; DS between ¶s
Top margin: default

1. Read the copy at right; learn to use the Paragraph Indent feature on your software.
2. Key the text at right with the indentions as shown (0.5");
3. Then, indent the first numbered item to match the second numbered item.
4. Center the text vertically.

The **Paragraph Indent** feature moves a complete paragraph a certain amount of space to the right. At line endings, text wraps *to the indention point*, instead of the left margin. On some software, the indention point is the first tab position. In other cases, the indent position is separate from tab settings. Indented paragraphs stand out from the rest, indicating that such paragraphs contain "special" text. For example, Paragraph Indent may be used to format long quotations and listed items within a report.

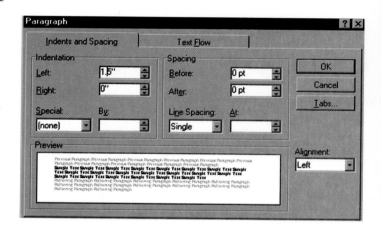

Follow the steps below as you begin to search the Internet.

1. Use the right tool for the job. Looking for a home page that sells books with a utility to find people is not going to work, no matter how good a searcher you are.

2. Learn how the search tool works. All search tools are not the same. Most are custom-designed to fit certain needs. Become familiar with the particular search engine by reading its instructions.

61D◆

Report with Numbered Items

1. Process the report at right and on p. 161 in unbound format (DS), all errors corrected.
   Notes: Do not underline the side headings.
   The text contains two grammar errors.
2. Indent the numbered paragraphs 0.5" from the left margin; SS and full-align them.
3. Key references below the body.
4. Change the font of the titles and side headings to Arial.
5. Italicize the first sentence of each numbered paragraph.

	words
THE VALUE OF	3
WORK EXPERIENCE	6

A summer or part-time job pays more than money. Even though the money earned is important, the work experience gained has a greater long-term value when one applies for a full-time job after graduation from school. Job application documents (the application blank and the personal data sheet) ask you to list jobs you have held and to list as references the names of individuals who supervised your work. (Gieseking and Plawin, 1994, 22)

As one young person was heard to remark, "You can't get a job without experience, and you can't get experience without a job." That dilemma can be overcome, however, by starting work early in life and by accepting simpler jobs that has no minimum age limit and do not require experience.

Jobs Teens Can Do

Begin early at jobs that may not pay especially well but help to establish a working track record: delivering newspapers, babysitting, mowing lawns, assisting with gardening, and the like. Use these work experiences as springboards for such later jobs as sales clerk, gas station attendant, fast-food worker, lifeguard, playground supervisor assistant, and office staff assistant (after you have developed basic office skills). As you progress through these work exploration experiences, try increasingly to

Word counts: 19, 33, 47, 61, 78, 92, 94, 108, 123, 137, 152, 156, 170, 185, 200, 215, 229, 244, 259

Lesson 61

14C◆ 17
New-Key Mastery

1. Key the lines once SS; DS between 2-line groups.
2. Key the lines again at a faster pace.

Technique goals
- reach *up* without moving hands away from you
- reach *down* without moving hands toward your body
- use quick-snap keystrokes

Goal: finger-action keystrokes; quiet hands and arms

reach review
1 vf p; xs mj ed yj ws nj rf ik tf ol cd hj gf uj bf
2 if lap jag own may she for but van cub sod six oak

3d/1st rows
3 by vie pen vim cup six but now man nor ton may pan
4 by six but now may cut bent me fine gems five reps

key words
5 with kept turn corn duty curl just have worn plans
6 name burn form when jury glad vote exit came eight

key phrases
7 if they|he kept|with us|of land|burn it|to name it
8 to plan|so sure|is glad|an exit|so much|to view it

all letters learned
9 Kevin does a top job on your flax farm with Craig.
10 Dixon flew blue jets eight times over a city park.

14D◆ 6
Technique: Shift Keys and Return

Key a 1' writing on each 2-line sentence SS; DS between sentences.

Goal
To reach the end of each *line* in 30".

Eyes on copy as you shift and as you return

		30"	1'
1	Marv is to choose a high goal	12	6
2	and to do his best to make it.	12	12
3	Vi said she had to key from a book	14	7
4	as one test she took for a top job.	14	14
5	Lexi knows it is good to keep your goal	16	8
6	in mind as you key each line of a drill.	16	16
7	Viv can do well many of the tasks she tries;	18	9
8	she sets top goals and makes them one by one.	18	18

Enrichment

1. Key each line once at a steady, easy pace to master reach-strokes.
2. Key each line again at a faster pace.

Technique goals
- keep fingers upright
- keep hands/arms steady

m/p
1 mj p; me up am pi jam apt ham pen map ape mop palm
2 Pam may pack plums and grapes for my trip to camp.

b/x
3 bf xs be ax by xi fix box but lax buy fox bit flax
4 Bix used the box of mix to fix bread for six boys.

y/v
5 yj vf buy vow boy vie soy vim very have your every
6 Vinny may have you buy very heavy silk and velvet.

60C (cont.)

3. Key the reference below the report body.
4. Make changes:
   a. Use your name in the byline.
   b. Replace underlines with italics.
   c. If you find appropriate synonyms using the Thesaurus feature, replace *optimistic* and *opulent* (¶ 3).
5. The report contains four errors (¶s 2, 3, 5, and 6). If the Grammar feature is available on your software, use it to help you find the errors. If you are using *Applied MicroType Pro* and are unable to find the errors, check with the *Teacher's Key.*
6. Proofread and correct any errors that remain.

forces Paul to leave his Uncle's home to find work on his own. 205

The behavior and work ethic of Joe Jr., who is born to wealth and 218

privilege in America, is juxtaposed with that of imigrant Paul. 231

The author pictures *Jakes portrays* Joe Jr. as spoiled and with out focus, especially 243

when compared to Pauls mature approach to life and work. 256

Jakes utilizes the character of Paul to introduce the reader 268

to the flegling business of moving pictures. Paul is facinated 281

with this new "art form which involves him in many adventures including 295

war, a brush with death, and marrying his first love. 307

This first novel of the Crown serejs does a credible job in 320

sitting the stage for future adventures of Paul Crown and his 332

budding new family. QS 336

REFERENCE 338

QS

Jakes, John. <u>Homeland</u>. New York: Bantam Books, 1994 349

(Paperback Edition). 353

Lesson 61 Numbered Lists in Reports

Objectives:

Approx. time: 115'

1. **To learn how to format listed items in reports.**
2. **To make reports more attractive and readable using software features.**
3. **To improve skill in processing reports.**

61A◆
Keyboard Mastery

Use Skill Builder 3, p. 153, lines 1, 6, and 9, or K on p. A7.

61B◆ FEATURE

Full Alignment (Justification)

1. Read the copy at right.
2. Learn to use the "Full" feature on your software; do Steps 1-4 at right.

Full justification, or **alignment**, is another way to align text on a page in relation to the margins. Use the Full Alignment feature to align text along both the left and right margins. The space between words is adjusted to make the right margin even.

In general, full justification makes text look good. With some fonts, though, it results in gaps between words that may be unattractive. Also, some people say that text is easier to read when the right margin is slightly "ragged."

1. Open the report in **60C** (above).
2. View the pages at a small percentage so that you can see a whole page at once. Note the general appearance of the report.
3. Stop viewing and use the Full Alignment feature for all paragraphs of the book report.
4. View the pages again at the same percentage, noting the difference in appearance.

Lesson 61

Lesson 15 New Keys: Q and , (Comma)

Objectives:
1. **To learn reach technique for Q and , (comma).**
2. **To combine smoothly Q and , (comma) with all other learned keys.**

15A♦ 7
Conditioning Practice

each line twice SS (slowly, then faster); DS between 2-line groups; if time permits, rekey the lines

all letters learned	1 do fix all cut via own buy for the jam cop ask dig
p/v	2 a map; a van; apt to; vie for; her plan; have five
all letters learned	3 Beth will pack sixty pints of guava jam for David.

15B♦ 20
New Keys: Q and , (Comma)

each line twice SS; DS between 2-line groups; if time permits, rekey lines 7-9

q *Left little* finger

, **(comma)**
Right middle finger

SPACING CUE:
Space once after , used as punctuation.

Follow the *Standard Plan for Learning New Keys* outlined on p. 9.

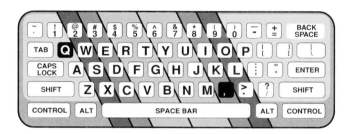

Learn q

1 a qa qa aq aq quo quo qt. qt. quad quad quit quits

2 qa quo quo qt. qt. quay quay aqua aqua quite quite

3 a qt.; pro quo; a quad; to quit; the quay; a squad

Learn , (comma)

4 k k ,k ,k kit, kit; Rick, Ike, or I will go, also.

5 a ski, a ski; a kit, a kit; a kite, a kite; a bike

6 Ike, I see, is here; Pam, I am told, will be late.

Combine q and , (comma)

7 Enter the words quo, quote, quit, quite, and aqua.

8 I have quit the squad, Quen; Raquel has quit, too.

9 Marquis, Quent, and Quig were quite quick to quit.

60B ◆ FEATURE

Grammar

1. Read the copy at right.
2. Learn to use Grammar if the feature is available on your software.
3. Using the default top margin, key the ¶ at right DS *without* changing the text.
4. Do Steps 1-3 below the ¶.

Use the **Grammar** feature to check text for grammar, punctuation, and spelling errors, and style flaws. You can determine how strictly the feature observes grammar and style rules by choosing the degree of formality (formal, casual, standard, strict [*all rules*]) to which your text will be compared. In some software, Grammar allows you to compare your text to writing styles considered acceptable for business letters, fiction, newspapers, reports, etc. When an error or style flaw is found, Grammar suggests how to correct or improve the sentence.

The impact it will have on office work is hard too predict. It may not be widely used in the vary near future, but I think your wise to question how it will effect office workers. We cannot afford to talk about it as a possibility. Its a reality! For anyone who prepares documents, it likely will increase the importance of finding, and correcting erors. For people who create memos an letters, planning there messages may become more critical. What is *it*? It is speech-recognition technology.

1. Use the Grammar feature; compare this ¶ to "standard business writing."
2. Correct all errors found by the Grammar feature;
3. make suggested style changes **if** you believe they will improve the ¶.
4. Proofread the document and make necessary changes not found by the Grammar feature.

60C ◆

Book Report

1. Review the proofreader's marks shown below.
2. Format/key the text at right and on p. 159 as an unbound report.

Proofreader's Marks

⋏, = insert comma

—— = underline

◠ = close up

⊬ = add space

⋏ = insert

⤼ = delete

≡ = capitalize

⋂ = transpose

/ *lc* = lowercase

∨ = insert apostrophe

(Directions continued on next page.)

words

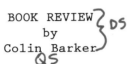

BOOK REVIEW   2
by   3
Colin Barker   6
QS

Homeland, John Jakes formidable novel about the final explo-   18
sive events of the nineteenth 19th century, is the first in a series that   32
will focus attention on a new "Jakes," family, the Crowns.   44
Multiple Many characters and settings is normal for Jakes, how-   55
ever, this story rivets focuses primary attention on Paul Crown, a young   68
german immigrant. Paul leaves behind a Germany of cholera, pov-   81
erty and political upheaval only to face problems of equal magni-   94
tude in america.   98
Undaunted by a dificult ocean crossing, Paul arrives at Ellis   111
island penniless but niavely optimistic about his future. He makes   124
his weary way to the opulant home of his uncle, Joe Crown, a well   137
established brewer in Chicago. Jakes used the Chicago setting as   151
a back drop for his "class struggle" motive which is central to   164
the plot of his story.   168
Paul's uncle, Joe, and cousin, Joe Jr., are foils in this   180
class struggle that ultimately fractures the Crown family and   192

Lesson 60

UNBOUND REPORT FROM ROUGH DRAFT

158

New-Key Mastery

1. Key the lines once SS; DS between 2-line groups.
2. Key the lines again at a faster pace.

Technique goals

- reach *up* without moving hands away from you
- reach *down* without moving hands toward your body
- use quick-snap keystrokes

Goal: finger-action keystrokes; quiet hands and arms

reach review
1 qa .l ws ,k ed nj rf mj tf p; xs ol cd ik vf hj bf
2 yj gf hj quo vie pay cut now buy sot mix vow forms

3d/1st rows
3 six may sun coy cue mud jar win via pick turn bike
4 to go|to win|for me|a peck|a quay|by then|the vote

key words
5 pa rub sit man for own fix jam via cod oak the got
6 by quo sub lay apt mix irk pay when rope give just

key phrases
7 an ox|of all|is to go|if he is|it is due|to pay us
8 if we pay|is of age|up to you|so we own|she saw me

all letters learned
9 Jevon will fix my pool deck if the big rain quits.
10 Verna did fly quick jets to map the six big towns.

Technique: Spacing with Punctuation

each line once DS

SPACING CUE:

Space once after , and ; used as punctuation.

Space once.

1 Aqua means water, Quen; also, it is a unique blue.
2 Quince, enter qt. for quart; also, sq. for square.
3 Ship the desk c.o.d. to Dr. Quig at La Quinta Inn.
4 Q. J. took squid and squash; Monique, roast quail.

Enrichment

each set of lines twice SS (once slowly; then again at a faster pace); DS between 6-line groups

Technique goals

Lines 1-3:
fingers upright

Lines 4-6:
hands/arms steady

Lines 7-9:
two quick taps of each doubled letter

Adjacent keys

1 re io as lk rt jk df op ds uy ew vc mn gf hj sa ui
2 as ore ask opt buy pew say art owe try oil gas her
3 Sandy said we ought to buy gifts at her new store.

Long direct reaches

4 ce un gr mu br ny rv ym rb my ice any mug orb grow
5 nice curb must brow much fume sync many dumb curve
6 Brian must bring the ice to the curb for my uncle.

Double letters

7 all off odd too see err boo lee add call heed good
8 door meek seen huff less will soon food leek offer
9 Lee will seek help to get all food cooked by noon.

2
DS

<u>Spreadsheet Software</u>
DS

A spreadsheet is an electronic worksheet made up of columns and rows of data. Spreadsheet software allows the user to "create, calculate, edit, retrieve, modify, and print graphs, charts, reports, and spreadsheets" necessary for current business operations and in planning for the future. (Fulton and Hanks, 1996, 156)

A review of newspaper advertisements shows the skills that employers expect for most jobs: competent use of word processing and spreadsheet software and familiarity with database applications.

QS (2 DS)

REFERENCES
QS

Fulton, Patsy J., and Joanna D. Hanks. <u>Procedures for the Office Professional</u>. 3d ed. Cincinnati: South-Western Publishing Co., 1996.

Tilton, Rita S., et al. <u>The Electronic Office: Procedures & Administration</u>. 11th ed. Cincinnati: South-Western Publishing Co., 1996.

Unbound Report with Textual Citations, Page 2

59F◆

Two-Page Unbound Report

1. Review the format guides on p. 154; study the model report as needed (p. 156 and above).

2. Key the model report (pages 1 and 2).
3. Proofread and correct errors.

Lesson 60 Unbound Report from Rough Draft

Objectives: | Approx. time: 75'

1. To key a book report in unbound report format.
2. To improve skill in keying from rough draft.
3. To edit and align text using word processing features.

60A◆

Keyboard Mastery

Use Skill Builder 3, p. 153, lines 1, 5, and 9, or J on p. A7.

Lesson 16

review

Objectives:
1. **To learn to key block paragraphs.**
2. **To improve keying technique and speed.**

**Fingers
properly
curved**

**Fingers
properly
aligned**

16A◆ 7
Conditioning Practice

each line twice SS (slowly, then faster); DS between 2-line groups; if time permits, practice each line again

reach review 1 Virgil plans to find that mosque by six with Jack.
shift keys 2 Pam, Van, and Quin have to be in New Hope by five.
easy 3 Vi is to aid the girl with the sign work at eight.

| 1 | 2 | 3 | 4 | 5 | 6 | 7 | 8 | 9 | 10 |

16B◆ 10
Block Paragraphs

each paragraph (¶) once SS; DS between ¶s; then key the ¶s again at a faster pace

 Your software will return automatically at the end of a line ("soft return"—also called "wordwrap"). So do not strike **Return/Enter** at the end of each line. Return twice at the end of ¶ 1 to leave a DS between ¶s. Your lines may end in a different place than the lines shown here.

Paragraph 1   1'

When you strike the return or enter key at the end   10
of a line to space down and start a new line, this   20
process is called a hard return.   27

Paragraph 2

If a machine returns at line ends for you, what is   10
known as a soft return or wordwrap is in use. You   20
must use a hard return, though, between paragraphs.   30

| 1 | 2 | 3 | 4 | 5 | 6 | 7 | 8 | 9 | 10 |

16C◆ 10
Speed Check

1. Key a 30" writing on each line. Your rate in gross words a minute *(gwam)* is shown word for word above the lines.
2. If time permits, key another 30" writing on each line. Try to increase your keying speed.

Goal: At least 18 *gwam*.

30" 2| 4| 6| 8| 10| 12| 14| 16| 18| 20|

1 I am to fix the sign for them.
2 Jaye held the key to the blue auto.
3 Todd is to go to the city dock for fish.
4 Vi paid the girl to make a big bowl of salad.
5 Kal may keep the urn he just won at the quay show.

| 2| | 4| | 6| | 8| | 10| | 12| | 14| | 16| | 18| | 20| |

If you finish a line before time is up and start over, your *gwam* is the figure at the end of the line PLUS the figure above or below the point at which you stopped.

Title

COMPUTER APPLICATIONS

QS (4 hard returns)

Report
body

Learning to key is of little value unless one applies it in preparing a useful document--a letter, a report, and so on. Three basic kinds of software (applications) are available to assist those with keying skill in applying that skill electronically. **DS**

Side
heading

Word Processing Software
DS

Textual
citation

Word processing software is specifically designed to assist in the document preparation needs of individuals or businesses. Word processing software permits the user to "create, edit, format, store, and print documents." (Fulton and Hanks, 1996, 152) The software can be used to process a wide variety of documents such as memos, letters, reports, and tables.

This software has editing and formatting features that reduce

1" LM

time and effort. It permits easy error detection and correction; merging of text with variables in another document or even another application (for example, database software); and graphic design of pages. These features increase efficiency while enhancing the appearance of documents.

1" RM

DS

Side
heading

Database Software
DS

A database is any collection of related items stored in computer memory. The data in a database may be about club members, employee payroll, company sales, and so on. Database software allows the user to enter data, sort it, retrieve and change it, or select certain data (such as an address) for use in word processing documents. (Tilton, et al, 1996, 112-113)

Textual
citation

At least 1 "

(continued on next page)

Unbound Report with Textual Citations

16D◆ 12
Technique: Space Bar and Shift Keys

each line twice SS; DS between 4-line groups

Goals
- ■ to reduce the pause between words
- ■ to reduce the time taken to shift/strike key/release when making capital letters

Down-and-in spacing

Out-and-down shifting

Space Bar (Space _immediately_ after each word.)

1 so an if us am by or ox he own jay pen yam own may
2 she is in|am to pay|if he may|by the man|in a firm

3 I am to keep the pens in a cup by a tan mail tray.
4 Fran may try to fix an old toy for the little boy.

Shift keys (Shift; strike key; release both quickly.)

5 J. V., Dr. or Mrs., Ph.D. or Ed.D., Fourth of July
6 Mrs. Maria Fuente; Dr. Mark V. Quin; Mr. T. C. Ott

7 B. J. Marx will go to St. Croix in March with Lex.
8 Mae has a Ph.D. from Miami; Dex will get his Ed.D.

16E◆ 11
Speed Building

each line twice SS (slowly, then faster); DS between 4-line groups

Technique goals
- ■ quick-snap keystrokes
- ■ quick joining of letters to form words
- ■ quick joining of words to form phrases

Key words and phrases (_Think_, _say_, and _key_ words and phrases.)

1 ox jam for oak rid pay got own the lap via sob cut
2 make than with them such they when both then their

3 to sit|an elf|by six|an oak|did go|for air|the jam
4 to vie|he owns|pay them|cut both|the quay|for they

Key sentences (Strike keys at a brisk, steady pace.)

all letters learned
5 I may have six quick jobs to get done for low pay.
6 Vicky packed the box with quail and jam for Signe.

all letters learned
7 Max can plan to bike for just five days with Quig.
8 Jim was quick to get the next top value for Debby.

Enrichment

1. Key each line once at a steady, easy pace.
2. Key each line again at a faster pace.

Technique goals
- ■ keep fingers upright
- ■ keep hands/arms steady

q/b
1 qa bf by quo but qt. quit both quad lube quid blow
2 Bob quickly won my squad over quip by brainy quip.

x/,
3 xs ,k sxs k,k ox ox, six six, flax flax, axle axle
4 I keyed ox, six, lox, mix, fox, fix, fax, and nix.

p/m
5 p; mj p.m. map amp pep mum mop imp camp ramp clump
6 Palma and her mom made peppy caps for my pep team.

v/y
7 vf yj ivy vary envy very wavy navy have many savvy
8 Levy may have to vary the way we serve and volley.

Lesson 59 Unbound Reports

O b j e c t i v e s :

| Approx. time: 115' |

1. **To learn features of unbound reports.**
2. **To learn a word processing feature for indenting copy.**
3. **To process a two-page unbound report.**

59A◆
Keyboard Mastery

Use Skill Builder 3, p. 153, lines 1, 4, and 9, or I on p. A7.

59B◆
Unbound Report

1. Read the format guides on p. 154; study the model report (page 1) on p. 156.
2. Key from the model, *stopping after the second ¶*.
3. Proofread and correct errors.
4. Key this text again at rough-draft speed to increase your input rate.

59C◆ **FEATURE**

Right Alignment (Justification)
line spacing: SS
top margin: default

1. Read the copy at right.
2. Learn to align copy at the right margin using your software.
3. Using the default top margin, do Steps 1-3 at the right, SS.

Most text is aligned at the left margin (**left alignment**). When text is centered, it is aligned between the left and right margins. Use the Right Alignment feature when you want a line of text to end even with the right margin. **Right alignment** can be done before or after text is keyed. If turned on before text is keyed, the text will "back up" from the right margin as you key. **Justification** is another word for alignment.

1. Turn on Right Alignment; then key each line.

This line is keyed with Right Alignment on.
This line uses right alignment so that it ends at the right.

2. Turn on Left Alignment; then key each line.

This line can be right-aligned after it is keyed.
Right alignment may be used for page numbers in reports.

3. Right-align the text in Step 2.

59D◆ **FEATURE**

Hanging Indent

1. Read the copy at right and learn to use the Hanging Indent feature in your software.
2. Below the lines of **59C**, do Steps 1-3 at right, SS.

Use the **Hanging Indent** feature to move all but the first line of a paragraph to the right. The first line begins at the left margin, but all other lines in the paragraph wrap around to the indention. (In some software, the indention is the same as the first tab position.)

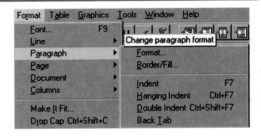

1. Turn on Hanging Indent; then key this paragraph.

This paragraph begins, as usual, at the left margin. When my text wraps to a second line, though, I can see that it is hanging indented.

2. Turn off Hanging Indent; then key this paragraph.

This paragraph is blocked at the left margin.   When I finish the paragraph, I will use Hanging Indent to move lines below the first line to the right.

3. Use Hanging Indent on the text in Step 2.

59E◆
Unbound Report

1. Read "Page Numbers" and "Reference List" in the format guides on p. 154; study the model report, page 2, on p. 157.
2. Key from the model, page 2, p. 157.
3. Proofread and correct errors.

Lesson 17 New Keys: Z and : (Colon)

Objectives:
1. **To learn reach technique for Z and : (colon).**
2. **To combine smoothly Z and : (colon) with all other learned keys.**

17A◆ 7
Conditioning Practice

each line twice SS; then a 1'
writing on line 3; find *gwam*

Note: Whenever directions in this book call for a timed writing, your teacher may time you, or direct you to use the count-down timer in *Applied MicroType Pro*.

all letters learned 1 Jim won the globe for six quick sky dives in Napa.

spacing 2 to own|is busy|if they|to town|by them|to the city

easy 3 She is to go to the city with us to sign the form.

| 1 | 2 | 3 | 4 | 5 | 6 | 7 | 8 | 9 | 10 |

17B◆ 18
New Keys: Z and : (Colon)

each line twice SS (slowly, then faster); DS between 2-line groups; if time permits, rekey lines 7-10

z *Left little* finger

: (colon) *Left Shift* then *right little* finger

SPACING/LANGUAGE SKILLS CUES:
Space twice after : used as punctuation. Capitalize the first word of a complete sentence following a colon.

Follow the *Standard Plan for Learning New Keys* outlined on p. 9.

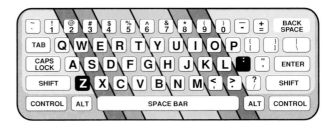

Learn z

1 a a za za zap zap zap zoo zoo zip zip zag zag zany

2 za za zap zap zed zed oz. oz. zoo zoo zip zip maze

3 zap it, zip it, an adz, to zap, the zoo, eight oz.

Learn : (colon)

4 ; ; :: :: Date: Time: Name: Room: From: File:

5 :; :; To: File: Reply to: Dear Al: Shift for :

6 Two spaces follow a colon, thus: Try these steps:

Combine z and : (colon)

7 Zelda has an old micro with : where ; ought to be.

8 Zoe, use as headings: To: Zone: Date: Subject:

9 Liza, please key these words: zap, maze, and zoo.

10 Zane read: Shift to enter : and then space twice.

Formatting Unbound Reports
Lessons 59-62

Unbound Report, Page 1

Unbound Report, Page 2

Note: The textual citation method has largely replaced the footnote method because it is easier and quicker to use.

Format Guides: Unbound Reports

Short reports are often prepared without covers or binders. If they consist of more than one page, the pages are usually fastened together in the upper left corner by a staple or paper clip. Such reports are called **unbound reports**.

Standard Margins

Unbound reports have standard margins.

First page:	
Top margin: 2"	
Side margins: 1" or default	
Bottom margin: at least 1"	
Second and subsequent pages:	
Top margin: 1"	
Side margins: 1" or default	
Bottom margin: at least 1"	

Note: Avoid placing the first line of a paragraph by itself at the bottom of a page. Avoid placing the last line of a paragraph by itself at the top of a new page. Hard returns may be inserted above text to force it onto a new page.

Page Numbers

Page numbers may be keyed at the top or bottom of a page, at the left margin, right margin, or center. The reports in these lessons show the page number at the top right. The page number is omitted from page 1.

Spacing of Reports

QS between the report title and first line of the body. DS multiple-line titles.

DS between side headings and following text, and between paragraphs. Key paragraphs DS unless directed otherwise.

DS between the page number and body on the second and subsequent pages.

Textual Citations

Information to give authors credit for material quoted or paraphrased in the report is given in the report body (in parentheses). **Textual citations** include the name(s) of the author(s), the year of publication, and the page number(s) of the material quoted.

Quotation marks are used around quotations of up to three lines within text. Longer quotations (four lines or more) are set apart from text. Key such long quotations SS. Indent them 0.5" from the left margin; run the lines to the right margin. Use an ellipsis (. . .) to indicate words omitted from a quotation:

> The ability to proofread accurately is one of the most important skills for . . . daily activities that involve working with written communication. (Jones and Kane, 1990, iii)

Reference List

All references (books, magazines, web sites, etc.) used in a report are listed alphabetically by author surnames at the end of a report (a QS below the body or on a separate page) under the heading REFERENCES (or BIBLIOGRAPHY or WORKS CITED). QS between the heading and the first reference.

For a separate reference page, use the same margins as for the first page of the report, but key a page number at the top right margin. SS each reference; DS between references. Begin the first line of each reference at the left margin; indent other lines 0.5".

17C◆ 15
New-Key Mastery

1. Key the lines once SS; DS between 2-line groups.
2. Key the lines again at a faster pace.

Technique goals
- curved, upright fingers
- quiet hands and arms
- steady keystroking pace

Fingers properly aligned

q/z
1 zoo qt. zap quo zeal quay zone quit maze quad hazy
2 Zeno amazed us all on the quiz but quit the squad.

p/x
3 apt six rip fix pens flex open flax drop next harp
4 Lex is apt to fix apple pie for the next six days.

v/m
5 vim mum van dim have move vamp more dive time five
6 Riva drove them to the mall in my vivid lemon van.

easy
7 Glen is to aid me with the work at the dog kennel.
8 Dodi is to go with the men to audit the six firms.

alphabet
9 Nigel saw a quick red fox jump over the lazy cubs.
10 Jacky can now give six big tips from the old quiz.

17D◆ 10
Block Paragraphs

1. Key each paragraph (¶) once SS; DS between them; then key them again faster.
2. Key a 1' writing on each ¶; find your *gwam*.

Paragraph 1   1'

The space bar is a vital tool, for every fifth or   10
sixth stroke is a space when you key. If you use   20
it with good form, it will aid you to build speed. 30

Paragraph 2

Just keep the thumb low over the space bar. Move   10
the thumb down and in quickly toward your palm to   20
get the prized stroke you need to build top skill. 30

| 1 | 2 | 3 | 4 | 5 | 6 | 7 | 8 | 9 | 10 |

Enrichment

1. Key each line once at a steady, easy pace.
2. Key each line again at a faster pace.

Technique goals
- keep fingers upright
- keep hands/arms steady

x/:
1 xs :; |fix mix|Max: Use TO: and FROM: as headings.
2 Read and key: oxen, exit, axle, sixty, and sixth.

q/,
3 qa ,k|aqa k,k|quo quo,|qt. qt.,|quite quite,|squat
4 Quen, key these: quit, aqua, equal, quiet, quick.

p/z
5 p; za|;p; zaza|zap zap|zip zip|size size|lazy lazy
6 Zip put hot pepper on his pizza at the zany plaza.

m/v
7 mj vf|jmj fvf|vim vim|vow vow|menu menu|move movie
8 Mavis vowed to move with a lot more vim and vigor.

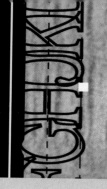

Skill Builder 3

1. Key lines 1-9 once at an easy, steady pace.
2. Key the lines again at a faster pace.
3. Key a 1' writing on each of lines 7-9; find *gwam* on each writing.

alphabet 1 Jukebox music puzzled eight visitors from that quiet valley town.
top row 2 Top-row checkup: 3#, 7&, 4$, 6, 5%, 8*, 9(, 0), 1/4, 1/2, 3 5/8.
keypad 3 1980- 1981-1990 1991-2000 2001-2010 2011-2020 2021-2030 2031-2040

3d/4th fingers 4 Paula saw six zebra eating waxy poppy pods in the quaint old zoo.
adjacent keys 5 Jeremy asked her to go to the theater to see a popular new opera.
long reaches 6 Celia brought my aunt to see a mural unveiled in my dance studio.

double letters 7 A little more effort lesson by lesson will boost my keying skill.
combination 8 In the opinion of a union man the pay rate of a few girls is bad.
balanced-hand 9 She is to sign the audit forms when she pays for the island land.

| 1 | 2 | 3 | 4 | 5 | 6 | 7 | 8 | 9 | 10 | 11 | 12 | 13 |

1. Key a 1' writing on ¶ 1; find *gwam*.
2. Add 4 *gwam* for a new goal rate. (See checkpoint chart below.)
3. Key two 1' *guided* writings on the ¶ to reach the checkpoint each 1/4'.
4. Key ¶ 2 in the same manner.
5. Key two 3' writings on ¶s 1-2 combined; find *gwam* and count errors on each.

Quarter-Minute Checkpoints				
gwam	1/4'	1/2'	3/4'	Time
20	5	10	15	20
24	6	12	18	24
28	7	14	21	28
32	8	16	24	32
36	9	18	27	36
40	10	20	30	40
44	11	22	33	44
48	12	24	36	48
52	13	26	39	52
56	14	28	42	56

a   all letters used

		3'	5'

Someone once said that how our ancestors came to this country does not matter; what does matter is what they achieved after they got here.   Similarly, it matters little who your parents are and what they do; what does count is how you develop your talents and abilities.   Many people sleepwalk through life without goals and do not realize a justifiable purpose to their actions.

	3'	5'
	4	2	33
	9	5	36
	13	8	38
	17	10	41
	22	13	44
	25	15	46

The goals and behavior habits you form now carry over to your later life.   The road to success is filled with many obstacles; to succeed, you must overcome them and not be overcome by them.   Think of each problem as an opportunity for growth through extra effort-- nothing worthwhile is easily won.   What makes our country unique is our freedom to work and develop to our highest potential.

	3'	5'
	29	18	48
	34	20	51
	38	23	54
	43	26	56
	47	28	59
	51	31	61

| 1 | 2 | 3 | 4 |
| 1 | 2 | 3 |

Lesson 18 New Keys: CAPS LOCK and ?

Objectives:

1. To learn reach technique for CAPS LOCK and ? (question mark).
2. To combine smoothly CAPS LOCK and ? (question mark) with other learned keys.

18A◆ 7
Conditioning Practice

each line twice SS; then a 1' writing on line 3; find *gwam*

alphabet 1 Lovak won the squad prize cup for sixty big jumps.

z/: 2 To: Ms. Mazie Pelzer; From: Dr. Eliza J. Piazzo.

easy 3 He is to go with me to the dock to do work for us.

| 1 | 2 | 3 | 4 | 5 | 6 | 7 | 8 | 9 | 10 |

18B◆ 16
New Keys: CAPS LOCK and ? (Question Mark)

each line twice SS (slowly, then faster); DS between 2-line groups; if time permits, rekey lines 7-9

CAPS LOCK
Left little finger

? (question mark)
Left Shift then
right little finger

> Depress CAPS LOCK to key a series of capital letters. To release CAPS LOCK to key lowercase letters, strike CAPS LOCK key again.

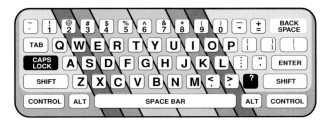

Learn CAPS LOCK

1 Hal read PENTAGON and ADVISE AND CONSENT by Drury.

2 Oki joined FBLA when her sister joined PBL at OSU.

3 Zoe now belongs to AMS and DPE as well as to NBEA.

Learn ? (question mark)

Space twice.

4 ; ; ?; ?; Who? What? When? Where? Why? Is it?

5 Who is it? Is it she? Did he go? Was she there?

6 Is it up to me? When is it? Did he key the line?

Combine CAPS LOCK and ?

7 Did he join a CPA firm? I will stay on with NASA.

8 Is her dad still CEO at BSFA? Or was he made COB?

9 Did you read HOMEWARD? If so, try WHIRLWIND next.

Lesson 18

LEARN **CAPS LOCK** AND **?** (QUESTION MARK) | **41**

1. Identify the rule(s) you need to review/practice.
2. **Read:** Study each rule.
3. **Learn:** Key the *Learn* line(s) beneath it, noting how the rule is applied.
4. **Apply:** Key the *Apply* line(s).
5. Check work with the *Teacher's Key*.

Internal punctuation: Parentheses

RULE 1: Use parentheses to enclose parenthetical or explanatory matter and added information. (Commas or dashes may be used instead.)

Learn 1 Senator Dole (a Republican) ran for the presidency in 1996.
Learn 2 The contracts (Exhibits C and D) need important revisions.
Apply 3 Sean Duncan the person with highest sales is being honored.
Apply 4 The Sixth Edition 2000 copyright date has been delivered.

RULE 2: Use parentheses to enclose identifying letters or figures of lists within a sentence.

Learn 5 Check for these errors: (1) keying, (2) spelling, and (3) grammar.
Apply 6 The focus group leaders are 1 Ramos, 2 Zahn, and 3 Pyle.
Apply 7 The order of emphasis is 1 technique and 2 speed of motions.

RULE 3: Use parentheses to enclose a name and date used as a reference.

Learn 8 Thousands of us heard the "I Have a Dream" speech (King, 1963).
Apply 9 He cited "The Gettysburg Address" Lincoln, 1863 in his report.
Apply 10 We read *The Old Curiosity Shop* Dickens, 1841 in class.

Internal punctuation: Dash

RULE 4: Use a dash (two hyphens with no space before or after) to set off clarifying or added information, especially when it interrupts the flow of the sentence.

Learn 11 The skater--in clown's disguise--dazzled with fancy footwork.
Apply 12 Our trade discounts 10%, 15%, and 20% are the best available.
Apply 13 The gown a copy of an Italian original sells for only $150.

RULE 5: Use a dash before the author's name after a poem or quotation.

Learn 14 "All the world's a stage . . . ." --William Shakespeare
Apply 15 "I have taken all knowledge to be my province." Francis Bacon

18C ◆ 18
New-Key Mastery

1. Key the lines once SS; DS between 2-line groups.
2. Key the lines again at a faster pace.
3. Key a 1' writing on line 11 and then on line 12; find *gwam* on each writing.

Technique goals
- reach *up* without moving hands away from you
- reach *down* without moving hands toward your body

TECHNIQUE CUE:
Use CAPS LOCK to make ALL CAPS.

To find 1' *gwam* : Add 10 for each line you completed to the scale figure beneath the point at which you stopped in a partial line.

Goal: finger-action keystrokes; quiet hands and arms

CAPS LOCK/? 1 Did she join OEA? Did she also join PSI and DECA?
2 Do you know the ARMA rules? Are they used by TVA?

z/v 3 Zahn, key these words: vim, zip, via, zoom, vote.
4 Veloz gave a zany party for Van and Roz in La Paz.

q/p 5 Paul put a quick quiz on top of the quaint podium.
6 Jacqi may pick a pink or aqua suit of unique silk.

key words 7 they quiz pick code next just more bone wove flags
8 name jack flax plug quit zinc wore busy vine third

key phrases 9 to fix it|is to pay|to aid us|or to cut|apt to own
10 is on the|if we did|to be fit|to my pay|due at six

alphabet 11 Lock may join the squad if we have six big prizes.
easy 12 I am apt to go to the lake dock to sign the forms.

| 1 | 2 | 3 | 4 | 5 | 6 | 7 | 8 | 9 | 10 |

18D ◆ 9
Block Paragraphs

1. Key each paragraph once, using soft returns. The lines you key will be longer than the lines shown if default side margins are used. DS between ¶s.
2. If time permits, key a 1' writing on one or two of the paragraphs.

Goal
Continuity (keep the insertion point moving steadily across the screen).

Insert at least four hard returns between 1' writings to avoid confusion when you find *gwam*.

1'

Paragraph 1
When you key lines of drills, strike the return or   10
enter key at the end of each line. That is, use a   20
hard return to space down for a new line.   29

Paragraph 2
When you key copy in this form, though, you do not   10
need to return at the end of each line because the   20
software ends every full line with a soft return.   30

Paragraph 3
Even though your software returns or wraps at line   10
endings, you do have to strike the enter or return   20
key at the end of a paragraph to have a blank line.   31

Paragraph 4
Learn now when you do not need to return at ends   10
of lines and when you must do so. Doing this now   20
will assure that your copy will be in proper form.   30

| 1 | 2 | 3 | 4 | 5 | 6 | 7 | 8 | 9 | 10 |

Language & Writing Skills 11

Activity 1:

1. Study the spelling/definitions of the words in the color block at right.
2. Key the *Learn* lines, noting word choices.
3. Key the *Apply* lines, selecting correct words.
4. Check work with the *Teacher's Key*.
5. Rekey lines in which you made word-choice errors.

Choose the right word

> **farther** *(adv)* greater distance
>
> **further** *(adv)* in greater depth, extent, or importance; additional
>
> **weather** *(n)* state of the atmosphere
>
> **whether** *(conj)* if

Learn 1 The farther I drive, the further my mind wanders.
Learn 2 The weather is dreadful, whether we like it or not.
Apply 3 With (farther, further) effort, I pulled (farther, further) ahead.
Apply 4 Carla asked (weather, whether) the (weather, whether) had improved.

Activity 2:

1. Key lines 1-10, inserting needed parentheses and dashes.
2. Check work with the *Teacher's Key*.
3. Note the rule number(s) at the left of each sentence in which you made an error.
4. Turn to page 152 and identify those rules for review/practice.
5. Use the Read/Learn/Apply plan for each rule to be reviewed.

Proofread & correct

RULE

1	1	The appendices Exhibits A and B utilize computer graphics.
2	2	The three areas are 1 ethical, 2 moral, and 3 legal.
2	3	Emphasize: 1 writing, 2 speaking, and 3 listening.
3	4	You cited the "Liberty or Death" speech Henry, 1775 twice.
4	5	The payment terms 2/10, n/30 are clearly shown on the invoice.
4	6	The article and I know you're interested is in *Newsweek.*
5	7	"The finger that turns the dial rules the air." Will Durant
1	8	The contract reads: "For the sum of $600 Six Hundred Dollars."
4	9	Albert Camus, as you know a Frenchman was an existentialist.
2	10	Her talk addressed two issues: A family values and B welfare.

Activity 3:

1. Key the ¶, correcting punctuation and word choice.
2. Check your work with the *Teacher's Key* and make any needed corrections.
3. Compose/key another ¶ to:
   (a) state the level of your self-image: high, low, or in-between;
   (b) identify factors that make it what it is;
   (c) identify factors that could improve it;
   (d) list any plans you have to raise it.

Compose (think) as you key

   Narcissus, a mythical young man saw his image reflected in a pool of water fell in love with his image, and starved to death admiring himself. Unlike Narcissus, our self-esteem or self-image should come not threw mirror reflections but buy analysis of what we are--inside. Farther, it is dependent upon weather others who's opinions we value see us as strong or week, good or bad positive or negative. No one is perfect, of course; but those, who develop a positive self-image, wait the factors that affect others views of them and work to improve those factors. Its time to start.

Lesson 19 Tab Key

Objectives:
1. **To learn to use the Tab key to indent paragraphs.**
2. **To improve and check keying speed.**

19A◆ 7
Conditioning Practice

each line twice SS; then a
1' writing on line 3; find *gwam*

CAPS LOCK affects only the
letter keys; shifted punctuation marks—such as : and
?—require the use of one of
the shift keys.

Fingers properly curved

alphabet 1 Zosha was quick to dive into my big pool for Jinx.

CAPS LOCK 2 Type ZIP Codes for PA, WV, VA, MD, DE, OH, and IN.

easy 3 Ian kept a pen and work forms handy for all of us.

| 1 | 2 | 3 | 4 | 5 | 6 | 7 | 8 | 9 | 10 |

19B◆ 12
Paragraph Indention

The **Tab key** is used to indent
copy. Software uses preset tabs
(called **default** tabs).

Usually, the first default tab is set
0.5" to the right of the left margin
and is used to indent ¶s (see
copy below right).

1. Locate the Tab key on your
   keyboard (usually at upper
   left of alphabetic keyboard).
2. Reach up to the Tab key with
   the left little finger; strike the
   key firmly and release it
   quickly. The insertion point
   will move 0.5" to the right.

3. Key each ¶ once SS, using
   soft returns; DS between ¶s.
   As you key, strike the Tab
   key firmly to indent the first
   line of each ¶.
4. If you complete all ¶s, rekey
   them as time permits.

Tab key *Left little* finger

Tab ⟶ The tab key is used to indent blocks of copy
such as these.

Tab ⟶ It should also be used for tables to arrange
data quickly and neatly into columns.

Tab ⟶ Learn now to use the tab key by touch; doing
so will add to your keying skill.

Tab ⟶ Strike the tab key firmly and release it very
quickly. Begin the line without a pause.

Tab ⟶ If you hold the tab key down, the cursor will
move from tab to tab across the line.

Above & Beyond
P R O J E C T

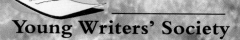

Young Writers' Society

Task 8

Career Day activities will include three workshops for anyone, regardless of career goals. Three presenters have been arranged. You will prepare letters to confirm these arrangements, using the basic message (body) at right and the specific information in the boxes. You will have to supply some details.

Suggestion: Before you start to key, read through the ¶s at right. Mentally, insert the missing letter parts and information from the Letter 1 box. Prepare Letter 1 as a personal-business letter. Then copy and paste it and make the changes needed for Letter 2 and Letter 3.

Use your school's address for the return address. Use next Monday's date. Center the workshop title. Bold the date and time. Use your name as sender. Omit reference initials. Center the letter vertically. Address a large envelope in USPS style.

Thank you for agreeing to present a workshop at [your school's] 30th Annual Career Day. Already, [number] students and teachers have signed up for your session at [time] on Friday, April 3. Many more people likely will enroll once we put up the posters announcing your topic: [centered title]

We would like for you to talk about [make up one or more ideas to be covered and/or questions to be answered for the title of the workshop]. Please include activities for all participants and allow time to answer questions.

Room [number] is the location. Please check in at the Main Office about 15 minutes before the workshop. Someone will escort you to the room. Parking will be available in spaces marked "Visitor" at the front of the building.

If you will need special equipment, please call [teacher's name] at [school telephone number]. After ensuring that the equipment you request works properly, we will set it up before you arrive.I Sincerely yours I [your full name] I Career Day Planning Committee

---

Name/Address:
Ms. Sabrina Wells
Biz–Write Services
900 Main St.
[Your City, ST 00000+0000]

Dear Ms. Wells

Number: 17

Time: 9:30–10:45

Title: "E–Mail Etiquette"

Room: 115

Letter 1

Name/Address:
Mr. Lyle Schaber
CSR Consultants
621 Mehring Way, Ste. 228
[Your City, ST 00000+0000]

Dear Mr. Schaber

Number: 12

Time: 11:00–12:15

Title: "Talking to Your Computer: Voice Recognition and Writing"

Room: 117

Letter 2

Name/Address:
Miss Mie-Yun Lee
Word Tailor
7320 Jager Ct.
[Your City, ST 00000+0000]

Dear Miss Lee

Number: 9

Time: 1:30-2:45

Title: "Step Write Up"

Room: 115

Letter 3

19C◆　　10
Technique: Space Bar, Shift Keys, and CAPS LOCK
each pair of lines twice SS; DS between 4-line groups

Fingers upright

space bar
1 an me so en if em by he ox go am do is no or in to
2 She may go to the city if he can fix the old auto.

shift keys
3 The best dancers are: Ana and Jose; Mag and Boyd.
4 Did Ms. Paxon send us the letter from Dr. LaRonde?

CAPS LOCK
5 Masami saw the game on ESPN; Krista saw it on NBC.
6 The AMS meeting is on Tuesday; the DPE, on Friday.

19D◆　　14
Speed Building

1. Key the lines once SS; DS between 2-line groups.
2. Key a 1' writing on each of lines 5-8; find *gwam* on each writing (1' *gwam* = total 5-stroke words keyed).
3. If time permits, key another 1' writing on line 7 and then on line 8 for speed.

Key words and phrases (*Think*, *say*, and *key* words and phrases.)

1 ad my we in be on at up as no are him was you gets
2 girl quay turn rush duty down maps rich laid spend

3 an ad|to fix|an oak|to get|the zoo|via jet|in turn
4 if they|to risk|by them|the duty|and paid|she kept

Key easy sentences (Key the words at a brisk, steady pace.)

5 He is to aid the girls with the work if they wish.
6 Jan may go to the city for the bid forms for them.

7 He may go to the lake by dusk to do the dock work.
8 I did all the work for the firm for the usual pay.

| 1 | 2 | 3 | 4 | 5 | 6 | 7 | 8 | 9 | 10 |

19E◆　　7
Speed Check

1. Key each ¶ once SS; DS between ¶s. Use wordwrap.
2. Key a 1' writing on each ¶; find *gwam* on each writing (1' *gwam* = figure above the last word keyed—the dots represent odd numbers).

Copy used to measure skill is triple-controlled for difficulty. An **e** shows that these ¶s are easy.

 all letters used

　　　　•　　　2　　　•　　　4　　　•　　　6　　　•　　　8　　　•
　　　Be quick to excel in form and speed. If you
　10　　•　　12　　　•　　14　　　•　　16　　　•　　18　　•
do, you can move back a word or two and watch the
　20　　•　　22　　　•　　24　　　•　　26　　　•　　28　　•
errors fall away. Keep this in mind as you work.

　　　　•　　　2　　　•　　　4　　　•　　　6　　　•　　　8　　　•
　　　You might be amazed how your speed will grow
　10　　•　　12　　　•　　14　　　•　　16　　　•　　18　　•
if you first push for speed and then level off to
　20　　•　　22　　　•　　24　　　•　　26　　　•　　28　　•
take control at just the right speed. Try it now.

58B ◆

Letter in Block Format

1. Set a 2" top margin. Take three 1' writings on the opening lines of the letter at right. Try to add 2 *gwam* on the second and third writings.
2. Take three 1' writings on the last ¶ and closing lines. Try to add 2 *gwam* on the second and third writings.
3. Key the letter rapidly (as you would a rough draft).
4. Correct all of your errors.

	words
(Today's date) │ Mrs. Glendora Ramos │ 3716 Rangely Dr. │ Raleigh, NC	13
27609-4116 │ Dear Mrs. Ramos	18

In these days of fancy office equipment, friendly contact with people is 33
sometimes overlooked. We want you to know that we appreciate this new 47
opportunity to serve you. 52

The enclosed acknowledgment shows the items you ordered a few days 65
ago. As usual, we will follow your instructions for processing and ship- 80
ping. 81

We appreciate receiving payment with an order, but prepayment is not 95
required. You may simply write your account number (see catalog 108
address label) on the order form, and we will send a bill later. 120

Cordially yours │ Miguel J. Maddox │ Mail Order Department │ xx │ 132
Enclosure 134

58C ◆

Personal-Business Letters

Letter 1

Key the copy at right as a personal-business letter, centered vertically (if feature is available). Correct all errors.

Letter 2

Copy Letter 1 and paste it on a new page. Change the letter address, salutation, and name of school (¶ 1):

Xavier C. Johnson, Ph.D.
Admissions Director
Missouri College of Music
314 Merriweather St.
Kansas City, MO 64109-3244
Dear Dr. Johnson

	words
7706 Circle Dr. │ St. Louis, MO 63121-4583 │	8
[Today's date] │ Dr. Yolanda Flores │ Director	17
of Admissions │ LaRhonde School of Music │	25
1035 Bellevue Ave. │ St. Louis, MO 63121-	33
2758 │ Dear Dr. Flores	37

Please send me an application form for admission to the LaRhonde School 51
of Music. I am to be graduated in June and hope to enter college in 65
September. 67

I shall appreciate information about scholarships that are available and 82
the procedure to follow in applying for one. If I am to enter college 96
in September, as I earnestly hope to do, some financial aid is needed. 110

If an audition is required, when should I plan to come to campus and 124
what records should I bring with me? 131

Sincerely yours │ Ivalee Moore 136

review

Objectives:

1. **To demonstrate level of technique mastery.**
2. **To demonstrate level of keying speed attained.**

20A◆ 7
Conditioning Practice

each line twice SS; then a 1'
writing on line 3; find *gwam*

alphabet 1 Quig just fixed prize vases he won at my key club.

spacing 2 Marcia works for HMS, Inc.; Juanita, for XYZ Corp.

easy 3 Su did vow to rid the town of the giant male duck.

| 1 | 2 | 3 | 4 | 5 | 6 | 7 | 8 | 9 | 10 |

20B◆ 20
Technique Check

each line twice SS; DS between
6-line groups

Fingers curved

Fingers upright

Finger-action key-stroking

Down-and-in spacing

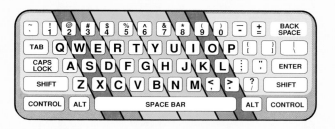

Reach review (Keep on home keys the fingers not used for reaching.)

1 old led kit six jay oft zap cod big laws five ribs

2 pro quo is just my firm was then may grow must try

3 Olga sews aqua and red silk to make six big kites.

Space Bar emphasis (*Think*, *say*, and *key* the words.)

4 en am an by ham fan buy jam pay may form span corn

5 I am a man an elm by any buy ham can plan try them

6 I am to form a plan to buy a firm in the old town.

Shift key emphasis (Reach *up* and reach *down* without moving the hands.)

7 Jan and I are to see Ms. Han. May Lana come, too?

8 Bob Epps lives in Rome; Vic Copa is in Rome, also.

9 Oates and Co. has a branch office in Boise, Idaho.

Easy sentences (*Think*, *say*, and *key* the words at a steady pace.)

10 Eight of the girls may go to the social with them.

11 Corla is to work with us to fix the big dock sign.

12 Keith is to pay the six men for the work they did.

| 1 | 2 | 3 | 4 | 5 | 6 | 7 | 8 | 9 | 10 |

57G◆

Personal-Business Letter with Envelope

1. Review guides for keying a return address in a letter (p. 141) and study the model below.
2. Key the letter at right with a 2" top margin. If the Thesaurus feature is available, look for a synonym to replace *choices* (¶ 2).
3. View, check spelling, proofread, and make all necessary corrections.
4. Address a large envelope in USPS style. Include the return address; add a POSTNET bar code if you can.

9248 Socorro Rd. — 3
El Paso, TX 79907-2366 — 8
(Today's date) — 11

Mrs. Susan L. Orr, Director / Graphic Arts Institute / — 21
2099 Calle Lorca / Santa Fe, NM 87505-3461 / — 30
Dear Mrs. Orr — 32

¶ A graduate of your school, Ms. San-li Chou, — 41
has suggested that I write to you because of — 50
my interest in graphic design. — 56

¶ To keep my choices open, I am taking a college- — 66
prep program. All my electives, though, are — 75
chosen from courses in art, design, and graphics-- — 85
including photography. I do unusually well — 94
in these courses. — 97

¶ Can you send me a catalog that outlines the graphics — 108
programs now being offered by your school. I will — 118
appreciate it. — 121

Cordially yours / Miguel Blanco — 126

Lesson 58   Block Letters: Mastery and Assessment

Objectives:

1. **To improve letter processing skill.**
2. **To process block letters and envelopes.**

| Approx. time: 50' |

58A◆
Keyboard Mastery

Use Skill Builder 2, p. 140, lines 1, 7, and 9, or H on p. A7.

20C◆ 8

Speed Check: Sentences

1. Key a 30" writing on each line. Your rate in *gwam* is shown word-for-word above the lines.
2. Key another 30" writing on each line. Try to increase your keying speed.

Goal

At least 22 *gwam*.

```
30" |    2|    4|    6|    8|   10|   12|   14|   16|   18|   20|   22|

1  He bid for the rich lake land.

2  Suzy may fish off the dock with us.

3  Pay the girls for all the work they did.

4  Quen is due by six and may then fix the sign.

5  Janie is to vie with six girls for the city title.

6  Duane is to go to the lake to fix the auto for the man.

   |    2|    4|    6|    8|   10|   12|   14|   16|   18|   20|   22|
```

If you finish a line before time is up and start over, your *gwam* is the figure at the end of the line PLUS the figure above or below the point at which you stopped.

20D◆ 15

Speed Check: Paragraphs

1. Key a 1' writing on each paragraph (¶); find *gwam* on each writing.
2. Using your better *gwam* as a base rate, select a goal rate and key two 1' guided writings on each ¶ as directed at bottom of page.

e all letters used   2'

```
          •     2     •     4     •     6     •     8     •
Tab → How you key is just as vital as the copy you    5
     10    •    12    •    14    •    16    •    18    •
work from or produce.  What you put on paper is a     10
     20    •    22    •    24    •    26    •    28    •
direct result of the way in which you do the job.     15
          •     2     •     4     •     6     •     8     •
Tab → If you expect to grow quickly in speed, take    19
     10    •    12    •    14    •    16    •    18    •
charge of your mind.  It will then tell your eyes     24
     20    •    22    •    24    •    26    •    28    •
and hands how to work through the maze of letters.    29

   |      1      |      2      |      3      |      4      |      5      |
```

Quarter-Minute Checkpoints				
gwam	1/4'	1/2'	3/4'	Time
16	4	8	12	16
20	5	10	15	20
24	6	12	18	24
28	7	14	21	28
32	8	16	24	32
36	9	18	27	36
40	10	20	30	40

Guided Writing Procedure

Set a practice goal

1. Key a 1' writing on ¶ 1 above.
2. Using the *gwam* as a base, add 4 *gwam* to determine your goal rate.
3. Choose from Column 1 of the table at the left the speed nearest your goal rate. At the right of that speed, note the 1/4' points in the copy you must reach to maintain your goal rate.
4. Determine the checkpoint for each 1/4' from the word-count dots and figures above the lines in ¶ 1. (**Example:** Checkpoints for 24 *gwam* are 6, 12, 18, and 24.)

Practice procedure

1. Key two 1' writings on ¶ 1 at your goal rate guided by the quarter-minute calls.

Goal: To reach one of your checkpoints just as the guide (one-quarter, one-half, three-quarters, or *stop*) is called.

2. Key two 1' writings on ¶ 2 in the same way.
3. If time permits, key a 2' writing on both ¶s together, without the guides.

Speed level of practice

When the purpose of practice is to reach out into new speed areas, use the *speed* level. Take the brakes off your fingers and experiment with new stroking patterns and new speeds. Do this by:

1. Reading 2 or 3 letters ahead of your keying to foresee stroking patterns.
2. Getting the fingers ready for the combinations of letters to be keyed.
3. Keeping your eyes on the copy in the book.

57E◆

Envelopes

1. Study the guides at right and the illustrations below.
2. Prepare a small (No. 6 3/4) and a large (No. 10) envelope for each address (3d column). Use your return address on the small envelopes. Assume that a return address is preprinted on the large envelope.

Return Address
Key the sender's (return) address if it is not preprinted on the envelope. Use block style, SS, and Caps/lowercase. Begin about 0.25" from top of envelope, and 0.25" from left edge.

Delivery Address
Set a tab at 4" for large envelope and at 2.5" for small envelope. Space down about 2". Begin the delivery address at the tab.

USPS (Postal Service) Style
Use block style, SS. Use ALL CAPS; omit punctuation. An address must contain at least three lines. Omit nonessential information to avoid more than six lines. Place ONLY the city name, 2-letter state abbreviation, and ZIP Code + 4 on the last address line. Space once between the state abbreviation and ZIP Code.

Standard Abbreviations
Use USPS standard abbreviations for states and street suffix names, such as AVE and BLVD. Never abbreviate the name of a city or country.

International Addresses
Omit postal (ZIP) codes from the last line of addresses outside the U.S. Show only the name of the country on the last line.

```
MISS ARNELLA WILSON
C/O OASIS MANOR
106 FREMONT ST
LAS VEGAS NV 89101-2277

MR PHONG HO MANAGER
ELECTRONIC PRODUCTS INC
8746 LA JOLLA PKWY
SAN DIEGO CA 92136-3927

MS INGE D FISCHER
HARTMANNSTRASSE 7
4209 BONN 5
FEDERAL
REPUBLIC OF GERMANY

MR HIRAM SANDERS
2121 CLEARWATER ST
OTTAWA ONKIA 0B1
CANADA
```

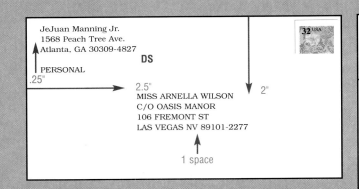

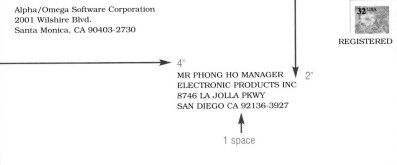

57F◆

Envelope

1. Read the copy at right.
2. Learn to prepare envelopes using the Envelope feature, if available on your software.
3. Open the files for **57B** and **57D** if not already open. Follow the directions at right (below).

The **Envelope** feature places addresses as described and shown above. If the feature is used while a letter is open, the software "reads" the letter address and places it on the envelope. Then the feature may allow you to add the address to its list of addresses. You may need to specify envelope size, type of paper, feed for your printer, your choice of font, and the like. You can choose to print a POSTNET bar code above or below the delivery address. A machine-readable form of ZIP Code + 4, bar codes speed mail sorting at the post office.

1. Use the Envelope feature to address a large envelope for **57B**. If the software "reads" the letter address, use it, though it is not USPS style. Include a POSTNET bar code *above* the delivery address if the software allows. Assume a return address is preprinted on the envelope.

2. Address a large envelope for **57D** in USPS style. Include a POSTNET bar code *below* the address if you can. Assume a return address is preprinted on the envelope.

Master Letter Keyboarding Technique

Lesson 21   Alphabetic Keying Technique

Objectives:
1. **To learn proper response-pattern technique to gain speed.**
2. **To improve technique/speed on alphabetic copy.**

21A◆   5
Conditioning Practice
each line twice SS; then a 1'
writing on line 3; find *gwam*

alphabet	1	Nat will vex the judge if she bucks my quiz group.
punctuation	2	Al, did you use these words: vie, zeal, and aqua?
easy	3	She owns the big dock, but they own the lake land.

| 1 | 2 | 3 | 4 | 5 | 6 | 7 | 8 | 9 | 10 |

Skillbuilding

21B◆   18
Technique: Response Patterns

1. Key each pair of lines twice SS; DS between 4-line groups.
2. Key a 1' writing on line 10 and then on line 12; find *gwam* (total words keyed) on each writing.
3. Key another 1' writing on the slower line to increase your speed on more difficult copy.

> A **balanced-hand** word is one in which the letters of each 2-letter combination are keyed by opposite hands. In a **one-hand** word, all of the letters are keyed with the same hand.

Letter response

Many one-hand words (as in lines 3-4) are not easy to key. Such words may be keyed letter-by-letter and with continuity (steadily without pauses).

Word response

Short, balanced-hand words (as in lines 1-2) are so easy to key that they can be keyed as words, not letter-by-letter. *Think* and *key* them at your top speed.

PRACTICE CUES:

Balanced-hand lines:
Think, say, and *key* the words by word response at a fast pace.
One-hand lines:
Think, say, and *key* the words by letter response at a steady but unhurried pace.

balanced-hand words	1	ah do so go he us if is of or to it an am me by ox
	2	ha for did own the for and due pay but men may box
one-hand words	3	as up we in at on be oh ax no ex my ad was you are
	4	ad ink get ilk far him few pop set pin far imp car
balanced-hand phrases	5	of it|he is|to us|or do|am to|an ox|or by|is to do
	6	do the|and for|she did|all six|the map|for the pay
one-hand phrases	7	as on|be in|at no|as my|be up|as in|at him|saw you
	8	you are|oil tax|pop art|you get|red ink|we saw him
balanced-hand sentences	9	The man is to go to the city and do the auto work.
	10	The girl is to go by bus to the lake for the fish.
one-hand sentences	11	Jimmy saw you feed a deer on a hill up at my mill.
	12	Molly sat on a junk in oily waters at a bare reef.

| 1 | 2 | 3 | 4 | 5 | 6 | 7 | 8 | 9 | 10 |

Thesaurus

1. Read the copy at right.
2. If your software has a Thesaurus feature, learn to use it.
3. Do the 5 steps at right.

The **Thesaurus** feature can make your writing more precise and varied. Use the feature to look for synonyms (words with the same or similar meaning) and antonyms (words with the opposite meaning) of certain words in your text. From the list of synonyms (or antonyms) displayed, you can select one to replace a word in your copy.

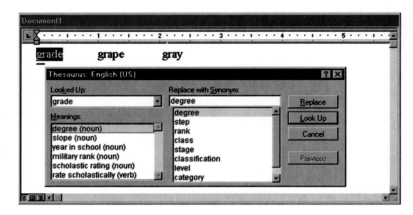

1. QS below the letter (**57B**); key these words: **grade** [tab] **grape** [tab] **gray**.
2. Use the Thesaurus feature to look up the word *grade*. How many nouns are listed as synonyms? How many verbs? Select one of the verbs and replace *grade* on your screen.
3. Use the Thesaurus feature to look up the word *grape*. Are any synonyms listed?
4. How many synonyms can you think of for the word *gray*? Use the Thesaurus to look up the word. If any antonyms are listed, choose one to replace *gray* on your screen.
5. In the letter, replace these words: *choosing* (¶ 1), *safe* (¶ 2). Delete text below the enclosure notation before closing the letter.

57D ◆

Letter with Changes in Wording

1. Format/key the letter (use today's date); center and view it.
2. Replace these words with a synonym if the Thesaurus feature is available:
   chance (¶ 1)
   exact (¶ 2)
   properly (¶ 3)
   signs (¶ 4)
   useful (¶ 5)
3. Make corrections as needed. Keep the letter open on your screen.

words

Miss Rikki Samuels, President | Business Education Club | 14

Sooner High School | 2165 Granada Ave. | San Diego, CA   24

92104-3710 | Dear Miss Samuels   30

Thank you for giving me the chance to tell you the main things we   43
look for in entry-level office workers.   51

First, we look for graduates who have the exact skills we need: in com-   65
munications, keyboarding, word/data processing, accounting, and   79
records management, to name a few. A detailed personal data sheet will   93
usually provide such information.   99

Next, we seek people who show pride in themselves--those who dress   112
properly and are well groomed and who speak positively as well as force-   127
fully about their educational background and related experiences.   140
Usually these behavior patterns are observed in the job interview.   153

Finally, we seek people who show signs that they can work well with   166
others. An effective application letter and data sheet will identify group   182
activities in which the applicant has participated successfully and in what   197
roles.   198

People with these qualifications have at least the potential to develop into   213
useful members of an office staff.   220

Sincerely yours | Miss Maryann Figueroa | Human   229

Services Director | xx   233

21C◆ 12

Speed Building

Line spacing: DS

1. Key one 1' unguided and two 1' *guided* writings on ¶ 1 as directed on p. 46.
2. Key ¶ 2 in the same way.
3. As time permits, key two 2' unguided writings on ¶s 1-2 together; find *gwam*.

1' *gwam* goals

▽ 17 = acceptable

⊡ 21 = average

⊙ 25 = good

◇ 29 = excellent

e all letters used   2'

Keep in home position all of the fingers not   5
being used to strike a key. Do not let them move   10
out of position for the next letters in your copy.   15
    Prize the control you have over the fingers.   19
See how quickly speed goes up when you learn that   24
you can make them do just what you expect of them.   29

21D◆ 15

Technique Mastery: Individual Letters

1. Key each line once; note the lines that caused you to slow down, hesitate, or stop altogether.
2. Key those lines two or three times to eliminate the hesitations and pauses.

Technique goals

■ curved, upright fingers

■ quick-snap keystrokes

■ quiet hands and arms

■ *finger* reaches with no finger "flyout"

A 1 Alan had half a sandwich and a small salad at two.

B 2 Bobbi bought a big blue bow and bright red ribbon.

C 3 Cici can cut yucca and cactus for a class project.

D 4 Dodd did a wild dance to take a second gold medal.

E 5 Eve led her team to a new record in the last meet.

F 6 Fifi filed a full staff report at my field office.

G 7 Gig is going with a good group on the golf outing.

H 8 Hugh has had a huge lead in homers all this month.

I 9 Irena is in high spirits and is in ideal position.

J 10 Jake adjusted a major jump just for the joy of it.

K 11 Kim baked cakes and cookies for a kooky ski party.

L 12 Lars blew his lead and finally fell to last place.

M 13 Mamie must make a major move for many amber items.

N 14 Nat never knew how many friends he could count on.

O 15 Orpha lost a gold locket she wore to the town zoo.

56G ◆

Business Letter

1. Format and key the letter at right. Center it vertically and use Hyphenation if features are available.
2. Preview the letter if you can, comparing the format with the model on p. 142; correct any formatting errors.
3. Replace misspelled words; correct any other errors you make. Leave the letter open.

Some software will change the dash in ¶ 2 from two hyphens to a solid character.

	words
(Today's date) │ Ms. Theresa Dinardo │ Chief Logan High School │ 129 Dorcas	14
St. │ Lewistown, PA 17044-1439 │ Dear Ms. Dinardo	22

You raised an important question. No guides exist for writing and formatting e-mail, but guides are needed. — 37, 43

Some people use formal letter style, which seems to defeat the purpose of e-mail--convenience and speed. Others post messages in the style and tone of memos. Still others suspend nearly all rules, writing in sentence fragments and omitting capitals (or using ALL CAPS) and most punctuation marks. — 58, 73, 88, 102, 103

As the volume of e-mail increases, rules for using it will come out of our need for efficient, effective communication. For now, I recommend a simple, direct "memo" style for your posts. — 118, 133, 141

Sincerely │ Mr. H. D. Brown, Client Services │ xx — 150

56H ◆ FEATURE

Undo and Redo

1. Read the copy at right.
2. Learn to use Undo and Redo (if available) in your software.
3. Follow the directions at right to change the letter on screen (56G).

Use the **Undo** feature to reverse the last change(s) you made in text. Undo restores deleted text to its original location, even if you move the insertion point to another position. The **Redo** feature, available in some word processing packages, reverses the action of Undo.

1. In ¶ 2, delete the dash and the three words after it; delete the parentheses and the four words in them.
2. In ¶ 3, delete *simple, direct*.
3. Use Undo to restore all three deletions.
4. Use Redo (if available) to delete this text again: *—convenience and speed.*

Lesson 57 Letters and Envelopes

Objectives:

1. **To review features of letters in block format.**
2. **To learn to address envelopes.**

Approx. time: 90'

57A ◆

Keyboard Mastery

Use Skill Builder 2, p. 140, lines 1, 5, and 9, or G on p. A6.

57B ◆

Letter in Block Format

1. Prepare the letter at the right. Use today's date; add your reference initials and an enclosure notation.
2. Center the letter and view it if the features are available.
3. Make needed format changes and correct spelling and other errors. Keep the letter open.

	words
Mr. Pablo J. Lobos │ 733 Marquette Ave. │ Minneapolis, MN 55402-2736 │	16
Dear Mr. Lobos	19

Congratulations! You are now the sole owner of the car you financed through our bank. We want to say thank you for choosing us to serve your credit needs. — 33, 47, 50

The original Certificate of Title and your Installment Loan Contract marked "Paid in Full" are enclosed. File the papers in a safe place with your other important records. — 66, 81, 85

You have a preferred credit rating with us. Please let us know when we may serve you again. — 99, 103

Sincerely yours │ Ms. Ilya Lindgren │ Auto Loan Department — 117

Lesson 22 Alphabetic Keying Technique

Objectives:
1. **To learn proper response to different kinds of copy.**
2. **To develop control and speed on script and straight copy.**

22A◆ 5
Conditioning Practice

each line twice SS; then a 1'
writing on line 3; find *gwam*

alphabet 1 Wusov amazed them by jumping quickly from the box.
spacing 2 am to|is an|by it|of us|an oak|is to pay|it is due
easy 3 It is right for the man to aid them with the sign.
| 1 | 2 | 3 | 4 | 5 | 6 | 7 | 8 | 9 | 10 |

Skillbuilding

22B◆ 18
Technique: Response Patterns

1. Key each set of 3 lines twice SS (slowly, then faster); DS between 6-line groups.
2. Key a 1' writing on line 10, on line 11, and on line 12; find *gwam* on each; compare rates.
3. If time permits, rekey the slowest line.

Combination response
Normal copy (as in lines 7-9) includes both word- and letter-response sequences, as described on p. 47. Use *top* speed for word response (easy words), *lower* speed for letter response (words that are harder to key).

letter response 1 be in as no we kin far you few pin age him get oil
2 see him|was nil|vex you|red ink|wet mop|as you saw
3 Milo saved a dazed polo pony as we sat on a knoll.

word response 4 ox if am to is may end big did own but and yam wit
5 do it|to cut|he got|for me|jam it|an owl|go by air
6 He is to go to the city and to do the work for me.

combination response 7 am at of my if on so as to be or we go up of no by
8 am in|so as|if no|is my|is up|to be|is at|is up to
9 Di was busy at the loom as you slept in the chair.

letter 10 Jon gazed at a phony scarab we gave him in a case.
combination 11 Pam was born in a small hill town at the big lake.
word 12 Keith is off to the lake to fish off the big dock.
| 1 | 2 | 3 | 4 | 5 | 6 | 7 | 8 | 9 | 10 |

22C◆ 5
Handwritten Copy (Script)

Key the lines once DS (2 hard returns); rekey the lines if time permits.

1 Script is copy that is written with pen or pencil.
2 Copy that is written poorly is often hard to read.
3 Read script a few words ahead of the keying point.
4 Doing so will help you produce copy free of error.
5 Leave proper spacing after punctuation marks, too.
6 With practice, you will key script at a good rate.

56E ◆

Business Letter

1. Format and key the letter at the right with the Hyphenation feature on (if available) as you key.
2. Center the letter between the top and bottom margins.
3. Check for misspelled words; proofread and correct any other errors you make. Keep the letter (file) open.

	words
(Today's date)	4
Mr. Nigel P. Byers	7
Central High School	11
65 Union Ave.	14
Memphis, TN 38103-2745	19

Dear Mr. Byers — 22

Your question about the effect of word processing equipment on the need — 36
for keying accuracy is a good one. — 43

Accuracy of documents processed is just as important now as ever before. — 58
The ease with which keying errors can now be corrected, however, has — 72
shifted the emphasis from number of input errors made to skill in finding — 87
and correcting these errors. — 93

A major weakness of those who take employment tests is their inability — 107
to detect and correct the errors they make. Therefore, we suggest that — 121
employee training should emphasize proofreading and error correction — 135
rather than error-free input. — 141

A grading system rewarding efficient proofreading and correction skills — 156
instead of penalizing errors of initial input is worthy of your serious — 171
consideration. — 174

Sincerely yours — 177

Ms. Leslie Bancroft, Office Manager | vk — 184

◆ FEATURE

56F ◆

View and Zoom

1. Read the copy at right.
2. Learn how to preview a document using your software.
3. Preview the letter on your screen (**56E**) to see how it will look on a printed page.

The **View**, or **Preview**, feature allows you to see what a document will look like on paper before you print it. Thus you will not waste time and paper printing a document that is not correct. The feature displays a small model of each page. In some software, you can choose whether you want to see full-sized pages, or half-size, quarter-size, etc. Choose a model large enough for you to judge whether margins and the spacing between document parts are appropriate. In some software, documents can be edited in the View mode. If needed, the Zoom feature can be used to enlarge specific parts of a document for a closer look.

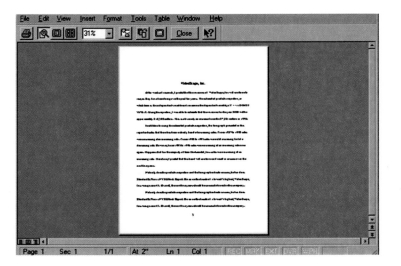

22D◆ 10
Speed Building

Line spacing: DS

1. Key one 1' unguided writing and two 1' guided writings on ¶ 1 as directed on p. 46.
2. Key ¶ 2 in the same way.
3. As time permits, key two 2' unguided writings on ¶s 1-2 together; find *gwam*.

Quarter-Minute Checkpoints			
gwam	1/4'	1/2'	3/4'	Time
16	4	8	12	16
20	5	10	15	20
24	6	12	18	24
28	7	14	21	28
32	8	16	24	32
36	9	18	27	36
40	10	20	30	40

e   all letters used   2'

Are you one of the people who often looks from   5
the copy to the screen and down at your hands? If   10
you are, you can be sure that you will not build a   15
speed to prize. Make eyes on copy your next goal.   20
When you move the eyes from the copy to check   24
the screen, you may lose your place and waste time   30
trying to find it. Lost time can lower your speed   35
quickly and in a major way, so do not look away.   39

22E◆ 12
Technique Mastery: Individual Letters

1. Key each line once; note the lines that caused you to slow down, hesitate, or stop altogether.
2. Key those lines two or three times to eliminate the hesitations and pauses.

Technique goals
- curved, upright fingers
- quick-snap keystrokes
- quiet hands and arms
- *finger* reaches with no finger "flyout"

P 1 Pepi popped up to a new pitcher but kept his cool.

Q 2 Qwen was quick to quote a quip to quiet the squad.

R 3 Rita wrote a big report for her course in history.

S 4 Sisi said she saw a flash before she heard a shot.

T 5 Toby took title to the truck after paying the tax.

U 6 Una is sure to turn a dull party into unusual fun.

V 7 Vic vexed five voters by vivid slogans on his van.

W 8 Wen will wash and wax two wagons for a new lawyer.

X 9 Xena fixed a taxi axle for sixty dollars plus tax.

Y 10 Yanny says he may fly to your zany birthday party.

Z 11 Zaza dazzled us with zany jokes and bizarre humor.

Lesson 56 Block Letters

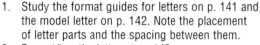

O b j e c t i v e s :

1. **To learn features of block-style letters.**
2. **To process business letters in block format.**
3. **To enhance appearance of letters using word processing features.**

Approx. time: 105'

56A◆

Keyboard Mastery

Use Skill Builder 2, p. 140, lines 1, 2, and 9, or F on p. A6.

56B◆

Business Letter in Block Format

1. Study the format guides for letters on p. 141 and the model letter on p. 142. Note the placement of letter parts and the spacing between them.
2. Format/key the letter on p. 142.
3. Check for misspelled words (Spelling feature), proofread your copy, and correct your errors. Keep the letter open on the screen.

56C◆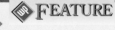

Vertical Center

1. Read the copy at right and study the screen.
2. Learn to center copy vertically using your software.
3. Starting at the date, select and copy the letter on your screen (**56B**); paste the letter on a new page.
4. Center the letter vertically.

Your software enables you to center lines of text between the top and bottom margins of a page. This feature leaves nearly an equal number of blank lines above and below the text.

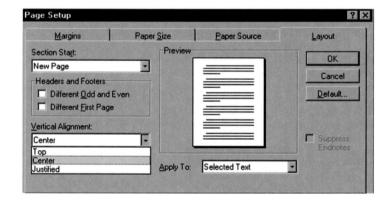

56D◆ FEATURE

Hyphenation

Line spacing: SS
Top margin: 1"

1. Read the copy at right.
2. Learn to use the Hyphenation feature (if available) in your software.
3. Key the text at the lower right with Hyphenation off; key the text again with Hyphenation on.

The **Hyphenation** feature divides (hyphenates) words that normally would wrap to the next line. The use of hyphenation makes a document more attractive by making the right margin more nearly even. In some software, a dialog box requires the operator to decide where to place some hyphens. You could choose to insert a hyphen where the feature has placed it or move the hyphen in the word. Other options may include inserting a space instead of a hyphen, ignoring a word (causing it to wrap to the next line), or suspending Hyphenation (turning it off temporarily).

A very useful feature in most of today's best word processing software packages is the feature that automatically hyphenates long words at the right margin. This feature will automatically divide such words rather than wrap them to the next line. By dividing these words automatically, the Hyphenation feature makes the right margin less "ragged."

Lesson 23 Alphabetic Keying Technique

Objectives:

1. **To improve response-pattern technique to increase speed.**
2. **To improve control and speed on script and straight copy.**

23A◆ 5
Conditioning Practice

each line twice SS; then a 1'
writing on line 3; find *gwam*

alphabet 1 Marjax made five quick plays to win the big prize.

CAPS LOCK 2 Did you say to send the cartons by UPS or by USPS?

easy 3 I am to pay the six men if they do the work right.

| 1 | 2 | 3 | 4 | 5 | 6 | 7 | 8 | 9 | 10 |

Skillbuilding

23B◆ 18
Technique: Response Patterns

1. Key each set of 3 lines twice SS; DS between 6-line groups.
2. Key a 1' writing on line 10, on line 11, and on line 12 to increase speed; find *gwam* on each.

Goal:
At least 24 *gwam* on line 12.

letter response
1 kilo beef yolk were only date upon gave milk rates
2 my car|oil tax|you are|was him|raw milk|as you see
3 We ate plump plum tarts in a pink cafe on a barge.

word response
4 also form town risk fuel auto goal pens iris visit
5 apt to|go for|is also|the goal|fix them|go for the
6 Roxie is also apt to go for the goal of good form.

combination response
7 an in of at is fix pop for him ham are pen far men
8 in the|at the|and tar|for him|due you|she saw them
9 An odor of wax and tar was in the air at the mill.

letter 10 Zac gave only a few facts in a case on wage taxes.
combination 11 He set off for the sea by dusk to see a rare loon.
word 12 It is right for them to audit the work of the men.

| 1 | 2 | 3 | 4 | 5 | 6 | 7 | 8 | 9 | 10 |

23C◆ 10
Speed Building

Line spacing: DS

1. Key one 1' unguided and two 1' *guided* writings on ¶ 1 and then on ¶ 2, as directed on p. 46.
2. Key two 2' unguided writings on ¶s 1-2 together; find *gwam* on each.

e all letters used   2'

      .   2   .   4   .   6   .   8   .
     The level of your skill is a major item when   5
10   .   12   .   14   .   16   .   18   .
you try to get a job. Just as vital, though, may 10
20   .   22   .   24   .   26   .   28   .
be how well you can express ideas in written form. 15

      .   2   .   4   .   6   .   8   .
     It might amaze you to learn what it is worth 19
10   .   12   .   14   .   16   .   18   .
to a company to find those who can write a letter 24
20   .   22   .   24   .   26   .   28   .
of quality as they key. Learn to do so in school. 29

| 1 | 2 | 3 | 4 | 5 |

NuTech Cellulars, Inc.

2" (Approximate)

Dateline April 15, (Current year)

QS (4 hard returns)

Letter address Mr. Jean M. Basanez, Manager
La Layfette's Restaurant
224 Saint Louis St.
Baton Rouge, LA 77802-3615

DS

Salutation Dear Jean DS

Your superb steak au poivre drew me back to La Layfette's yesterday. My guests and I were taken promptly to our table, but we waited over ten minutes before menus were presented to us.

DS

(1")
Body Several times I provided clues to the server that I was hosting the luncheon. Without noting these clues or asking who should receive the check, the server gave it to the person across from me. Had the check been placed upside down in the middle of the table, my client wouldn't have been "put on the spot."

DS

Several times a week someone from my company entertains clients at La Layfette's Restaurant. Will you talk with your staff about presenting menus in a timely manner and about handling checks properly. But please, Jean, don't disturb the chef!

DS

Complimentary close Cordially

QS (4 hard returns)

Luanne Chang

Writer Mrs. Luanne Chang, President

DS

Reference initials mt

(1")

Shown in Times New Roman 12-point type, 2" top margin, 1" side margins, photoreduced.

Block Letter

738 Main Street • Baton Rouge, LA 77802-3827
PHONE: 504-555-1288 • FAX: 504-555-1997 • E-MAIL: nutech@brouge.com

23D ◆ 11

Difficult-Reach Mastery

1. Key each set of 4 lines once SS; DS between 4-line groups.
2. Note the lines that caused you difficulty; practice them again to develop a steady pace.

Adjacent (side-by-side) keys (as in lines 1-4) can be the source of many errors unless the fingers are kept in an upright position and precise motions are used.

Long direct reaches (as in lines 5-8) reduce speed unless they are made without moving the hands forward or downward.

Reaches with the outside fingers (as in lines 9-12) are troublesome unless made without twisting the hands in and out at the wrist.

Fingers properly curved

Fingers properly aligned

Adjacent-key letter combinations

1 Rena saw her buy a red suit at a new shop in town.
2 Opal will try to stop a fast break down the court.
3 Jeremy knew that we had to pool our points to win.
4 Her posh party on their new patio was a real bash.

Long direct reaches with the same finger

5 Herb is under the gun to excel in the second race.
6 My fervor for gym events was once my unique trait.
7 Music as a unique force is no myth in any century.
8 Lynda has since found many facts we must now face.

Reaches with 3d and 4th fingers

9 The poet will opt for a top spot in our port town.
10 Sam said the cash price for gas went up last week.
11 Zane played a zany tune that amazed the jazz band.
12 My squad set a quarter quota to equal our request.

23E ◆ 6

Handwritten Copy (Script)

1. Key a 1' writing on each ¶; find *gwam*.
2. Key a 2' writing on ¶s 1-2 together; find *gwam*.

	1'	2'
If you do not make your goal the first time,	9	5
do not give up or quit. Size up the task and try	19	10
it again in a new way. Try to focus on what will	29	15
help you make your rate the next time.	37	18
It may be that you need just to slow down in	9	23
order to speed up. That is to say, do not try so	19	28
hard to force your speed. Relax, read with care,	29	33
and just let the words flow from your fingers.	38	37

Block Letter

Personal-Business Letter

Format Guides: Block Letters

When all parts of a letter begin at the left margin, as shown in the models at left, the document is arranged in block format (style). Block format is widely used for business and personal letters.

Letter Margins

Top margin: 2"*
Side margins: default (1")
Bottom margin: at least 1"

*Note: Instead of a 2" top margin, letters may be centered vertically, using a software feature.

Basic Parts of Letters

Letter parts are described below in order of their occurrence.

Date: Key or insert the date at the top margin in business letters. In personal-business letters, key the date below the return address.

Letter address: Key the first line of the letter address a QS below the date. Use a personal title (Miss, Mr., Mrs., Ms.) or professional title (Dr., Lt., Senator) before the receiver's name.

Salutation: Key the salutation (greeting) a DS below the letter address.

Body: Begin the letter body (message) a DS below the salutation. SS and block paragraphs with a DS between them.

Complimentary close: Key the complimentary close (farewell) a DS below the last line of the body.

Name of sender: Key the name of the sender a QS below the complimentary close. A personal title (Miss, Mrs., Ms.) may precede the name to show the title a woman prefers. If a man has a name that does not clearly indicate his gender (Kim, Leslie, Pat, for example), the title Mr. may precede his name. A job title or department name may be keyed on the line with the sender's name, separated by a comma; or it may be keyed on the next line at the left margin.

Special Parts of Letters

Return address: In personal-business letters, the return (sender's) address consists of a line for the street address (keyed at the top margin) and one for the city, state, and ZIP Code. The date is keyed a SS below the return address.

Attention line: If a letter is addressed to a company, the address may include an attention line (the first line of the address) to get the attention of a certain department or person having a certain job title.

Example: Attention Human Resources Director

Subject line: A subject line may be used to alert reader(s) to what the letter is about. A subject line may be keyed in ALL CAPS or Caps/lowercase a DS below the salutation.

Reference initials: If someone other than the writer of the letter keys it, the keyboard operator's initials are keyed in lowercase letters a DS below the writer's name, title, or department.

Attachment/Enclosure notation: If another document is attached to or enclosed with a letter, the word *Attachment* or *Enclosure* is keyed a DS below the reference initials. If reference initials are not used, the notation is keyed a DS below the writer's name or title.

Lesson 24 Alphabetic Keying Technique

Objectives:
1. To demonstrate/assess proper keying technique.
2. To demonstrate/assess skill on various kinds of copy.

24A♦ 5
Conditioning Practice

each line twice SS; then a 1'
writing on line 3; find *gwam*

alphabet 1 Jack viewed unique forms by the puzzled tax agent.

? 2 Where is Elena? Did she call? Is she to go, too?

easy 3 Title to all of the lake land is held by the city.

| 1 | 2 | 3 | 4 | 5 | 6 | 7 | 8 | 9 | 10 |

Skillbuilding

24B♦ 10
Speed Building

1. Key the lines once SS with a DS between 2-line groups.
2. If time permits, key the lines again to improve keying ease and speed.

Technique goals
- reach *up* without moving hands away from you
- reach *down* without moving hands toward your body
- use quick-snap keystrokes

ed/de 1 ed de led ode need made used side vied slide guide
2 Ned said the guide used video slides for her talk.

ju/ft 3 ju ft jug oft jut aft jug lift just soft jury loft
4 Judy left fifty jugs of juice on a raft as a gift.

ol/lo 5 ol lo old lot lob lox log sold loan fold long told
6 Lou told me that her local school loans old books.

ws/sw 7 ws sw was swat laws rows cows vows swam sway swing
8 Swin swims at my swim club and shows no big flaws.

ik/ki 9 ik ki kit ski kin kid kip bike kick like kiwi hike
10 The kid can hike or ride his bike to the ski lake.

za/az 11 za az zap adz haze zany lazy jazz hazy maze pizzas
12 A zany jazz band played with pizzazz at the plaza.

alphabet 13 Olive Fenz packed my bag with six quarts of juice.
14 Jud aims next to play a quick game with Bev Fritz.

| 1 | 2 | 3 | 4 | 5 | 6 | 7 | 8 | 9 | 10 |

24C♦ 14
Speed Check: Straight Copy

Line spacing: DS

1. Key one 1' unguided and two 1' *guided* writings on ¶ 1 and then on ¶ 2, as directed on p. 46.
2. Key two 2' unguided writings on ¶s 1-2 together; find *gwam* on each.

Goals
1': At least 22 *gwam*.
2': At least 20 *gwam*.

e all letters used   2'

$\quad$.   2   .   4   .   6   .   8
You must realize by now that learning to key   5
  10   .   12   .   14   .   16   .   18
requires work. However, you will soon be able to   10
  20   .   22   .   24   .   26   .   28
key at a higher speed than you can write just now.   15
         .   2   .   4   .   6   .   8
You will also learn to do neater work on the   19
  10   .   12   .   14   .   16   .   18
machine than you can do by hand. Quality work at   24
  20   .   22   .   24   .   26   .   28
higher speeds is a good goal for you to have next.   29

| 1 | 2 | 3 | 4 | 5 |

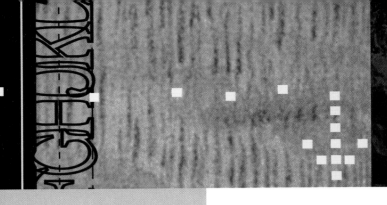

1. Key lines 1-9 once at an easy, steady pace.
2. Key the lines again at a faster pace.
3. Key a 1' writing on each of lines 7-9; find *gwam* on each writing.

alphabet 1 Marj is quite pleased with a snazzy jewelry box we got for Vicki.
top row 2 Ramos & Cho used an * to identify "best buys": #17285*; #30496*.
keypad 3 -- 631-2805 941-1700 271-8655 321-6947 891-3716 871-4302 711-5529

space bar 4 The boys and the girls will do their very best every day and win.
shift keys 5 Maria Spinoza and Nancy Spahn sailed to Spain and Italy in April.
CAPS LOCK 6 Melinda used THE WORLD ALMANAC 1999 as the source for her tables.

one-hand 7 John saw him join my best union crew at my mill as we were aware.
combination 8 Handle the gas with care and test it when you get it into a pump.
balanced-hand 9 They wish to go to the city hall to visit the busy field auditor.

| 1 | 2 | 3 | 4 | 5 | 6 | 7 | 8 | 9 | 10 | 11 | 12 | 13 |

---

1. Key a 1' writing on ¶ 1; find *gwam*.
2. Add 4 *gwam* for a new goal rate. (See checkpoint chart below.)
3. Key two 1' *guided* writings on the ¶ to reach the checkpoint each 1/4'. (See p. 46.)
4. Key ¶ 2 in the same manner.
5. Key two 3' writings on ¶s 1-2 combined; find *gwam* and count errors on each.

Quarter-Minute Checkpoints

gwam	1/4'	1/2'	3/4'	Time
20	5	10	15	20
24	6	12	18	24
28	7	14	21	28
32	8	16	24	32
36	9	18	27	36
40	10	20	30	40
44	11	22	33	44
48	12	24	36	48
52	13	26	39	52
56	14	28	42	56

a all letters used

		3'	5'

One of the great hazards in social and medical science lies in — 4 | 3 | 31

pretending that we know exactly what is best for an individual, a — 9 | 5 | 33

couple, or a group. People vary so much that the utmost we can ex- — 13 | 8 | 36

pect is a series of general or specific guidelines that have been — 17 | 10 | 39

tested and proven quite effective in careful research with large — 22 | 13 | 41

numbers of individuals. — 23 | 14 | 42

Education is a social science, and teaching people how to key — 27 | 16 | 45

is not an exception. Good teaching, like developing solid learning — 32 | 19 | 47

material, depends upon a set of major guides or rules that are — 36 | 22 | 50

based on the findings of careful research into how learners acquire — 41 | 24 | 53

a skill most easily. This is why a teacher knows best what and how — 45 | 27 | 55

a student should practice. — 47 | 28 | 56

| 1 | 2 | 3 | 4 |
| 1 | 2 | 3 |

24D◆ 8
Corrected Copy (Rough Draft)

1. Study the proofreader's marks illustrated below and in the sentences.
2. Key each sentence DS, making all handwritten changes.
3. Rekey the lines to improve your correcting speed.

Proofreader's Marks

≡ = capitalize
∧ = insert
⟊ = delete
ᴎ = transpose
= add space
⌒ = close up
⊙ = insert period

---

1 Rough draft is ~~typed work~~ keyed copy with hand written changes.

2 Special marks are ~~may be~~ used to show changes tobe # made.

3 First read a sentence notᴵing changes; then ~~type~~ key it.

4 Next, check to see that ~~if~~ you made the changes correctly properly⊙

5 If not correct your ~~copy~~ work or key the that sentence again.

6 Read rough draft slightly ~~a bit~~ ahead of ~~your~~ the keying p⌒oint.

7 Doing so ~~this~~ will help you make to ~~all~~ the changⴺe right.

8 You soon will key often from script and rough draft⊙ ~~copy~~

24E◆ 13
Skill Transfer: Straight Copy to Script and Rough Draft

1. Key each ¶ once SS; DS between ¶s.
2. Key a 1' writing on each ¶; find *gwam* on each writing; compare the three rates.

   Your highest speed should be on ¶ 1 (straight copy); next highest on ¶ 2 (script); lowest on ¶ 3 (rough draft).

3. Key one or two more 1' writings on the two slowest ¶s to improve skill transfer.

Recall

1' *gwam* = total words keyed

A standard word = 5 strokes (characters and spaces)

Straight copy   1'

No matter what form the copy takes, keep the eyes on it   11
as you key. If you look away from the copy, you lose a second   24
or two. If you look away too often, your speed will drop by   36
a word or two.   39

Script

Fix your eyes on the copy now and keep them   9
there as you key this copy. Be quick to recognize   19
that looking away from the copy drops your speed.   29

Rough draft

Reád script and rough draft with real great care to avoⅰd a   11
major error in keying, typing. Read slightly a bit ahead of where your the fingers   23
are key⌒ing; that helps too.   29

ALPHABETIC KEYING TECHNIQUE   54

1. Identify the rule(s) you need to review/practice.
2. **Read:** Study each rule.
3. **Learn:** Key the *Learn* line(s) beneath it, noting how the rule is applied.
4. **Apply:** Key the *Apply* line(s).
5. Check work with the *Teacher's Key*.

Internal punctuation: Quotation marks

RULE 1:	Use quotation marks to enclose direct quotations. **Note**: When a question mark applies to the entire sentence, place it outside the quotation marks.

Learn 1 Professor Dye asked, "Are you spending the summer in Europe?"
Learn 2 Was it Emerson who said, "To have a friend is to be one"?
Apply 3 Marcella asked, May I borrow your class notes from yesterday?
Apply 4 Did John Donne say, No man is an island, entire of itself?

RULE 2:	Use quotation marks to enclose titles of articles, films/movies, poems, songs, television programs, and unpublished works, such as theses and dissertations.

Learn 5 Kari read aloud the poem "Fog" from Sandburg's <u>Selected Poems</u>.
Apply 6 The song Getting to Know You is from The King and I.
Apply 7 The title of his term paper is PC Software for Grade 4.

RULE 3:	Use quotation marks to enclose special words or phrases used for emphasis or for coined words (words not in dictionary usage).

Learn 8 My problem: I have "limited resources" and "unlimited wants."
Apply 9 His talk was filled with phrases like ah and you know.
Apply 10 She said that the words phony and braggart describe him.

RULE 4:	Use a single quotation mark (the apostrophe) to indicate a quotation within a quotation (including titles and words as indicated in Rules 2 and 3, above).

Learn 11 I wrote, "We must have, as Tillich said, 'the courage to be.'"
Apply 12 I said, "As Milton wrote, he is 'sober, steadfast, and demure."
Apply 13 I say, "Don't lie, for Swift said, facts are stubborn things."

Internal punctuation: Hyphen

RULE 5:	Use a hyphen to join compound numbers from twenty-one to ninety-nine that are keyed as words.

Learn 14 The youngest member is twenty-one; the oldest fifty-seven.
Apply 15 Anita invited thirty five guests to her twenty-first birthday party.
Apply 16 Thirty four delegates went to the national convention.

RULE 6:	Use a hyphen to join compound adjectives preceding a noun they modify as a unit.

Learn 17 End-of-term grades will be posted outside the classroom.
Apply 18 The most up to date fashions are featured in the store window.
Apply 19 Their new computer programs feature state of the art graphics.

Language & Writing Skills 1

Activity 1:

1. Study the spelling/definitions of the words in the color block at right.
2. Key line 1 (the *Learn* line), noting the proper choice of words.
3. Key lines 2-3 (the *Apply* lines), choosing the right words to complete the lines.
4. Key the remaining lines in the same way.
5. Check your accuracy; rekey lines containing errors.

Choose the right word

do *(vb)* to bring about; to carry out	**hear** *(vb)* to gain knowledge of by the ear
due *(adj)* owed or owing as a debt; having reached the date for payment	**here** *(adv)* in or at this place; at this point; in this case; on this point

Learn 1 If you do pay when it is due, the cost will be less.
Apply 2 (Do, Due) you expect the plane to arrive when it is (do, due)?
Apply 3 (Do, Due) you want me to indicate the (do, due) date of the invoice?

Learn 4 Did you hear the sirens while you were here in the cellar?
Apply 5 (Hear, Here) is the new CD you said you wanted to (hear, here).
Apply 6 To (hear, here) well, we should see if we can get seats (hear, here).

Activity 2:

1. Key lines 1-10 at right, supplying capital letters as needed.
2. Check work with the *Teacher's Key*.
3. Note the rule numbers at the left of each sentence in which you made a capitalization error.
4. Turn to page 56 and identify those rules for review.
5. Follow the Read/Learn/Apply plan for each rule to be reviewed.

Proofread & correct

RULES
1,6   1   has dr. holt moved his offices to hopewell medical center?
1,3,5   2   pam has made plans to spend thanksgiving day in fort wayne.
1,2,8   3   j. c. hauck will receive a d.d.s. degree from usc in june.
1,4,6   4   is tech services, inc., located at fifth street and elm?
1,2,7   5   i heard senator dole make his acceptance speech on thursday.
1,3,8   6   did mrs. alma s. banks apply for a job with butler county?
1,3   7   she knew that albany, not new york city, is the capital.
1,3   8   eldon and cindy marks now live in santa fe, new mexico.
1,6   9   are you going to the marx theater in mount adams tonight?
1,2,6   10   on friday, the first of july, we move to keystone plaza.

Activity 3:

1. Read Sentence 1 to decide the word to supply in the blank.
2. Key Sentence 1, inserting the word that correctly completes the sentence.
3. Follow Steps 1-2 to complete the other sentences.
4. Check the accuracy of your work with the teacher; correct any errors you made.

Compose (think) as you key

1 All that glitters is not _____.

2 Do not cry over spilt _____.

3 A friend in need is a friend _____.

4 A new broom always sweeps _____.

5 A penny saved is a penny _____.

Language & Writing Skills 10

Activity 1:

1. Study the spelling/definitions of the words in the color block at right.
2. Key the *Learn* lines, noting word choices.
3. Key the *Apply* lines, selecting correct words.
4. Check work with the *Teacher's Key.*
5. Rekey lines in which you made word-choice errors.

Choose the right word

wait *(vb / n)* to stay in place; to pause; to serve as a waiter; act of waiting	**weak** *(adj)* lacking in strength, skill, or proficiency
weight *(n)* amount something weighs	**week** *(n)* a series of seven days; series of days within seven-day period

Learn 1 Opal wants to wait until her weight loss is complete.
Learn 2 For more than a week, his performance was weak.
Apply 3 I'll gain more (wait, weight) the longer I (wait, weight).
Apply 4 Mel was too (weak, week) to practice last (weak, week).

Activity 2:

1. Key lines 1-10, inserting needed single and double quotation marks and hyphens.
2. Check work with the *Teacher's Key.*
3. Note the rule number(s) at the left of each sentence in which you made an error.
4. Turn to page 139 and identify those rules for review/practice.
5. Use the Read/Learn/Apply plan for each rule to be reviewed.

Proofread & correct

RULES

1	1	The coach asked, How many of you practiced during the summer?
1	2	Didn't Browne say, "There is no road or ready way to virtue?"
2	3	Do you and your sister regularly watch The Nanny on TV?
2	4	My mom's column, Speak Up, appears in the local newspaper.
3	5	You have trouble deciding when to use affect and effect.
1,4	6	I said, I must take, as Frost wrote, 'the road less traveled.
5	7	Jae boasted, "I'm almost twenty one; you're thirty two."
6	8	My older self confident cousin sells life insurance door to door.
6	9	The weekly best seller list appears in Sunday's newspaper.
6	10	Over the counter sales showed a great increase last month.

Activity 3:

1. Key the ¶, correcting the word-choice errors it contains. (Every line contains at least 1 error; some contain as many as 4 errors.)
2. Check your work with the *Teacher's Key.*
3. Finally, compose/key a second ¶ to:
   (a) express your viewpoint about special treatment of "stars."
   (b) state your view about whether *same offense/same penalty* should apply to everyone alike.

Compose (think) as you key

Some people think that because their good at sum sport, music, or other activity, there entitled to respect and forgiveness for anything else they choose to do in the passed. Its not uncommon, than, when such people break the law or violate sum code of conduct, four them to expect such behavior to be overlooked buy those who's job it is to enforce the law or to uphold an established code of conduct. Sum parents, as well as others in hour society, think that a "star's" misbehavior ought too be treated less harshly because of that person's vary impressive "celebrity" status; but all people should be treated equally under and threw the law.

1. Identify the rule(s) you need to review/practice.
2. **Read:** Study each rule.
3. **Learn:** Key the *Learn* line(s) beneath it, noting how the rule is applied.
4. **Apply:** Key the *Apply* line(s), supplying the needed capital letters.
5. Check work with the *Teacher's Key*.

Capitalization

| **RULE 1:** | Capitalize the first word of a sentence, personal titles, and names of people. |

Learn   1   Ask Ms. King if she and Mr. Valdez will sponsor our club.
Apply   2   did you see mrs. watts and gloria at the school play?

| **RULE 2:** | Capitalize days of the week and months of the year. |

Learn   3   He said that school starts on the first Monday in September.
Apply   4   my birthday is on the third thursday of march this year.

| **RULE 3:** | Capitalize cities, states, countries, and specific geographic features. |

Learn   5   When you were recently in Nevada, did you visit Lake Tahoe?
Apply   6   when in france, we saw paris from atop the eiffel tower.

| **RULE 4:** | Capitalize names of clubs, schools, companies, and other organizations. |

Learn   7   The Voices of Harmony will perform at Music Hall next week.
Apply   8   lennox corp. owns the hyde park athletic club in boston.

| **RULE 5:** | Capitalize historic periods, holidays, and events. |

Learn   9   The Fourth of July celebrates the signing of the Declaration of Independence.
Apply   10   henri asked if memorial day is an american holiday.

| **RULE 6:** | Capitalize streets, buildings, and other specific structures. |

Learn   11   Jemel lives at Bay Shores near Golden Gate Bridge.
Apply   12   dubois tower is on fountain square at fifth and walnut.

| **RULE 7:** | Capitalize an official title when it precedes a name and elsewhere if it is a title of high distinction. |

Learn   13   In what year did Juan Carlos become King of Spain?
Learn   14   Masami Chou, our class president, made the scholastic awards.
Apply   15   did the president speak to the nation from the rose garden?
Apply   16   mr. chavez, our company president, chairs two major panels.

| **RULE 8:** | Capitalize initials; also, letters in abbreviations if the letters would be capitalized when the words are spelled out. |

Learn   17   Does Dr. R. J. Anderson have an Ed.D. or a Ph.D.?
Learn   18   She said that UPS stands for United Parcel Service.
Apply   19   we have a letter from ms. anna m. bucks of washington, dc.
Apply   20   m.d. means Doctor of Medicine, not medical doctor.

Above & Beyond
PROJECT

Young Writers' Society

Project Tasks

Read the text at the right; then complete each task outlined below.

Task 6

Prepare a memo to the Career Day panel.

TO: Career Day Panel

FROM: [Your Name], Young Writers' Society

DATE: [Today's date]

SUBJECT: WRITING ON THE JOB

Tell the panel: **The list below may help you prepare for Career Day. Members of Young Writers' Society said that taking the actions on this list helped them to write better. Do you do these things in your writing? What other actions can we take to improve our writing?**

Now list and center the actions (shaded in the memos). You may word the actions differently.

Example: *Pretend that you are talking to the reader(s).*

Task 7

1. Write a memo to your keyboarding teacher. State how using word processing software has helped you with your school work OR how it may help you later. Name a class activity that helps you to learn or build skill.

2. Include a question about writing or word processing that you would ask the Career Day panel to discuss.

Students filled out and returned the Career Day questionnaire you prepared (p. 125). Of the three program ideas, students favored the panel discussion about writing on the job.

The panel will include people who work at your school and other organizations in your area. To help them prepare, you will send them information about the writing problems of students in YWS.

At your request, most members sent a memo to YWS' writing coach telling him (1) ways in which their writing improved last term and (2) what action(s) helped them improve (highlighted words). Here are a few of their memos.

• •

Task 6

Student Memo 1

TO:	Mr. Roger Holloway
FROM:	Marissa Simms
DATE:	January 18, ----
SUBJECT:	BETTER WRITING

My writing has improved in two ways: I make fewer "false starts" than I used to, and I give my written work a "finished" look. Here are two ways that you have helped me: You said, "pretend that you are talking to the person or people who will read your writing." Also, you showed me how to format my text so that it looks nice and is easy to read.

Student Memo 2

TO:	Mr. Holloway
FROM:	Michael Sanders
DATE:	January 18, ----
SUBJECT:	HOW MY WRITING HAS IMPROVED

My writing *flows* smoother these days. Your almost-constant reminders to "ignore errors!" while drafting text is the main thing that made this happen.

Student Memo 3

TO:	Roger Holloway
FROM:	Jensen Zhao
DATE:	January 18, ----
SUBJECT:	HOW MY WRITING HAS IMPROVED

People who read my writing don't ask as many questions as they used to. My writing must be clearer--easier to understand. Your advice about the four C's of good writing helped me, I think. Every time, I ask myself, "Is it clear? Is it complete? Is it concise? Is it courteous?"

Learn Top-Row Technique: Figures
Lesson 25   New Keys: 8 and 1

Objectives:
1. To learn reach technique for 8 and 1.
2. To improve skill on straight copy, script, and rough draft.

25A◆   5
Conditioning Practice
Line spacing: SS
Side margins: default

each line twice (slowly, then faster); a 1' writing on line 3; find *gwam*

alphabet 1 Max was quick to fly a big jet plane over the frozen desert.

spacing 2 Any of them can aim for a top goal and reach it if they try.

easy 3 Nan is to go to the city hall to sign the land forms for us.

| 1 | 2 | 3 | 4 | 5 | 6 | 7 | 8 | 9 | 10 | 11 | 12 |

25B◆   16
New Keys: 8 and 1

each line twice (slowly, then faster); DS between 2-line groups; if time permits, key lines 5-7 again to build skill

8 *Right middle* finger

1 *Left little* finger

Follow the *Standard Plan for Learning New Keys* outlined on p. 9.

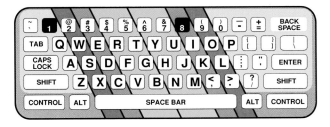

Learn 8
1 k k 8k 8k kk 88 k8k k8k 88k 88k Reach up for 8, 88, and 888.
2 Key the figures 8, 88, and 888. Please open Room 88 or 888.

Learn 1
3 a a 1a 1a aa 11 a1a a1a 11a 11a Reach up for 1, 11, and 111.
4 Add the figures 1, 11, and 111. Has just 1 of 111 finished?

Combine 8 and 1
5 Key 11, 18, 81, and 88. Just 11 of the 18 skiers have left.
6 Reach with the fingers to key 18 and 188 as well as 1 and 8.
7 The stock person counted 11 coats, 18 slacks, and 88 shirts.

55D ◆

Memo Assessment

Memo 1

1. Prepare the copy at right as a memo. Bold the words in ¶ 4 as you key.
2. Add your initials as the keyboard operator.
3. Correct all errors.

TO: Student Council Officers   6

FROM: Lenore M. Fielding, Principal   13

DATE: **(Today's date)**   18

SUBJECT: STUDENT BEHAVIOR AT ATHLETIC EVENTS   27

Reports from a number of faculty and parents suggest that the behavior of   42
a few of our students at two recent athletic events violated the Code of   57
Student Conduct.   60

Only a few students were involved, and only three incidents were reported.   76
Even so, the reported behavior does not create the image Lakeview wants   90
to portray to members of our community or visitors from other commu-   104
nities.   105

Because you along with your fellow council officers monitor such events   120
and participate in the evaluation of Code of Student Conduct violations, I   135
want to meet with you and the assistant principals to review these reports   150
and their impact on our school's image.   158

This meeting is scheduled for **2:30 this Thursday afternoon in Conference** 174
Room B. Be prepared to tell us what you know about any such incidents   187
and what action you think we should take. | xx   196

· ·

words

Memo 2

1. Key the text at right as a memo. Change the heading lines to ALL CAPS. Add an enclosure notation.
2. Correct all errors.

Memo 3

1. Copy Memo 2; paste it on a new page.
2. TO: **All Guidance Counselors**.
3. Delete the last ¶ and enclosure notation.
4. In ¶ 2, replace *many* with **13**; delete *telephone*; replace *several* with **3**.

To: Manuel Delgado, Community Services Coordinator   10

From: Lenore M. Fielding, Principal   18

Date: November 18, (Current year)   23

Subject: Community Clean-up Campaign   30

Congratulations to you and your junior/senior workers on a   42
successful Community Clean-up Campaign.   50

I have received many telephone calls and several letters from   63
people in the community conveying their thanks to and admira-   75
tion for these students. They freely gave their time and   86
effort to help the elderly and others in the community who   98
were physically unable to perform the needed work themselves.   111

Please share our compliments and gratitude with your work-   122
force. Their attitude and conduct during this campaign have   135
enhanced our image in the community.   142

I am enclosing an envelope containing some telephone messages   155
and letters for you to share with the students who partici-   166
pated. | xx   169

25C◆ 16
New-Key Mastery

1. Key lines 1-12 once SS; DS between 2-line groups.
2. Key a 1' writing on line 13, then on line 14; find *gwam* on each writing.
3. If time permits, key a 1' writing on line 8 and then on line 12, trying to maintain your better rate in Step 2.

Technique goals

■ reach *up* without moving the hand forward

■ reach *down* without twisting the wrists or moving the elbows in and out

Row emphasis

figures
1 The quiz on the 18th will be on pages 11 to 18 and 81 to 88.
2 Just 11 of the 118 boys got 81 of the 88 quiz answers right.

home/1st
3 hand axe| lava gas| can mask| jazz band| lack cash| a small flask
4 Ms. Hamm can call a cab, and Max can flag a small black van.

home/3d
5 she quit| with just| that play| fair goal| will help| they did go
6 Dru said you should try for the goal of top speed this week.

Response patterns

letter response
7 as in re on we no ax up gas oil red mop fee hum are you were
8 You, in fact, saw him on a pump barge up at my mill at noon.

word response
9 if so is do id go us me am by an ox and the for men end form
10 She is to go by the zoo to sign a work form for the six men.

combination response
11 if as so in is re do on go we us no me ax am up by pi an kin
12 If she is at the inn, we may go by car to see a poppy field.

easy
13 Ty is to pay for the eight pens she laid by the audit forms.
14 Keith is to row with us to the lake to fix six of the signs.

| 1 | 2 | 3 | 4 | 5 | 6 | 7 | 8 | 9 | 10 | 11 | 12 |

Skillbuilding

25D◆ 13
Speed Building

1. Key a 1' writing on each ¶; find *gwam* on each writing.
2. Add 2-4 *gwam* to better rate in Step 1 for a new goal.
3. Key three 1' guided writings on each ¶ at new goal rate. (See p. 46 for procedure.)

Quarter-Minute Checkpoints			
gwam	1/4'	1/2'	3/4'	Time
16	4	8	12	16
20	5	10	15	20
24	6	12	18	24
28	7	14	21	28
32	8	16	24	32
36	9	18	27	36
40	10	20	30	40

e all letters used

Do you think that someone is going to wait around just for a chance to key your reports? Do you believe that when you work in an office there will be someone to key your documents for you? Think again. The world does not work that way.

Even a person in an important office position, such as the head of a business, now uses a computer to send and get data. Be quick to realize that you can get more done at work when you learn to key with great skill. Try to excel at this and move up in your career.

| 1 | 2 | 3 | 4 | 5 | 6 | 7 | 8 | 9 | 10 | 11 | 12 |

Lesson 55 Memos: Mastery and Assessment

O b j e c t i v e s :
1. **To check your knowledge of memo format.**
2. **To check the level of your memo processing skill.**

Approx. time: 60'

55A◆
Keyboard Mastery

Use Skill Builder 1, p. 128, lines 1, 7, and 9, or E on p. A6.

55B◆
Review

1. Key all lines as shown DS.
2. Change lines 1-4: use c/lc, bold, and the Arial font. Move line 2 to line 5; move line 3 to line 9; move line 4 to line 13.
3. Delete underlines; use italic instead.
4. Change newspaper titles (lines 11-13) to uppercase.
5. Bold http:// in each web site address (lines 14-16).
6. Center all lines.

1 BOOKS/PUBLISHERS
2 MAGAZINES
3 NEWSPAPERS
4 WEB SITES
5 A Reporter's Life/Knopf
6 Snow Falling on Cedars/Vintage
7 Simple Abundance/Warner
8 Modern Maturity
9 Outdoor Life
10 Seventeen
11 Bay News
12 Boston Globe
13 Erie Sentinel
14 http://games.net
15 http://plch.lib.oh.us/kidspace
16 http://www.smithsonianmag.si.edu

55C◆
Memo Mastery

1. Using the default top margin, take three 1' writings on the opening lines of this memo; QS between writings. Try to key 2 more words (10 characters and spaces) on the second and third writings.
2. Format and key all the copy at right as a memo. Italicize the word *Periscope* (¶ 2) as you key. Add an attachment notation.
3. Check spelling and replace or correct all misspelled words. Correct all other errors, too.

words

TO:	Jonathon Eagle	4
FROM:	Jacque Jordan	8
DATE:	(Today's date)	12
SUBJECT:	ARTICLE FOR PERISCOPE	19

Attached is an annotated guide sheet for the preparation of your article | 33
reviewing the native American art exhibit at Lakeview. | 44

Because space in *Periscope* is limited, we allocate that space before | 58
articles are written so that you, rather than the editor, hone your copy to | 73
fit the space. | 76

As the guide sheet indicates, you may use 2 columns of 34 lines each | 90
plus the equivalent of 6 lines across the 2 columns for the title and by- | 104
line. So you have 68 lines of approximately 40 characters each for your | 119
story. If you key your copy using this line length, a quick line count will | 134
indicate whether cutting or expanding is needed. | 146

Lesson 26 New Keys: 9 and 4

Objectives:

1. **To learn reach technique for 9 and 4.**
2. **To improve skill on straight copy, script, and rough draft.**

26A ◆ 5
Conditioning Practice

Line spacing: SS
Side margins: default

each line twice; then a 1' writing on line 3; find *gwam*

alphabet 1 Joby quickly fixed a glass vase and amazed the proud owners.

spacing 2 She told us to add the figures 11, 88, 18, 81, 118, and 881.

easy 3 Ciel may make a bid on the ivory forks they got in the city.

| 1 | 2 | 3 | 4 | 5 | 6 | 7 | 8 | 9 | 10 | 11 | 12 |

26B ◆ 18
New Keys: 9 and 4

each line twice SS (slowly, then faster); DS between 2-line groups; if time permits, key lines 5-7 again

9 *Right ring* finger

4 *Left index* finger

Follow the *Standard Plan for Learning New Keys* outlined on p. 9.

Learn 9

use the letter "l"

1 l l 9l 9l ll 99 l9l l9l 99l 99l Reach up for 9, 99, and 999.

2 Key the figures 9, 99, and 999. Did only 9 of 99 finish it?

Learn 4

3 f f 4f 4f ff 44 f4f f4f 44f 44f Reach up for 4, 44, and 444.

4 Add the figures 4, 44, and 444. Please study pages 4 to 44.

Combine 9 and 4

5 Key 44, 49, 94, and 99. Only 49 of the 94 joggers are here.

6 Reach with the fingers to key 49 and 499 as well as 4 and 9.

7 My goal is to sell 44 pizzas, 99 tacos, and 9 cases of cola.

26C ◆ 5
New-Key Mastery

1. Key each of lines 1-3 twice SS (slowly, then faster); DS between 2-line groups.
2. If time permits, key each line again for speed.

Figure sentences

use the figure "1"

1 Keep the fingers low as you key 11, 18, 19, 48, 94, and 849.

2 On March 8, 1994, 14 people took the 4 tests for the 8 jobs.

3 He based his May 1 report on pages 449 to 488 of Chapter 19.

54E ◆

Memo

1. Prepare the message at right in memo format. The memo goes to **Andrea Valdez** from **Marcus Ellerbee.** The subject is **MEETING WITH ALAN WASHBURN'S PARENTS.** Use today's date and your reference initials.
2. Make these additional changes: In ¶ 1, cut the second sentence; combine the first and second ¶s. Change *a disorder that results from* to *a result of.* Cut the word *immediately* and move it to the end of the sentence.
3. Check for spelling errors and replace misspelled words. Proofread and correct any other errors you find. Keep the memo open.

Wednesday's meting with Alan Washburn's prents is can- 33

celed. His dad called me this morning. 40

Alan's doctor examined him recently and diagnosed <u>diabetes</u> *ital.* 52

insipidus a disorder that results from an "underactive" 64

pituitary gland. Alan immediately begin a doctor- 74

supervised treatment plan. 79

I agree with Alan's parents that we should weight until *wait* 90

he's had for to six weeks of medicle treatment. Then we *four* *medical* *can* 102

reconcider theneed for haveing Alan tested and observed at 114

the clinical Learning Center. In the mean time, Ill keep 125

tabs on Alan's progress in school 133

54F ◆ wp FEATURE

Drawing (Lines)

1. Read the copy at right and study the screen.
2. Learn how to draw a horizontal line using your software.
3. With Memo **54E** (above) on your screen, draw a thick line (about 4-point) from the left margin to the right margin between the headings and the body.
4. Copy the line and paste it at the end of the page (about 9.5"—insert hard returns).
5. Change the style of the line at the bottom margin to a thinner line (2-point).

The **Drawing (Lines)** feature is a quick and easy way to add horizontal lines to your documents. You can draw lines in different styles (....., ———) and choose the position, length, thickness, and even the color. After you draw a line, you can move, size, and change it.

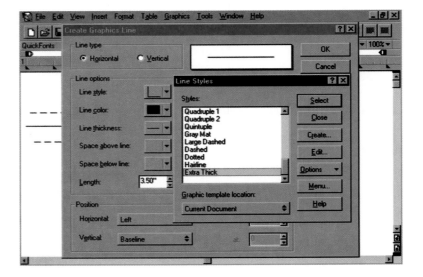

26D◆ 12
Script and Rough-Draft Copy

Line spacing: DS
Side margins: default

1. Key each line once DS (2 hard returns between lines).
2. Rekey the rough-draft lines if time permits.

Proofreader's Marks

≡	= capitalize
∧	= insert
⌿	= delete
⌒	= transpose
ℐ#	= delete space
#	= add space
lc	= lowercase
⌒	= close up

Script

1 Proofread: Compare copy word for word with the original.
2 Compare all figures digit by digit with your source copy.
3 Be sure to check for spacing and punctuation marks, also.
4 Copy in script or rough draft may not show exact spacing.
5 It is your job to insert correct spacing as you key copy.
6 Soon you will learn how to correct your errors on screen.

Rough draft

7 cap the first word and all proper nouns in each every sentence.
8 For example: pablo Mendez is from San juan, Puerto rico.
9 Ami Qwan and her parents will return to Taipie this fall summer.
10 our coffee comes is from Columbia; tea, from England or china.
11 How many of you have Ethnic origins in a for eign country?
12 Did Do you know which of the our states once were part of mexico?

26E◆ 10
Speed Building

1. Key a 1' unguided writing on each ¶. Then key a 1' *guided* writing on each ¶ (see p. 46 for procedure).
2. Key a 2' writing on ¶s 1-2 together; find *gwam*.

Quarter-Minute Checkpoints

gwam	1/4'	1/2'	3/4'	Time
16	4	8	12	16
20	5	10	15	20
24	6	12	18	24
28	7	14	21	28
32	8	16	24	32
36	9	18	27	36
40	10	20	30	40

e all letters used   2'

How much time does it take you to return at the end of   6
the line? Do you return with a lazy or a quick reach? Try   12
not to stop at the end of the line; instead, return quickly   18
and move down to the next line of copy.   21

How much time does it take you to strike the shift key   27
and the letter to make a capital? Just a bit more practice   33
will help you cut by half the time you are now using. When   39
you cut the time, you increase your speed.   43

54C ◆ FEATURE

Spelling

1. Read the copy at right and study the screen.
2. Learn to use the Spelling tool in your software.
3. Use the feature to check for misspelled words in the memo on the screen (54B). Correct all errors found by editing or selecting a replacement offered by the Spelling feature.
4. Proofread after Spelling is used to check for other kinds of errors in your copy, such as a missing word or substitution error (**example**: *of* in place of *if*). Correct any errors you see.

The **Spelling** feature is useful for finding misspelled words in a sentence, paragraph, page, document, or selected block. The tool checks spelling by comparing each word of your text to words in its dictionary(ies). If the feature finds a word in your text that is not identical to one in its dictionary, that word is flagged as "misspelled." (A red wavy line may appear under a misspelled word as it is keyed, or it may appear in a dialog box only after you activate the Spelling feature.) The Spelling feature usually lists one or more words similar to the "misspelled" word

that may be used to replace it. You may (1) keep the spelling as is and add the word to the Spelling dictionary, (2) replace a misspelled word with a correctly spelled word on the list, or (3) replace a misspelled word by editing it if the correct spelling is not on the list.

The Spelling feature may also flag repeated words and words with irregular capitalization. The Spelling tool does not flag other kinds of errors (**examples**: *use* in place of *used, user,* or *uses*; *except* in place of *accept*; *there* in place of *their* or *they're*).

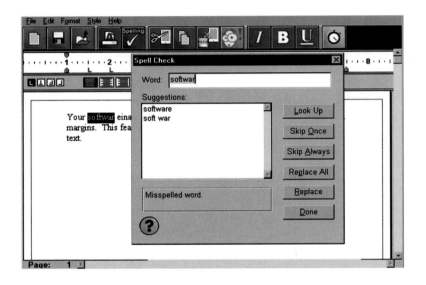

54D ◆

Memo

1. Key the memo at right.
2. Change the subject line to uppercase. In ¶ 3, move the last sentence to become the first sentence of the ¶. Bold the place, time, and day suggested for the meeting.
3. Use Spelling to find misspelled words.
4. Proofread and correct all errors.

		words
TO:	Andrea Valdez, Head of Special Programs	9
FROM:	Marcus Ellerbee, Counselor	16
DATE:	**(Today's date)**	21
SUBJECT:	Alan Washburn	25

After several informal testing activities with Alan Washburn, Ms. Davilos 40
and I believe he should be sent to the Clinical Learning Center at the 54
university for special testing and observation. 64

It appears to us that Alan exhibits not only deficient reading skills but 79
also short attention span and low motivation. Any one of these factors 93
can result in poor performance. Two or three of them in combination 107
certainly do. 110

Can you be available for a meeting in the Guidance Office at 4:30 next 124
Wednesday? The Washburns are available at that time. Before we can 138
make a referral, we must meet with Alan's parents and get their approval. 154
  xx 155

Lesson 27 New Keys: 0 and 5

Objectives:
1. **To learn reach technique for 0 and 5.**
2. **To improve technique/speed on straight-copy sentences/paragraphs.**

27A◆ 5
Conditioning Practice

Line spacing: SS
Side margins: default

each line twice (slowly, then faster); DS between 2-line groups; then a 1' writing on line 3

alphabet 1 Roz may put a vivid sign next to the low aqua boat for Jack.
figures 2 Please review Figure 8 on page 94 and Figure 14 on page 189.
easy 3 Tien may fix the bus panel for the city if the pay is right.

| 1 | 2 | 3 | 4 | 5 | 6 | 7 | 8 | 9 | 10 | 11 | 12 |

27B◆ 18
New Keys: 0 and 5

each line twice (slowly, then faster); DS between 2-line groups; if time permits, key lines 5-7 again

0 *Right little* finger

5 *Left index* finger

Follow the *Standard Plan for Learning New Keys* outlined on p. 9.

Learn 0 (zero)
1 ; ; 0; 0; ;; 00 ;0; ;0; 00; 00; Reach up for 0, 00, and 000.
2 Snap the finger off the 0. I used 0, 00, and 000 sandpaper.

Learn 5
3 f f 5f 5f ff 55 f5f f5f 55f 55f Reach up for 5, 55, and 555.
4 Reach up to 5 and back to f. Did he say to order 55 or 555?

Combine 0 and 5
5 Reach with the fingers to key 50 and 500 as well as 5 and 0.
6 We asked for prices on these models: 50, 55, 500, and 5500.
7 On May 5, I got 5 boxes each of 0 and 00 steel wool for her.

27C◆ 5
New-Key Mastery

each line once DS (2 hard returns between lines)

LANGUAGE SKILLS CUES:
- No space is left before or after : when used with figures to express time.
- Most nouns before numbers are capitalized; exceptions include *page* and *line*.

No space

1 Flight 1049 is on time; it should be at Gate 48 at 5:50 p.m.
2 The club meeting on April 5 will be in Room 549 at 8:10 a.m.
3 Of our 108 workers in 1994, 14 had gone to new jobs by 1995.
4 I used Chapter 19, pages 449 to 458, for my March 10 report.
5 Can you meet us at 1954 Maple Avenue at 8:05 a.m. August 10?
6 Of the 59 students, 18 keyed at least 40 w.a.m. by April 18.

53F ◆
Memo

1. Key the memo shown at the right. Show your initials below the last line.
2. Make the following changes: In ¶ 2, select and delete the words *interact and to work together.* Replace them with the word **collaborate**. Use italic instead of underline for *Periscope* (3 times). Change the theme to initial caps, center it on a separate line, and delete the period following it. Bold the time, day, date, and room number in ¶ 3. Cut the second sentence of ¶ 3 and move it a DS below the last sentence to make it ¶ 4. Underline *ideas* and *suggestions.*
3. Proofread your copy; correct errors.

		words
TO:	All Class and Club Presidents	7
FROM:	Joseph Costa, Editor-in-Chief	14
DATE:	(Today's date)	18
SUBJECT:	MEETING TO DISCUSS MIDWINTER ISSUE OF <u>PERISCOPE</u>	29

The proposed theme for "Current Focus" in the midwinter issue of <u>Periscope</u> is HARMONY THROUGH INTERACTION. — 42 / 50

The goal is to highlight recent activities that you believe helped to foster harmony among diverse groups in our school by getting them to interact and to work together. We would also like to report your suggestions for future activities with this focus. — 66 / 80 / 95 / 102

You are encouraged to attend a <u>Periscope</u> staff meeting at two o'clock on Wednesday, (next Wednesday's date), in Room AC 8 of the Activities Center to help in this effort. Please come and bring your ideas and suggestions with you. In addition to a brief Guest Editorial, we want to include three or four articles on this topic by some of you. — 116 / 129 / 146 / 160 / 170

Lesson 54 Memo Format

Objectives:
1. To process memos from semiarranged copy.
2. To use a word processing feature to check spelling.
3. To use a word processing feature to insert a horizontal line.

Approx. time: 90'

54A ◆
Keyboard Mastery

Use Skill Builder 1, p. 128, lines 1, 5, and 9, or D on p. A6.

54B ◆
Memo

1. Key the memo shown at the right. Use your initials as the keyboard operator.
2. Make these changes in ¶ 1: Cut the word *quite;* move the word *often* after *is;* and delete the second occurrence of *slightly.*
3. Make these changes in ¶ 2: Delete *when called up;* move the second sentence so that it is the last sentence in ¶ 2. Keep the memo open.

		words
TO:	Lenore M. Fielding, Principal	7
FROM:	Jevon Hardaway, Business Department	15
DATE:	(Today's date)	19
SUBJECT:	NEW MEMO PROCESSING PROCEDURE	28

I have used the plain-paper memo format for several years. I have found it quite satisfactory. In fact, keying the headings is easier, quicker, and more attractive than aligning copy on preprinted forms. (Keyed copy often is slightly above or slightly below the printed headings no matter what line spacing I use.) — 43 / 57 / 72 / 87 / 92

You may want to use a *template* that when called up will take you automatically to the points of copy entry. I'm enclosing a disk containing such a template for you to try. You may wish to consider doing this if several people have difficulty with the new format. — 106 / 121 / 127 / 145

Enclosure — 147

27D ◆ 12
Skill Transfer: Straight Copy, Script, Rough Draft

1. Key each ¶ once SS; DS between ¶s.
2. Key a 1' writing on each ¶; find *gwam* on each writing; compare the three rates.
3. Key one or two more 1' writings on the two slowest ¶s to improve skill transfer.

Your *gwam* on script will be lower than your rate on straight copy; your *gwam* on rough draft likely will be still lower. Improving skill transfer means trying to close the gap between your straight-copy *gwam* and the other rates, though the rates will rarely be the same.

Proofreader's Marks

stet	= no change
∧	= insert
⋏	= delete
#	= add space
⌒	= close up
∼	= transpose
⊙	= insert period

27E ◆ 10
Speed Building

1. Key a 1' unguided and a 1' *guided* writing on each ¶ (see p. 46 for procedure).
2. Key a 2' writing on ¶s 1-2 together; find *gwam* for each writing.

Straight copy 1'

   It is up to you to proofread the copy you produce to 11
find any mistakes you may have made. It is also up to you 22
to correct all the errors you find if the copy is to serve 34
a purpose other than to show that you have done the work. 46

| 1 | 2 | 3 | 4 | 5 | 6 | 7 | 8 | 9 | 10 | 11 | 12 |

Script

It is vital to check your copy word for word against 11
the source copy from which you keyed. The words should 22
be in the same order, and each word must be spelled right. 34
A space should be left after each word or punctuation mark. 46

Rough draft

Be *stet* quick to ~~discover~~ find your errors even though if you will not 11
correct them all just now. ~~As soon as~~ When you begin to apply your 22
skill you ~~may~~ will be taught easy ways to correct errors. For now, 35
learn to excell in marking and finding them⊙ 44

 all letters used 2'

     •   2   •   4   •   6   •   8   •   10   •

   I am now trying to learn to vary my keying rate to fit 5
the job of keying the words. When I learn to speed up more 11
of the easy words, I can take time to break the longer ones 17
into small parts and handle them quickly. 22

   With a bit more practice, I shall be able to handle by 27
word response more of the shorter ones that just now I must 33
analyze and key letter by letter. As I learn to do more of 39
these words as units, I shall become more expert. 44

| 1 | 2 | 3 | 4 | 5 | 6 |

53D ◆

Memo with Date Text

1. Key the memo shown at right. Use the Date Text feature, if available, to insert today's date. As the keyboard operator, replace *xx* with your initials.
2. Center the article title on a separate line. Delete the period following it.
3. Italicize the word *Periscope* (both places); change the article title to initial caps.
4. Proofread your copy; correct all errors. Leave the memo on the screen for use in **53E**.

<table>
<tr><td></td><td></td><td>words</td></tr>
<tr><td>TO:</td><td>Sandra Alexander, Reporter</td><td>6</td></tr>
<tr><td>FROM:</td><td>Marcella Del Rio, Associate Editor</td><td>14</td></tr>
<tr><td>DATE:</td><td>**(Today's date)**</td><td>19</td></tr>
<tr><td>SUBJECT:</td><td>PERISCOPE ARTICLE</td><td>24</td></tr>
</table>

Your proposed article for the midwinter issue of Periscope should be a | 38
winner. I like the title INCLUSION VS. EXCLUSION. | 48

The article is a few lines too long for the allocated space. I have marked | 63
some suggested cuts on the enclosed copy. Please consider these cuts | 79
along with the few other minor changes as you key your final copy. | 91

xx | 91

Enclosure | 94

53E ◆ ⬦ FEATURE

Cut/Copy and Paste

1. Read the copy at the right and study the screen.
2. Find the Cut, Copy, and Paste buttons on the toolbar or learn the keyboard commands for the features.
3. With Memo **53D** (above) on the screen, make the changes indicated at the right below.

> **wp**
> ■ Do you know how to select a word, sentence, or paragraph without dragging the mouse over it? If not, now is a good time to learn how.
> ■ Don't delete a block of words unless you're sure you won't want to use the text in your document later. Instead of deleting it, cut the text and paste it at the top of the page. You can move it into your document later if you want to, or simply delete it at that time.

After you select a block of text (**51D**), you can erase the text, move the text, or copy it. Once text is selected, tapping the Delete key erases the block. The **Cut** feature also removes selected text; the **Paste** feature allows text that has been cut to be moved to another location. (Text removed with the Delete key cannot be pasted.)

The **Copy** feature duplicates (copies) selected text. The Paste feature allows you to place copied text in another location, without moving the original text.

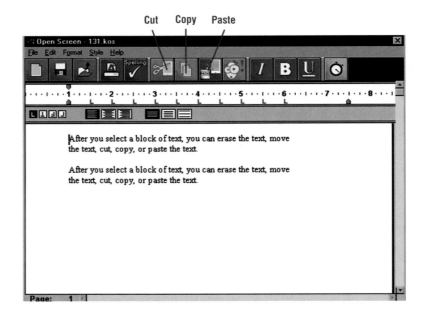

1. Select and delete the centered article title and extra line spaces; insert a period after the sentence.
2. In ¶ 2, use Cut and Paste to move the first sentence; make it the second sentence.
3. Select and copy all of the memo, even the headings.
4. DS below the enclosure notation; paste the copied text here.
5. On the copy, select and delete the name and title after TO:. Then key this name and title after TO: **Jason McKinley, Correspondent**.

Lesson 28 New Keys: 7 and 3

1. **To learn reach technique for 7 and 3.**
2. **To improve/assess skill on straight-copy sentences/paragraphs.**

28A◆ 5
Conditioning Practice
Line spacing: SS
Side margins: default

each line twice; DS between 2-line groups; then a 1' writing on line 3

alphabet 1 Gavin made a quick fall trip by jet to Zurich six weeks ago.
figures 2 Key 1 and 4 and 5 and 8 and 9 and 0 and 190 and 504 and 958.
easy 3 The man is to fix the big sign by the field for a city firm.

| 1 | 2 | 3 | 4 | 5 | 6 | 7 | 8 | 9 | 10 | 11 | 12 |

28B◆ 18
New Keys: 7 and 3

each line twice SS (slowly, then faster); DS between 2-line groups; if time permits, key lines 5-7 again

7 *Right index* **finger**

3 *Left middle* **finger**

Follow the *Standard Plan for Learning New Keys* outlined on p. 9.

Learn 7
1 j j 7j 7j jj 77 j7j j7j 77j 77j Reach up for 7, 77, and 777.
2 Key the figures 7, 77, and 777.   She checked Rooms 7 and 77.

Learn 3
3 d d 3d 3d dd 33 d3d d3d 33d 33d Reach up for 3, 33, and 333.
4 Add the figures 3, 33, and 333.   Read pages 3 to 33 tonight.

Combine 7 and 3
5 Key 33, 37, 73, and 77.   Just 37 of the 77 skiers have come.
6 Please order 7 Model 337 computers and 3 Model 737 printers.
7 On August 7, the 33 bikers left on a long trip of 377 miles.

Skillbuilding

28C◆ 7
Technique:
Response Patterns

1. Key each pair of lines once SS; DS between 2-line groups.
2. Key a 1' writing on line 2 and then on line 4; find *gwam* on each. Rekey the slower line if time permits.

letter response 1 face pump ever milk area jump vast only save upon safe union
2 As we were in a junk, we saw a rare loon feast on a crawdad.

word response 3 quay hand also body lend hang mane down envy risk corn whale
4 Tisha is to go to the lake with us if she is to do the work.

combination response 5 with only | they join | half safe | born free | firm look | goal rates
6 I sat on the airy lanai with my gaze on the sea to the east.

| 1 | 2 | 3 | 4 | 5 | 6 | 7 | 8 | 9 | 10 | 11 | 12 |

TO: TAB TAB Faculty and Staff DS (2 hard returns)

FROM: TAB Lenore M. Fielding, Principal

DATE: TAB November 15, (Current year)
DS

SUBJECT:TABMEMO FORMAT
DS

At a recent meeting, department heads recommended that memos be processed on plain paper instead of preprinted forms. The recommendation is a cost-cutting measure that requires only a little more effort on the part of the keyboard operators. DS

The customary margins are used: 2" (approximate) top margin; default (near 1") side margins; at least a 1" bottom margin. DS

Double spacing separates memo parts, including paragraphs, which are individually single-spaced. If someone other than the writer keys the memo, that person's initials should be keyed at the left margin a double space below the message. If an attachment or enclosure is included, Attachment or Enclosure should be keyed at the left margin a double space below the message or the keyboard operator's initials (if any). DS

Headings begin at the left margin. After To: tab twice to key the name; after From: tab once to key the name; after Date: tab once to insert the date; after Subject: tab once to enter the subject (may be bold/Cap and lowercase or ALL CAPS). DS

Please use this format for several days; then let me know if you experienced any difficulties. DS

tbh

Note: Some word processing software will show quotation marks (") that differ from the "curly quotes" shown in this memo.

Shown in Times New Roman 12-point type, 2" top margin, 1" side margins, photoreduced.

Memo

28D◆ 8
Speed Check

Line spacing: DS

1. Key a 1' writing on ¶ 1 and then on ¶ 2; find *gwam* on each ¶.
2. Key two 2' writings on ¶s 1-2 together; find *gwam* on each writing.

1' *gwam* goals

▽ 21 = acceptable
⊡ 25 = average
⊙ 29 = good
◇ 33 = excellent

 all letters used   2'

      •   2   •   4   •   6   •   8   •   10   •
Time and motion are major items in building our keying   6
  12   •   14   •   16   •   18   •   20 ▽ 22   •
power. As we make each move through space to a letter or a   12
  24   ⊡   26   •   28   ⊙   30   •   32 ◇ 34   •
figure, we use time. So we want to be sure that every move   18
  36   •   38   •   40   •   42   •   44   •   46   •
is quick and direct. We cut time and aid speed in this way.   24
      •   2   •   4   •   6   •   8   •   10   •
A good way to reduce motion and thus save time is just   29
  12   •   14   •   16   •   18   •   20 ▽ 22   •
to keep the hands in home position as you make the reach to   35
  24   ⊡   26   •   28   ⊙   30   •   32 ◇ 34   •
a letter or figure. Fix your gaze on the copy; then, reach   41
  36   •   38   •   40   •   42   •   44   •   46   •
to each key with a direct, low move at your very best speed.   47

| 1 | 2 | 3 | 4 | 5 | 6 |

28E◆ 12
Technique Mastery

1. Key each line once at an easy, steady pace; try to improve your technique.
2. Key each line again; try to increase your speed.

TECHNIQUE CUES:

- space quickly with down-and-in motion
- shift without moving hands down or elbows in or out
- keep fingers upright (not slanting) on home keys
- adjust speed to fit difficulty of words

Spacing

1 an am by pan ham any born slam gory then them they torn slam

2 I am | is on | go by | if any | by then | of them | is torn | if they sign

3 Stan is to go by the inn to sign the work form for the firm.

Shifting

4 Janette or Spiro | Apps and Kahn | J. A. Wolf Co. | March or April

5 FBLA meets on Tuesday, January 18, in Room 39 of Mason Hall.

6 Marvel and Sons is to build Fair Oaks Center on Sparks Lake.

Adjacent keys

7 rent sail mask riot last trim fort coin stop port more ruins

8 we try | as rent | we knew | her last | has more | new coin | mere hopes

9 Hoping that her old coins were a real buy, we made an offer.

Response patterns

10 so we if as pen was may far lay gas firm plum make gear with

combination response   11 if we | so as | the mop | may set | and get | they jump | she was to pay

12 He was to see if the dock crew was paid a good rate to work.

| 1 | 2 | 3 | 4 | 5 | 6 | 7 | 8 | 9 | 10 | 11 | 12 |

Formatting Memos

Lesson 53   Memo Format

Objectives:
1. **To learn to format memos.**
2. **To revise and enhance text using word processing features.**

Approx. time: 75'

53A◆
Keyboard Mastery

Use Skill Builder 1, p. 128, lines 1, 2, and 9, or C on p. A6.

53B◆

Memos

TO: Faculty and Staff
FROM: Lenore M. Fielding, Principal
DATE: November 15, (Current year)
SUBJECT: MEMO FORMAT

At a recent meeting, department heads recommended that memos be processed on plain paper instead of preprinted forms. The recommendation is a cost-cutting measure that requires only a little more effort on the part of the keyboard operators.

The customary margins are used: 2" (approximate) top margin; default (near 1") side margins; at least a 1" bottom margin.

Double spacing separates memo parts, including paragraphs, which are individually single-spaced. If someone other than the writer keys the memo, that person's initials should be keyed at the left margin a double space below the message. If an attachment or enclosure is included, Attachment or Enclosure should be keyed at the left margin a double space below the message or the keyboard operator's initials (if any).

Headings begin at the left margin. After T to: tab twice to key the name; after From: tab once to key the name; after Date: ab once to insert the date; after Subject: tab once to enter the subject (may be bold/Cap and lowercase or ALL CAPS).

Please use this format for several days; then let me know if you experienced any difficulties.

fb

Memo

Note: Insert hard returns (about 6) to leave a 2" (approximate) top margin, instead of changing the margin setting/page setup.

Format Guides: Memos
Memorandums (memos) are written messages used by individuals within an organization to communicate with one another. They are much like letters, but memos have fewer parts. Use these margins for memos:

| Top margin: 2" |
| Side margins: 1" or default |
| Bottom margin: at least 1" |

Begin all lines, including headings, at the left margin unless otherwise indicated. (A word, phrase, or sentence may be centered to draw attention to it.)

Double-space (DS) between *all* memo parts. Study the model memo on p. 130.

TO:	Tab *twice* to key name.	**DS**
FROM:	Tab *once* to key name.	**DS**
DATE:	Tab *once* to key date.	**DS**
SUBJECT:	Tab *once* to key subject.	**DS**

1. Study the format guides above and the model memo on p. 130. Note the vertical and horizontal placement of memo parts and the spacing between them.
2. Format/key the memo (p. 130).

3. Make the following changes: Italicize *Attachment* and *Enclosure* in ¶ 3; in ¶ 4, change To:, From:, Date:, and Subject: to uppercase. Change the subject line to initial caps and bold.

53C◆ **FEATURE**

Date Text
1. Read the copy at right.
2. Learn to use the Date Text feature if available on your software.

The **Date Text** feature inserts the current date. The date and time on your computer must be accurate for the date to be correct.

Several date styles are included. Only the Month Day, Year style should be used on memos and most other documents.

Lesson 29 New Keys: 6 and 2

Objectives:

1. To learn reach technique for 6 and 2.
2. To improve/assess skill on straight-copy sentences/paragraphs.

29A◆ 5
Conditioning Practice
Line spacing: SS
Side margins: default
each line twice; DS between 2-line groups; then a 1' writing on line 3

alphabet 1 Jared helped Mazy quickly fix the big wood stove in the den.

figures 2 Bella lives at 1847 Oak Street; Jessi, at 5039 Duard Circle.

easy 3 They may make their goals if they work with the usual vigor.

| 1 | 2 | 3 | 4 | 5 | 6 | 7 | 8 | 9 | 10 | 11 | 12 |

29B◆ 18
New Keys: 6 and 2

each line twice (slowly, then faster); DS between 2-line groups; if time permits, key lines 5-8 again

6 *Right index* finger

2 *Left ring* finger

Follow the *Standard Plan for Learning New Keys* outlined on p. 9.

Learn 6

1 j j 6j 6j jj 66 j6j j6j 66j 66j Reach up for 6, 66, and 666.
2 Key the figures 6, 66, and 666.   Did just 6 of 66 finish it?

Learn 2

3 s s 2s 2s ss 22 s2s s2s 22s 22s Reach up for 2, 22, and 222.
4 Add the figures 2, 22, and 222.   Review pages 2 to 22 today.

Combine 6, 2, and other figures

5 Key 22, 26, 62, and 66.   Just 22 of the 66 scouts were here.
6 Reach with the fingers to key 26 and 262 as well as 2 and 6.

7 Key figures as units: 18, 26, 37, 49, 50, 62, 162, and 268.
8 The proxy dated April 26, 1997, was vital in Case No. 30584.

29C◆ 7
New-Key Mastery
each line once SS

1 Lee has sold 16 elm, 28 ash, 37 oak, 49 pine, and 50 shrubs.

2 Flights 201 and 384 will be replaced by Flights 625 and 749.

3 Key as a unit: 10, 29, 38, 47, 56; two units, 162 and 4837.

4 In 1996, 26 of our 384 workers were moved to 507 Pecos Lane.

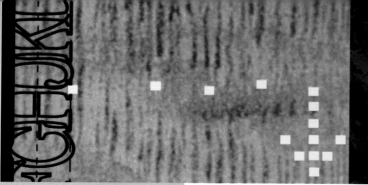

1. Key lines 1-9 once at an easy, steady pace.
2. Key the lines again at a faster pace.
3. Key a 1' writing on each of lines 7-9; find *gwam* on each writing.

alphabet	1	Virgil fixed two unique bronze sculptures he got at my junk shop.
top row	2	Didn't she say that Invoice #9480 was for $376 (plus 5 1/2% tax)?
keypad	3	417- 528- 528-639 639-174 456-789 654-123 981-654 321-789 582-693
CAPS LOCK	4	Check John Bartlett's FAMILIAR QUOTATIONS under TRUTH or HONESTY.
hyphen	5	A compound adjective such as 4-star or 12-foot also requires a -.
parentheses	6	Is the spacing after . following initials (a) 1, (b) 2, or (c) 3?
one-hand	7	We saw a few plump rats in a battered crate in my vacated garage.
combination	8	Jay may get an award for the extra work he did on the stage sets.
balanced-hand	9	The busy man did rush the six bus panels to the auto firm by air.

| 1 | 2 | 3 | 4 | 5 | 6 | 7 | 8 | 9 | 10 | 11 | 12 | 13 |

1. Key a 1' writing on ¶ 1; find *gwam.*
2. Add 4 *gwam* for a new goal rate. (See checkpoint chart below.)
3. Key two 1' *guided* writings on the ¶ to reach the checkpoint each 1/4'. (See p. 46.)
4. Key ¶ 2 in the same manner.
5. Key two 3' writings on ¶s 1-2 combined; find *gwam* and count errors on each.

Quarter-Minute Checkpoints

gwam	1/4'	1/2'	3/4'	Time
20	5	10	15	20
24	6	12	18	24
28	7	14	21	28
32	8	16	24	32
36	9	18	27	36
40	10	20	30	40
44	11	22	33	44
48	12	24	36	48
52	13	26	39	52
56	14	28	42	56

a all letters used

		3'	5'

People who take part in activities like tennis, cards, golf,   4 | 2 | 30

or ballet work to increase their skill. An excellent performance   8 | 5 | 33

for many of them may be just as critical as the final score. So   13 | 8 | 35

before their next game, they practice some tactics that may help   17 | 10 | 38

to increase their acuity, fluency, or another facet. Many also do   22 | 13 | 41

this in keyboarding.   23 | 14 | 42

     If you have developed a speed of thirty to forty words a min-   27 | 16 | 44

ute with good technique and acceptable accuracy, begin a vigorous   31 | 19 | 47

drive for speed. You have the potential for new growth; you should   36 | 22 | 49

not be satisfied with your current level of developed speed. Good   40 | 24 | 52

for now, it is merely a milestone to a level you will readily prize   45 | 27 | 55

throughout your life.   46 | 28 | 56

| 1 | 2 | 3 | 4 |
| 1 | 2 | 3 |

Skillbuilding

29D◆ 8
Technique: Keying, Spacing, Shifting

1. Key each line once SS; DS between 2-line groups.
2. Key a 1' writing on line 7 and then on line 8 if time permits; find *gwam* on each.

quick-snap keystrokes	1 Ella may go to the soap firm for title to all the lake land.
	2 Did the bugle corps toot with the usual vigor for the queen?
down-and-in spacing	3 Coy is in the city to buy an oak chair he wants for his den.
	4 Jan may go to town by bus to sign a work form for a new job.
out-and-down shifting	5 Robb and Ty are in Madrid to spend a week with Jae and Aldo.
	6 Are you going in April or in May? Elena is leaving in July.
easy	7 Rick paid for both the visual aid and the sign for the firm.
	8 Glena kept all the work forms on the shelf by the big chair.

| 1 | 2 | 3 | 4 | 5 | 6 | 7 | 8 | 9 | 10 | 11 | 12 |

29E◆ 12
Speed Check

Line spacing: DS
Side margins: default

1. Key two 1' writings on each ¶; find *gwam* on each writing.
2. Key a 2' writing on ¶s 1-2 combined; find *gwam*.
3. Key a 3' writing on ¶s 1-2 combined; find *gwam*.

Goals
1': At least 24 *gwam*.
2': At least 23 *gwam*.
3': At least 22 *gwam*.

e all letters used

	2'	3'
Success does not mean the same thing to everyone. For	6	4
some, it means to get to the top at all costs: in power, in	12	8
fame, and in income. For others, it means just to fulfill	18	12
their basic needs or wants with as little effort as required.	24	16
Most people fall within the two extremes. They work quite	30	20
hard to better their lives at home, at work, and in the social	36	24
world. They realize that success for them is not in being at	42	28
the top but rather in trying to improve their quality of life.	48	32

| 1 | 2 | 3 | 4 | 5 | 6 |
| 1 | 2 | 3 | 4 |

Enrichment

Proofreading

1. Print the 3' writing you keyed in 29E.
2. Note the kinds of errors marked in the ¶ at right.
3. Note how proofreader's marks above the copy are used to mark errors for correction.
4. Proofread the printout of your 3' writing; mark each error for correction, using proofreader's marks.

 = space   ∧ = insert   ⊂ = close up   ℓ = delete   ∿ = transpose (tr)

Sucess① does not mean the#same② thing to every⌢one③. For some, it means to get to①the top atℓ② all costs:#③ in power, in fame, and in income①. For others,② it means juts③ to fulfill their basic needs or or① wants wint)② as little effortas③ required.

Line 1	Line 2	Line 3	Line 4
1 Omitted letter	1 Omitted word	1 Misstroke	1 Added word
2 Failure to space	2 Added letter	2 Omitted comma	2 Transposition
3 Faulty spacing	3 Faulty spacing	3 Transposition	3 Omitted word

1. Identify the rule(s) you need to review/practice.
2. **Read:** Study each rule.
3. **Learn:** Key the *Learn* line(s) beneath it, noting how the rule is applied.
4. **Apply:** Key the *Apply* line(s).
5. Check work with the *Teacher's Key*.

Internal punctuation: Apostrophe

RULE 1: Use an apostrophe as a symbol to represent feet or minutes. (Quotation marks may be used to signify inches or seconds.)

Learn 1 Floyd bought twenty-four 2" x 4" x 12" studs for the new deck.
Learn 2 Shawnelle scored the 3-pointer with only 1' 08" left to go.
Apply 3 The new computer lab at my school is 18 ft. 6 in. x 30 ft.
Apply 4 The students were told to key a 3' writing on 8 1/2" x 11" paper.

RULE 2: Use an apostrophe as a symbol to indicate the omission of letters or figures (as in contractions).

Learn 5 Didn't you enjoy the "Spirit of '76" segment of the pageant?
Apply 6 I dont know why he doesnt take advantage of our new terms.
Apply 7 Last years reunion combined the classes of 97, 98, and 99.

RULE 3: Use an apostrophe plus *s* (*'s*) to form the plural of most figures, letters, and words used as words rather than for their meaning *(6's, A's, five's)*. In stock quotations and to refer to decades or centuries, form the plural of figures by adding *s* only.

Learn 8 She studied hard and earned A's throughout the 1990s.
Learn 9 Add Century As and 4s; show the Cosco 45s in boldface.
Apply 10 Correct the outline by changing the As, Bs, and Cs to CAPS.
Apply 11 My broker urged that I buy Apache 76's in the 1980's.

RULE 4: To show possession, use an apostrophe plus *s* after (1) a singular noun and (2) a plural noun that does not end in *s*.

Learn 12 Jerrod's store had a great sale on men's and women's apparel.
Apply 13 Ritas class ring was lost under the stands in the schools gym.
Apply 14 Our back-to-school sale on childrens clothes is in progress.

RULE 5: To show possession, use an apostrophe plus *s* (*'s*) after a proper name of one syllable that ends in *s*.

Learn 15 Jon Hess's next art exhibit will be held at the Aranoff Center.
Apply 16 Rena Haas new play will premier at the Emery Theater.
Apply 17 Jo Parks ACT scores were superb; Ed Sims SAT scores, mediocre.

RULE 6: To show possession, use only an apostrophe after (1) plural nouns ending in *s* and (2) a proper name of more than one syllable that ends in *s* or *z*.

Learn 18 The girls' new coach will visit at the Duclos' home next week.
Apply 19 The new shipment of ladies sportswear will arrive on Friday.
Apply 20 Lt. Santos plan for the officers annual ball was outstanding.

Language & Writing Skills 2

Activity 1:

1. Study the spelling/definitions of the words in the color block.
2. Key line 1 (the *Learn* line), noting proper choice of words.
3. Key lines 2-3 (the *Apply* lines), choosing the right words to complete the sentences correctly.
4. Study/practice the other words in the same way.
5. Check your accuracy; rekey lines containing errors.

Choose the right word

> **hour** *(n)* the 24th part of a day; a particular time
>
> **our** *(adj)* of or relating to ourselves as possessors
>
> **know** *(vb)* to be aware of the truth of; to have understanding of
>
> **no** *(adv / adj / n)* in no respect or degree; not so; indicates denial or refusal

Learn 1 It is our intention to complete the work in an hour or two.
Apply 2 If I drive steadily, we should reach (hour, our) house in an (hour, our).
Apply 3 We should earn one credit (hour, our) for (hour, our) computer class.

Learn 4 Did you know that there are to be no quizzes this week?
Apply 5 If you (know, no) the chapter, you should have (know, no) fear of a quiz.
Apply 6 Did you (know, no) that they scored (know, no) touchdowns in the game?

Activity 2:

1. Key lines 1-10 at right, expressing numbers correctly (words or figures).
2. Check work with the *Teacher's Key*.
3. Note the rule numbers at the left of each sentence in which you made a number expression error.
4. Turn to page 68 and identify those rules for review.
5. Follow the Read/Learn/Apply plan for each rule to be reviewed.

Proofread & correct

RULES

1	1	20 members have already voted, but 15 have yet to do so.
2	2	Only twelve of the hikers are here; six have not returned.
3	3	Do you know if the eight fifteen Klondike flight is on time?
3,4	4	We should be at 1 Brooks Road no later than eleven thirty a.m.
5	5	This oriental carpet measures eight ft. by 10 ft.
5	6	The carton is two ft. square and weighs six lbs. eight oz.
6	7	Have you read pages 45 to 62 of Chapter two that he assigned?
7	8	She usually rides the bus from 6th Street to 1st Avenue.
8	9	Nearly 1/2 of the team is here; that is about 15.
8	10	A late fee of over 15 percent is charged after the 30th day.

Activity 3:

Key each line once SS. In place of the blank line at the end of each sentence, key the word(s) that correctly complete(s) the sentence.

Compose (think) as you key

1 A small mass of land surrounded by water is a/an _____.
2 A large mass of land surrounded by water is a/an _____.
3 The earth rotates on what is called its _____.
4 When the sun comes up over the horizon, we say it _____.

5 When the sun goes down over the horizon, we say it _____.
6 A device used to display temperature is a/an _____.
7 A device used to display atmospheric pressure is a/an _____.
8 A device used to display time is a/an _____.

Language & Writing Skills 9

Activity 1:

1. Study the spelling/definitions of the words in the color block at right.
2. Key the *Learn* line(s), noting word choices.
3. Key the *Apply* lines(s), selecting correct words.
4. Check work with the *Teacher's Key*.
5. Rekey lines in which you made word-choice errors.

Choose the right word

whose *(adj)* of or to whom something belongs	**threw** *(vb)* past tense of throw; to toss
who's *(cont)* who is	**through** *(prep/adj)* beginning to end of; finished

Learn 1 Who's to say whose fault it is that we lost?
Learn 2 Greg threw perfectly through two quarters.
Apply 3 (Whose, Who's) ski is it, and (whose, who's) to fix it?
Apply 4 When they were (threw, through), I (threw, through) a party.

Activity 2:

1. Key lines 1-10, inserting needed apostrophes and quotation marks.
2. Check work with the *Teacher's Key*.
3. Note the rule number(s) at the left of each sentence in which you made an error.
4. Turn to page 127 and identify those rules for review/practice.
5. Use the Read/Learn/Apply plan for each rule to be reviewed.

Proofread & correct

RULES

1	1	Jay Corbin played 12 min. 30 sec.; Jack Odom, 26 min. 20 sec.
1	2	My desk is 3 ft. x 5 ft. 6 in.; the credenza is 2 ft. x 6 ft.
2	3	Didnt O'Brien prepare a sales comparison for 98 and 99?
3	4	Major changes in technology occurred in the 1980's and 1990s.
3	5	Dr. Knox gave mostly As and Bs, but he gave a few Cs and Ds.
2,4	6	Didnt you go to the big sale on childrens items?
5	7	Tess escort gave her a wrist corsage of exquisite violets.
6	8	The boys and girls teams appreciated Dr. Morris compliments.
6	9	Do you know whether the ladies swim coach is in her office?
2,6	10	Didnt you ask if the cast is set for Miss Winters new play?

Activity 3:

1. Key the ¶, correcting the word-choice errors it contains. (Every line contains at least 1 error; same lines contain 2 or 3 errors.)
2. Check your work with the *Teacher's Key*.
3. Compose/key a second ¶ to:
   (a) define what "respect" means to you;
   (b) identify kinds of behavior that help one earn respect;
   (c) identify kinds of behavior that cause the loss of respect.

Compose (think) as you key

That all individuals want others too respect them is not surprising. What is surprising is that sum people think their do respect even when there own behavior has been unacceptable or even illegal. Key two the issue is that we respect others <u>because</u> of certain behavior, rather then in spite of it. Its vital, than, to no that what people due and say determines the level of respect there given buy others. In that regard, than, respect has to be earned; its not hour unquestioned right to demand it. All of you hear and now should begin to chose behaviors that will led others to respect you. Its you're choice.

1. Identify the rule(s) you need to review/practice.
2. **Read:** Study each rule.
3. **Learn:** Key the *Learn* line(s) beneath it, noting how the rule is applied.
4. **Apply:** Key the *Apply* line(s), expressing the numbers correctly.
5. Check work with the *Teacher's Key*.

Number expression

RULE 1: Spell a number that begins a sentence even when other numbers in the sentence are shown in figures.

Learn 1 Twelve of the new shrubs have died; 48 are doing quite well.
Apply 2 14 members have paid their dues, but 89 have not done so.

RULE 2: Use figures for numbers above ten, and for numbers from one to ten when they are used with numbers above ten.

Learn 3 She ordered 8 word processors, 14 computers, and 4 printers.
Apply 4 Did he say they need ten or 14 sets of Z18 and Z19 diskettes?

RULE 3: Use figures to express date and time (unless followed by o'clock).

Learn 5 He will arrive on Paygo Flight 418 at 9:48 a.m. on March 14.
Apply 6 Candidates must be in Ivy Hall at eight forty a.m. on May one.

RULE 4: Use figures for house numbers except house number One.

Learn 7 My home is at 8 Vernon Drive; my office, at One Weber Plaza.
Apply 8 The Nelsons moved from 4059 Pyle Avenue to 1 Maple Circle.

RULE 5: Use figures to express measures and weights.

Learn 9 Glenda Redford is 5 ft. 4 in. tall and weighs 118 lbs. 9 oz.
Apply 10 This carton measures one ft. by nine in. and weighs five lbs.

RULE 6: Use figures for numbers following nouns.

Learn 11 Review Rules 1 to 18 in Chapter 5, pages 149 and 150, today.
Apply 12 Case 1849 is reviewed in Volume five, pages nine and ten.

RULE 7: Spell (and capitalize) names of small-numbered streets (ten and under).

Learn 13 I walked several blocks along Third Avenue to 54th Street.
Apply 14 At 7th Street she took a taxi to his home on 43d Avenue.

RULE 8: Spell indefinite numbers.

Learn 15 Joe owns one acre of Parcel A; that is almost fifty percent.
Learn 16 Nearly seventy members voted; that is nearly a fourth.
Apply 17 Over 20 percent of the students are out with the flu.
Apply 18 Just under 1/2 of the voters cast ballots for the issue.

Above & Beyond

P R O J E C T

Young Writers' Society

Line spacing: DS (unless noted)
Top and side margins: 1"

Read the text at the right. Then do each task below.

Task 1 Centered List

1. Prepare the list at the right below, each line centered. Insert hard return(s) after each line as shown. SS within a numbered item; DS between items.
2. Use any learned features— bold, italic, underline, case, or font—to improve the text's appearance.

Task 2 List

1. Prepare the list, each line centered.
2. Leave 4 or 5 blank lines between the items for noting new information.

Task 3 Announcement

1. Prepare this Career Day announcement for school bulletin boards, all lines centered.
2. Change appearance of the text using the features listed for Task 1 above.
3. Save this text for use later.

Task 4 Announcement

1. Prepare this "early" announcement of the Job Explo, all lines centered.
2. Add bold and other special effects.

Task 5 Questionnaire

1. Create a student questionnaire; list all 3 program ideas in Task 1.
2. Use two fonts; use bold, etc., to make some words stand out.

You're a member of Young Writers' Society (YWS), a student organization. At a recent YWS meeting, the group agreed that writing careers should be featured during the school's Career Day, set for April 3.

After last year's 29th Annual Career Day, you volunteered for this year's planning committee. Every committee member works hard to make this year's event bigger and better than any before it. As Young Writers' "rep" on the committee, you'll do your share—starting with tasks on this page. As your skills grow, you'll be asked to do more, sometimes writing the text yourself.

Later this year the national Chamber of Commerce will post a discussion list called Job Explo on the Internet. Interested students can join the list to explore many careers.

• •

Task 1

Career Day Program Suggestions

Prepared by Young Writers' Society

1. Talk by former student who writes for a living.

2. Panel discussion about writing on the job.

3. Demonstration of *Writer's Helper* software.

Task 2

Speaker's Career/←

Attorney/12 —4

Children's author/9

Copyrighter/22
~~wri~~

Editor/7 —5

Fund raiser/10

Manger/11
~~a~~

Reporter/16

Student Requests

Task 3

30th Annual Career Day

All-Day, Schoolwide Program

Friday, April 3

Speakers - Panels - Demos

Workshops - Q&A - Exhibits

Blue-Collar & White-Collar Careers

Check it out: www.GoWork.fhsd.edu

Task 4

Partners in Progress

Present

< JOB EXPLO FORUM >

Coming Soon (May 15)

to a Computer Near You

Chats - Library - Job News

Message Board - Seminars

Task 5 *2" top and side margins* STUDENT QUESTIONNAIRE

Directions: Rank these Career Day ideas (1-2-3). Write 1 for the idea you like best. *center items below*

____Talk by former student who writes for a living.

Master Alphanumeric Keyboarding Technique
Lesson 30   Alphanumeric Keying Skills

Objectives:
1. To improve technique on individual letters.
2. To improve keying speed on 1', 2', and 3' writings.

30A◆   5

Conditioning Practice

each line twice SS; then a 1'
writing on line 3; find *gwam*

alphabet	1	Lopez knew our squad could just slip by the next five games.
figures	2	Check Numbers 267, 298, 304, and 315 were still outstanding.
easy	3	Dixie works with vigor to make the theory work for a profit.

| 1 | 2 | 3 | 4 | 5 | 6 | 7 | 8 | 9 | 10 | 11 | 12 |

Skillbuilding

30B◆   30

**Technique Mastery:
Individual Letters**

1. Key each line twice SS; DS between 2-line groups. Note the lines that were difficult for you.
2. Key those lines again.

Technique goals
- curved, upright fingers
- quick-snap keystrokes
- quiet hands and arms

A	1	Ana ate a salami sandwich and some papaya after a quick nap.
B	2	Bobby bought a beach ball and big balloons for the big bash.
C	3	Cora can serve cake and coffee to the cold campers at lunch.
D	4	David did all he could to dazzle the crowd with wild dances.
E	5	Elaine left her new sled in an old shed near the grey house.
F	6	Frank found a file folder his father had left in the office.
G	7	Gloria got the giggles when the juggler dropped his oranges.
H	8	Hugh helped his big brother haul in the fishing net for her.
I	9	Inez sings in a trio that is part of a big choir at college.
J	10	Jason just joined the jury to judge the major jazz festival.
K	11	Kurt makes kapok pillows for kayaks and ketches at the dock.
L	12	Lola left her doll collection for a village gallery to sell.
M	13	Myna asked her mom to make more malted milk for the mission.
N	14	Nadine knew her aunt made lemonade and sun tea this morning.
O	15	Owen took the book from the shelf to copy his favorite poem.
P	16	Pamela added a pinch of pepper and paprika to a pot of soup.
Q	17	Quent posed quick quiz questions to his quiet croquet squad.
R	18	Risa used a rubber raft to rescue four girls from the river.
S	19	Silas said his sister has won six medals in just four meets.
T	20	Trisha told a tall tale about three little kittens in a tub.
U	21	Ursula asked the usual questions about four issues you face.
V	22	Vinny voted for five very vital issues of value to everyone.
W	23	Wilt wants to walk in the walkathon next week and show well.
X	24	Xania next expects them to fix the extra fax machine by six.
Y	25	Yuri said your yellow yacht was the envy of every yachtsman.
Z	26	Zoella and a zany friend ate a sizzling pizza in the piazza.

ALPHANUMERIC KEYING SKILLS   **69**

52C ◆ FEATURE

Change (Convert) Case

1. Read the copy at the right and study the screen.
2. Learn to change case in your software.
3. In the 4 announcements you keyed in **52B**, change ALL CAPS lines to initial caps; change the last line in each one to uppercase. Keep the text on screen.

Case refers to letter characters. **Uppercase** is the same as ALL CAPS; **lowercase** means "small letters." Most text involves both capitals and small letters, or "caps/lowercase"(c/lc). The Case feature allows you to switch text you have keyed from lower to uppercase and vice versa. Other options may include *sentence case* (first letter of line capitalized) and *title case* or *initial capitals* (first letter of each word capitalized).

Change (Convert) Case

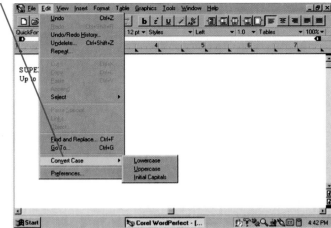

52D ◆ FEATURE

Change Font

1. Read the copy at the right and study the screen.
2. Learn to change fonts in your software.
3. In Announcements 3 and 4, change the font on lines 1, 3, and 8 (suggested: Arial, Century Gothic, or Modern).

Besides changing the case (lower, upper) and style (bold, italic, underlined) of text, you can give text a different look by changing its design, or **font**. Three common fonts are named Arial, Courier New, and Times New Roman (each name is shown in the font it represents). Use your software's default font unless the book or your teacher suggests another font to use.

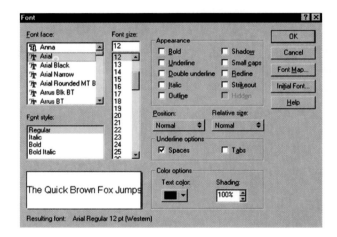

52E ◆

Center Menus

Line spacing: DS
Top margin: 1"

1. Format and key Menus 1 and 2, each on a separate page. Center all lines.
2. Before removing text from screen, make the changes listed below.

Menus 1 and 2

Change the font on line 1 to Arial or Modern; change case in lines 3, 5, 7, 9, and 11 to initial caps. Italicize line 2; bold lines 3, 5, 7, 9, and 11.

Menu 1

RESTAURANTE LA BAMBA
Salon Buganvilea
ENTREMES
Queso Fundido con Chorizo Cantimpalo
SOPA
Crema de Elotes con Rajas
ENSALADA
Coliflor a la Vinagreta
ENTRADA
Camarones Gigantes al Mojo de Ajo
POSTRE
Rollo de Nuez con Crema

Menu 2

LA BAMBA RESTAURANT
Bougainvillea Room
APPETIZER
Grilled Cheese with Cantimpalo Sausage
SOUP
Cream of Corn with Green Chili Strips
SALAD
Cauliflower a la Vinaigrette
ENTREE
Grilled Jumbo Shrimp with Garlic
DESSERT
Nut Roll in Cream Sauce

Speed Building: Guided Writing

1. Key one 1' unguided and two 1' *guided* writings on ¶ 1 and then on ¶ 2.
2. Key two 2' unguided writings on ¶s 1-2 combined; find *gwam* on each.
3. Key a 3' writing on ¶s 1-2 combined; find *gwam*.

1' *gwam* goals

▽ 23 = acceptable
⊡ 27 = average
⊙ 31 = good
◇ 35 = excellent

The **la** above these ¶s shows that they are low average difficulty—a bit more difficult than the ¶s in previous lessons.

 all letters used

2' | 3'

When saying hello to someone is the correct thing to do, 6 | 4
make direct eye contact and greet the person with vitality 12 | 8
in your voice. Do not look down or away or speak only in a 18 | 12
whisper. Make the person feel happy for having seen you, and 24 | 16
you will feel much better about yourself as a consequence. 30 | 20

Similarly, when you shake hands with another person, 35 | 23
look that person in the eye and offer a firm but not crushing 41 | 27
shake of the hand. Just a firm shake or two will do. Next 47 | 31
time you meet a new person, do not puzzle about whether to 53 | 35
shake hands. Quickly offer your firm hand with confidence. 59 | 39

Technique Mastery

1. Key each line once at an easy, steady pace.
2. Key each line again at a faster pace; try to force your speed.

Figure-technique mastery (quiet hands; *finger* reaches)

1 it 85 do 39 if 84 so 29 an 16 am 17 of 94 us 72 go 50 he 630
2 I was 17 on May 20, 1998; 6 ft. tall; weighed 153 lbs. 4 oz.

3 as 12 we 23 up 70 in 86 at 15 no 69 be 53 on 96 ax 12 re 433
4 In our last 3 games, we won 60 to 54, 71 to 69, and 32 to 8.

5 make 7183 kept 8305 work 2948 half 6194 gush 5726 fish 48263
6 Key these numbers: 305, 1492, 1776, 1862, 1914, 1929, 1946.

Response-pattern mastery (Change speed to fit word difficulty.)

7 a in be on we up as my at no was you are him get few see set
letter response
8 at no|as my|on you|we are|get him|at best|in fact|as you saw
9 As you see, you are free only after you get a case date set.

10 of is it he to by or us an so if do am go me the six and but
word response
11 to me|of us|and may|pay for|big box|the six|but due|own them
12 The city is to pay for the field work both men did for them.

13 of we to in or on is be it as by no if at us up an my he was
combination response
14 is in|if we do|is up to|may get all|she was off|pay you then
15 Tish saw you sign the tax form after you paid the city fees.

Lesson 52 Announcements and Menus

Objectives:
1. **To center documents and emphasize text.**
2. **To convert case and change fonts.**

52A◆
Keyboard Mastery

Use Conditioning Practice, p. 115, or B, p. A6.

52B◆
Center Announcements

Line spacing: DS; QS between announcements
Top margin: 1"

Announcements 1-2 on 1 page
Announcements 3-4 on 1 page

1. Center horizontally each line of each announcement.
2. Make the changes listed below.

Announcement 1
Change the day and date to *Friday, March 9.* Bold line 6; italicize the last line.

Announcement 2
Change 35% to 40%. Bold the shop name; underline line 2.

Announcement 3
Bold lines 4-7; underline lines 1 and 8.

Announcement 4
Bold and italicize line 1; underline line 7; bold the telephone number.

3. Keep all announcements open.

Announcement 1

ANNUAL FUND AUCTION

Student Activity Center

Lakeshore High School

Saturday, March 10

Dinner at 6:30 p.m.

Auction at 8:00 p.m.

Admission & Dinner: $17.50

Reservations: 555-4739

Announcement 2

SUPER SAVER SALE

Up to 35% off

Rings, Necklaces, Bracelets

at

THE GEM SHOP

December 1 Through 15

10 a.m. - 6 p.m.

Towne Shopping Center

Announcement 3

Louisville Public Theatre
Auditions for
SCHOOLHOUSE ROCK LIVE
Saturday, February 21
Noon to 2 p.m.
Thursday, February 26
6 p.m. to 9 p.m.
Turpin H.S. Auditorium

Announcement 4

Outside In III

Now Showing

KZF Gallery

655 Eden Park Drive, Suite 750

Paintings - Drawings - Pastels

Mixed Media - Sculptures

Runs Through May

Information: 126-6211

Lesson 31 Alphanumeric Keying Skills

Objectives:
1. **To improve skill on sentence and paragraph writings.**
2. **To improve speed on 1', 2', and 3' writings.**

31A◆ 5
Conditioning Practice

each line twice SS; then a
1' writing on line 3; find *gwam*

alphabet	1	Jung quickly baked extra pizzas for the film festival crowd.
figures	2	I moved from 3748 Oak Street to 1059 Jaymar Drive on May 26.
easy	3	She paid the big man for the field work he did for the city.

| 1 | 2 | 3 | 4 | 5 | 6 | 7 | 8 | 9 | 10 | 11 | 12 |

Skillbuilding

31B◆ 30
Technique Emphasis

1. Key the lines once SS as shown—DS between 3-line groups.
2. Key the lines again at a faster pace.
3. If time permits, key a 1' writing on each of lines 22, 23, and 24; find *gwam*.

Technique goals
- quick down-and-in spacing
- out-and-down reaches to shift keys
- curved, upright fingers
- quiet hands and arms
- unused fingers low over home keys

figures	1	a l ; 0 g 5 us 72 or 94 am 17 is 82 do 39 by 56 go 59 up 70;
	2	On June 17, 1998, 30 of them took a bus trip of 2,465 miles.
	3	We were billed for 3,650 bulbs, 1,278 shrubs, and 495 trees.
space bar	4	When you reach a goal you have set, set one a little higher.
	5	Kevin may sign the audit form in the city when he checks it.
	6	She said to turn in our term papers by the end of next week.
shift keys & CAPS LOCK	7	Did you see LA BOHEME at the Metropolitan Opera in New York?
	8	Mary Ann saw a new production of CAROUSEL at Lincoln Center.
	9	Chien read LINCOLN by Vidal; Kermit read MEXICO by Michener.
double letters	10	Nell took a small drill from the tool box to drill the hole.
	11	Ann took off the desk a book of odd poems to keep at school.
	12	Tommy will tell the class how a little more effort paid off.
adjacent keys	13	Kerry opted to rent a silk suit instead of buying a new one.
	14	If we buy her coffee shop, should we buy the gift shop, too?
	15	We spent a quiet week at the shore prior to the open season.
long direct reaches	16	Jenny spun on the ice, jumped the curb, and broke her thumb.
	17	We once had many mussels but not since your recent harvests.
	18	My niece has a chance to bring the bronze trophy back to us.
alphabetic sentences	19	Mae was quickly given the bronze trophy by six fussy judges.
	20	Quinto got six big jigsaw puzzles from the very daffy clerk.
	21	Roz fixed the crisp okra, while Jane made unique beef gravy.
easy sentences	22	Alfie is to go to work for the city to fix bus sign emblems.
	23	Did he rush the rotor of the giant robot to the island firm?
	24	The busy girl works with a fury to fix the signals by eight.

| 1 | 2 | 3 | 4 | 5 | 6 | 7 | 8 | 9 | 10 | 11 | 12 |

Center Lists and Announcements

Line spacing: DS; QS between items
Top margin: 1"

Items 1-3 on one page
Items 4 and 5 on one page
Item 6 on a separate page

1. Key Items 1-3 as shown, centering each line and adding underline, bold, and italic *as you key*.
2. Key Items 4 and 5 as shown; then center each line; add these special effects:
   - Item 4: Underline the second line. Bold the fourth line and the date.
   - Item 5: Bold the first line and date. Italicize the last line.
3. Key Item 6. You may center the lines and add special effects as you key OR afterwards.

Proofreader's Marks

∧	= Insert
⊓ OR *tr*	= Transpose
˜	= Delete and close
≡	= Capitalize
⋕	= Insert a space
⋀⋀⋀ OR *bf*	= Bold

LANGUAGE CUES:
- The word *italic* is abbreviated *ital.*
- Italic often replaces the underline since underlined text is not easy to read.

Item 1

National Honor Society
Joseph I. Emerik
Yuka Ito
Ricardo J. Mendoza
Billye Jean Peters
Christopher A. Thompson

Item 2
ENGLISH TO SPANISH

house: *casa*

hotel: *hostal*

airport: *aeropuerto*

bank: *banco*

train station: *tren estacion*

Item 3
SPANISH TO ENGLISH

por favor: *please*

gracias: *thank you*

da nada: *you are welcome*

hasta luego: *see you later*

hasta la vista: *I'll see you*

Item 4

ANNOUNCING

Student Auditions

for

Holiday Assembly Program

in

Student Activity Center

November 9

Actors at 9:00 a.m.

Vocalists at 10:30 a.m.

Instrumentalists at 1:00 p.m.

Item 5

Health Service Center

announces

Make-Up Flu Vaccination

November 24

8:30-10:30 a.m.

Special Events Dining Room

Item 6

School of Performing Arts

presents

"The Mouse that Roared" *bf*

on

January 21 and 22

2:30 and 8:00 p.m.

Marx Theatre

ital. Matinee: $4.50; Evening: $5.50

Speed Building: Guided Writing

1. Key one 1' unguided and two 1' *guided* writings on each ¶.
2. Key two 2' unguided writings on ¶s 1-2 combined; find *gwam* on each.
3. Key a 3' writing on ¶s 1-2 combined; find *gwam*.

| Quarter-Minute Checkpoints |				
gwam	1/4'	1/2'	3/4'	Time
16	4	8	12	16
20	5	10	15	20
24	6	12	18	24
28	7	14	21	28
32	8	16	24	32
36	9	18	27	36
40	10	20	30	40

Ia all letters used

When you need to adjust to a new situation in which new

people are involved, be quick to recognize that at first it

is you who must adapt. This is especially true in an office

where the roles of workers have already been established. It

is your job to fit into the team structure with harmony.

Learn the rules of the game and who the key players are;

then play according to those rules at first. Do not expect

to have the rules modified to fit your concept of what the

team structure and your role in it should be. Only after you

become a valuable member should you suggest major changes.

Enrichment

Key Rough Draft (Corrected Copy)

1. Review the proofreader's marks shown below.
2. Read the ¶s at right, noting marked changes.
3. Key the ¶s, making the changes as marked.
4. Key a 1' writing on each ¶ and a 2' writing on the 2 ¶s combined; find *gwam* on each writing.

Proofreader's Marks

∧ = insert
𝒶 = delete
◯ = close up
= add space
⊙ = insert period
∪ = transpose
∧ = insert comma

e all letters used

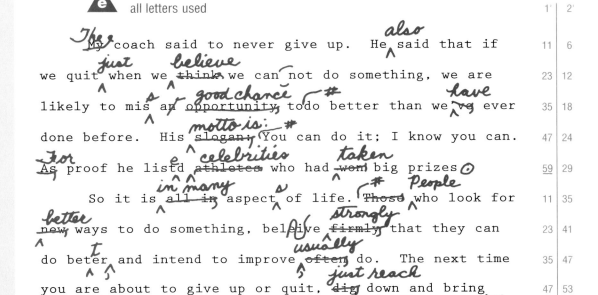

Bold, Italic, and Underline

Line spacing: DS
Top margin: 1"

1. Read the copy at the right.
2. Learn how to bold, italicize, and underline copy with your software. Learn keyboard commands for the features besides locating the toolbar buttons (see illustration).
3. Key Drills 1-3 DS on one page, using bold, italic, or underline as you key (as shown below). Center each line; QS between drills.

The **Bold** feature prints text **darker** than other (plain) copy. The **Italic** feature prints characters that slope up toward the right, as in *these words*. The **Underline** feature prints <u>a line</u> under copy. Each feature may be used as you key or to change the look of words in copy you have already keyed.

Follow the textbook to know when to use these features. Remember that bold, italic, or underline features are not "special" if used too much.

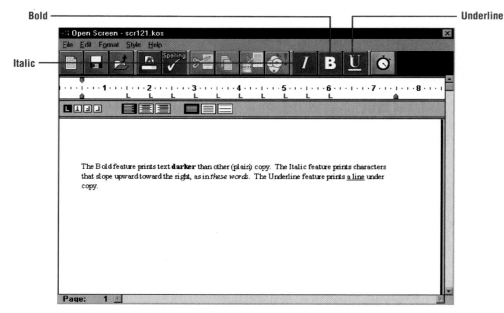

Drill 1	Drill 2	Drill 3
CITIES	**READING LIST**	**SPELLING LIST**
Havana	*Lord of the Flies*	accom<u>mo</u>date
Capetown	*Pride and Prejudice*	com<u>mittee</u>
Port-au-Prince	*To Kill a Mockingbird*	ju<u>dg</u>ment
Sault Sainte Marie	*Red Badge of Courage*	reco<u>mm</u>endation

Block Text

Line spacing: DS
Top margin: 1"

1. Read the copy at the right and study the screen in **51C** (above).
2. Learn to block text in your software.
3. Rekey Drills 1-3 in **51C**. As you key, omit bold, italic, and underline. Then, add them to the keyed copy.

The **Block Text** feature has no use by itself; in fact, you may not think of it as a feature at all. When you *block* text, you mark, or select, copy that you want to center or bold or italicize or underline. (Soon you will use Block Text for other reasons, too.)

To make copy bold, italic, or underlined after you key it, block or select the character, word, or line that you want to highlight; then, click the Bold, Italic, or Underline button (**51C**). To change bold, italic, or underlined text to plain text, block it; then, click each button again.

Lesson 32 Alphanumeric Keying Skills

Objectives:
1. **To improve technique on individual letters.**
2. **To increase speed on 1', 2', and 3' writings.**

32A◆ 5
Conditioning Practice

each line once SS; DS; each line again

alphabet 1 Bonzi may pick kumquats if Jorge will drive the old ox cart.

figures 2 On August 20 we had 84 copies of T37; 95 of B16; 32 of M247.

easy 3 They work with good form and vigor to make it to their goal.

| 1 | 2 | 3 | 4 | 5 | 6 | 7 | 8 | 9 | 10 | 11 | 12 |

Skillbuilding

32B◆ 30
Keyboard Mastery

each line once SS; DS; difficult lines again as time permits

A 1 Ada made good marks in all her classes and led her gym team.

B 2 Bubba dribbles the ball before he bounces it beyond a guard.

C 3 Cincy quickly cut the corn off the cob for her uncle to can.

D 4 Danny was added to the squad after an end dropped out today.

E 5 Euris felt the need to see her teacher about an oral report.

F 6 Ford left for the ski lift after a snack of fish and coffee.

G 7 Giget bought a bright green organza gown with an orange bow.

H 8 Harl feels he has had a bad time if he has had to work hard.

I 9 Iona is in line for a big raise in pay if given the new job.

J 10 Jo just jumped for joy as a judge gave her a major jury job.

K 11 Kiko asked the clerk to work quickly to check in the skiers.

L 12 Lolita will file a claim for a small parcel of my lake land.

M 13 Max may miss most of the game if the swim team misses a bus.

N 14 Nancy knew that her son had gone to the tennis court at ten.

O 15 Ossido opted to go to the opera instead of the opening game.

P 16 Patsy has put too much pepper in the soup pot for my palate.

Q 17 Quade uses quick quiet quips to quell squash squad quarrels.

R 18 Rosa read her story to thirty rapt students in third period.

S 19 Steve said his plans to improve the system met with success.

T 20 Netty meant to take a little time for thought before acting.

U 21 Uri quickly turned our bus around and drove up the mountain.

V 22 Viv used vim and vigor to have voters approve a savings tax.

W 23 Walter now wants to write news items for a weekly news show.

X 24 Xenia next faxed us six tax bills as extra extreme examples.

Y 25 Yancy saw your yellow yacht motor by a buoy in a nearby bay.

Z 26 Zelda, gazing at a hazy horizon, was puzzled by fuzzy ships.

Centering Documents

Lesson 51   Lists and Announcements

O b j e c t i v e s :

Approx. time: 75'

1. **To center lines of copy horizontally (side to side).**
2. **To highlight text with bold, italic, and underline.**

51A◆

Keyboard Mastery

Use Conditioning Practice, p. 113, or A, p. A6.

51B◆ **FEATURE**

Center ⬛

Line spacing: DS
Top margin: 1"

1. Read the copy at the right and study the screen.
2. Learn to use the Center feature in your software. Learn the keyboard command for centering as you key; also locate the toolbar button (see illustration).
3. Key Drills 1-3 DS on one page, each line centered horizontally as you key; QS between drills.

Some word processing features presented in Part 2 may not be available on your software.

⬛ If you are using *Applied MicroType Pro*, this "Open Screen" icon indicates that the feature is available.

☑ This icon indicates that the feature is available in *Applied MicroType Pro* and additionally the special Document Checker program can be used to check the accuracy of the text.

The **Center** feature puts text between the left and right margins, with the same number of spaces on each side of it.

To center a line, turn on the feature and key the copy. Turn off the Center feature to make text begin at the left margin.

Center

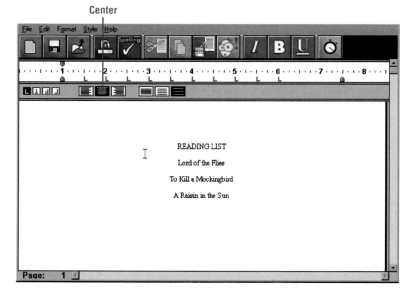

Drill 1	Drill 2	Drill 3
is	a	I
they	for	when
social	gowns	profit
problems	foreign	quality
amendments	processor	quantity

Check Speed: Guided Writing

1. Key a 1' writing on each ¶; find *gwam*.
2. Key a 2' and a 3' writing on ¶s 1-2 combined; find *gwam*.
3. As time permits, key 1' *guided* writings (p. 46) on each ¶ to build keying speed.

gwam	1/4'	1/2'	3/4'	Time
16	4	8	12	16
20	5	10	15	20
24	6	12	18	24
28	7	14	21	28
32	8	16	24	32
36	9	18	27	36
40	10	20	30	40

Quarter-Minute Checkpoints

la   all letters used   2' | 3'

A vital difference exists between a job done right and   6 | 4
one done just about right.   One is given approval while the   12 | 8
other is not.   To receive full approval of the jobs you do,   18 | 12
recognize that just about right is not adequate.   Attempt   23 | 16
now to do every task just right.   27 | 18

Before long you will try problems in which are applied   32 | 21
the seemingly little things that are crucial in learning to   38 | 25
key.   Mastery of little things now is certain to make the   44 | 29
big jobs easier to do just right a little later.   Knowledge,   50 | 33
skill, and purpose are the keys to your success.   55 | 36

Enrichment

Technique Mastery

1. Key each line once at an easy, steady pace.
2. Key each line again at a faster pace; try to force your speed.

Figure-technique mastery (quiet hands; *finger* reaches)

1 for 494 may 617 sir 284 lap 910 rod 493 got 505 the 563 firm
2 On August 20, 1998, we moved from 3746 Oak St. to 50 Elm Ct.

3 card 3143 only 9696 fact 5135 upon 7096 case 3123 limp 98706
4 Order Nos. 56173 and 62840 must be paid no later than May 9.

5 with 2856 quay 1716 door 3994 girl 5849 flap 4910 slam 29175
6 We need to order Stock Nos. 1056, 2948, and 3746 by March 1.

Response-pattern mastery (Change speed to fit word difficulty.)

letter response
7 you get mop car ply far pump area null ever junk after nylon
8 you were| few ever| tax only| oil case| act upon| after you trade
9 Get him my extra tax card only after you set up a case date.

word response
10 when also such form both with then city name than paid their
11 also work| with them| paid both| they held| soap firm| such forms
12 Six of the firms may also make a bid for the city dock work.

combination response
13 the oil for you may act due him she sat did get but red wish
14 she was| the mop| for him| may get| they are| big jump| to aid you
15 Kent was to get a pump for the small oil firm on the island.

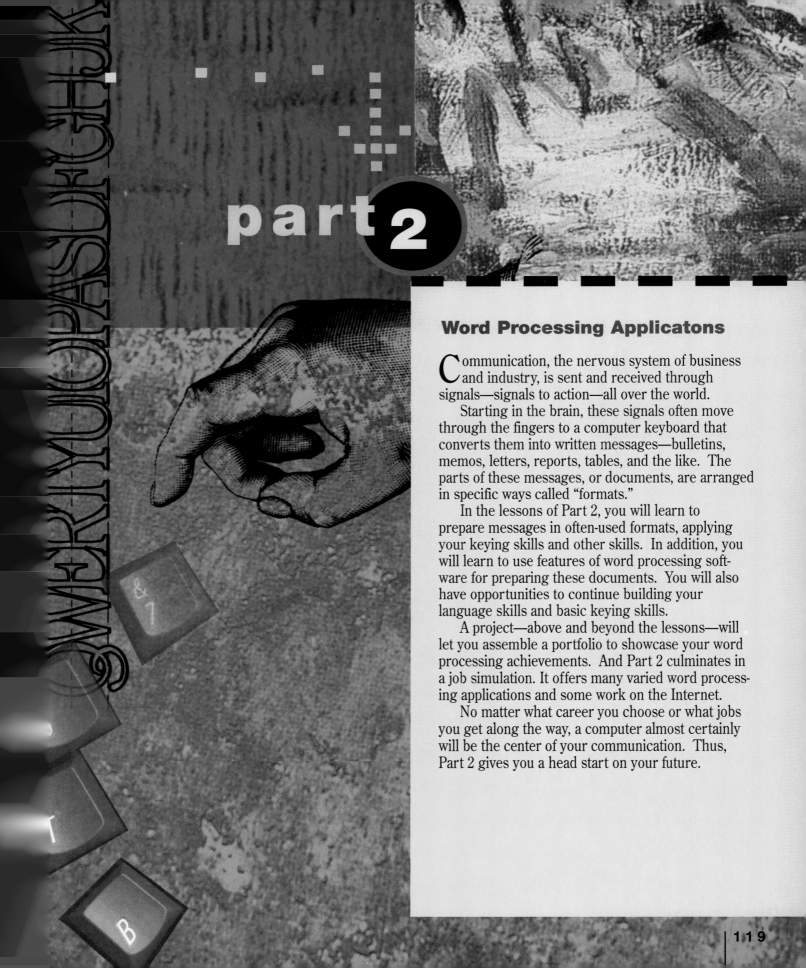

part 2

Word Processing Applicatons

Communication, the nervous system of business and industry, is sent and received through signals—signals to action—all over the world.

Starting in the brain, these signals often move through the fingers to a computer keyboard that converts them into written messages—bulletins, memos, letters, reports, tables, and the like. The parts of these messages, or documents, are arranged in specific ways called "formats."

In the lessons of Part 2, you will learn to prepare messages in often-used formats, applying your keying skills and other skills. In addition, you will learn to use features of word processing software for preparing these documents. You will also have opportunities to continue building your language skills and basic keying skills.

A project—above and beyond the lessons—will let you assemble a portfolio to showcase your word processing achievements. And Part 2 culminates in a job simulation. It offers many varied word processing applications and some work on the Internet.

No matter what career you choose or what jobs you get along the way, a computer almost certainly will be the center of your communication. Thus, Part 2 gives you a head start on your future.

Language & Writing Skills 3

Activity 1:

1. Study the spelling/definitions of the words in the color block at right.
2. Key line 1 (the *Learn* line), noting the proper choice of words.
3. Key lines 2-3 (the *Apply* lines), choosing the right words to complete the lines correctly.
4. Key the remaining lines in the same way.
5. Check your accuracy; rekey lines containing word-choice errors.

Choose the right word

lead *(vb)* to guide or direct; to be first	**choose** *(vb)* to select; to decide on
led *(vb)* the past tense of *lead*	**chose** *(vb)* the past tense of *choose*

Learn 1 Max is to lead the parade; Pam led it last year.
Apply 2 The Falcons (lead, led) now; the Friars (lead, led) at the half.
Apply 3 Marj (lead, led) at the ninth hole, but she does not (lead, led) now.

Learn 4 Jose chose a Eureka computer; I may choose a Futura.
Apply 5 After he (choose, chose) a red cap, I told him to (choose, chose) blue.
Apply 6 Mae (choose, chose) you as a partner; Janice may (choose, chose) me.

Activity 2:

1. Key lines 1-10 using the correct pronouns.
2. Check work with the *Teacher's Key.*
3. Note the rule number(s) at the left of each sentence in which you made a pronoun agreement error.
4. Turn to page 76 and identify those rules for review/practice.
5. Use the Read/Learn/Apply plan for each rule to be reviewed.

Proofread & correct

RULE

1 1 Suzy knew that (he, she, they) should do her best at all times.
3 2 People who entered the contest say (he, she, they) are confident.
3 3 As soon as class is over, I like to transcribe (our, my) notes.
3 4 Mrs. Kelso gave (her, his, their) lecture in Royce Hall.
2 5 The yacht moved slowly around (her, his, its) anchor.
1 6 As you practice the drills, (his, your) skill increases.
1 7 I played my new clarinet in (my, their, your) last recital.
3 8 The editors planned quickly for (its, their) next luncheon.
4 9 The women's volleyball team won (its, their) tenth game today.
4 10 Our family will take (its, their) annual trip in August.

Activity 3:

Key each line once SS. At the end of each line, supply the information (noted in parentheses) needed to complete the sentence. In lines 3 and 6, also choose the correct article (*a* or *an*) to precede the information you supply.

Compose (think) as you key

1 My full name is **(first/middle/last).**

2 I attend **(name of school).**

3 I am learning to key on a/an **(brand of computer/typewriter).**

4 My main goal has been to develop **(technique/speed/accuracy).**

5 My favorite class in school is **(name of subject).**

6 My career goal is to be a/an **(name of job).**

7 My main hobby is **(name of hobby).**

8 I spend most of my free time **(name of activity).**

1. Identify the rule(s) you need to review/practice.
2. **Read:** Study each rule.
3. **Learn:** Key the *Learn* line(s) beneath it, noting how the rule is applied.
4. **Apply:** Key the *Apply* line(s), adding semicolons and underlines as needed.
5. Check work with the *Teacher's Key*.

Internal punctuation: Semicolon

RULE 1:	Use a semicolon to separate two or more independent clauses in a compound sentence when the conjunction is omitted.

Learn 1 Ms. Willis is a superb manager; she can really motivate workers.
Apply 2 His dad is a corporate lawyer his law degree is from Columbia.
Apply 3 Orin is at the Air Force Academy Margo is at the Naval Academy.

RULE 2:	Use a semicolon to separate independent clauses when they are joined by a conjunctive adverb *(however, therefore, consequently*, etc.).

Learn 4 Patricia lives in Minneapolis; however, she works in St. Paul.
Apply 5 No discounts are available now consequently, I'll buy in July.
Apply 6 I work mornings therefore, I prefer an afternoon interview.

RULE 3:	Use a semicolon to separate a series of phrases or clauses (especially if they contain commas) that are introduced by a colon.

Learn 7 Al spoke in these cities: Denver, CO; Erie, PA; and Troy, NY.
Apply 8 Overdue accounts follow: Ayn, 30 da. Lowe, 60 da. Shu, 90 da.
Apply 9 I paid these amounts: April, $375 May, $250 and June, $195.

RULE 4:	Place the semicolon outside the closing quotation mark. (A period and a comma are placed *inside* the closing quotation mark.)

Learn 10 Miss Trent spoke about "leaders"; Mr. Sanyo, about "followers."
Apply 11 The coach said, "Do your very best" Paula said, "I'll try"
Apply 12 He said, "It's your own fault" she said, "With your help"

Internal punctuation: Underline

RULE 5:	Use an underline to indicate titles of books and names of magazines and newspapers. (Titles may be keyed in ALL CAPS or italics without the underline.)

Learn 13 <u>The World Almanac</u> lists <u>Reader's Digest</u> as the top seller.
Apply 14 I read the review of Runaway Jury in the New York Times.
Apply 15 He quoted from an article in Newsweek or the Chicago Sun-Times.

RULE 6:	Use an underline to call attention to words or phrases (or use quotation marks). **Note:** Use a continuous underline (see line 13 above) unless each word is to be considered separately as shown below.

Learn 16 Students often use <u>then</u> for <u>than</u> and <u>its</u> for <u>it's</u>.
Apply 17 I had to select the correct word from their, there, and they're.
Apply 18 He emphasized that we should stand up, speak up, then sit down.

1. Identify the rule(s) you need to review/practice.
2. **Read:** Study each rule.
3. **Learn:** Key the *Learn* line(s) beneath it, noting how the rule is applied.
4. **Apply:** Key the *Apply* line(s), choosing the correct pronouns.
5. Check work with the *Teacher's Key*.

Pronoun agreement

RULE 1: A personal pronoun (*I, we, you, he, she, it, their,* etc.) agrees in **person** (first, second, or third) with the noun or other pronoun it represents.

first person	I, we	represents the speaker(s) or writer(s)
second person	you	represents the person(s) spoken/written to
third person	he, she, it, they	represents the person(s) spoken/written about

Learn 1 We can win the game if we all give each play our best effort. **(1st person)**
Learn 2 You may play softball only after you finish all your homework. **(2nd person)**
Learn 3 Andrea said that she will drive her car to the shopping mall. **(3rd person)**
Apply 4 Those who saw the exhibit said that (he, she, they) were impressed.
Apply 5 After you run for a few days, (my, your) muscles are less sore.
Apply 6 Before I take the test, I want to review (our, my) class notes.

RULE 2: A personal pronoun agrees in **gender** (feminine, masculine, or neuter) with the noun or other pronoun it represents.

Learn 7 Miss Kimoto will give her talk after the announcements. **(feminine)**
Learn 8 The small boat lost its way in the dense fog. **(neuter)**
Apply 9 Each winner will get a corsage as she receives (her, its) award.
Apply 10 The ball circled the rim before (he, it) dropped through the hoop.

RULE 3: A personal pronoun agrees in **number** (singular or plural) with the noun or other pronoun it represents.

Learn 11 Celine drove her new car to Del Rio, Texas, last week. **(singular)**
Learn 12 The club officers made careful plans for their next meeting. **(plural)**
Apply 13 All workers must submit (his, their) vacation requests.
Apply 14 The sloop lost (its, their) headsail in the windstorm.

RULE 4: A personal pronoun that represents a collective noun (*team, committee, family,* etc.) may be singular or plural, depending on the meaning of the collective noun.

Learn 15 Our men's soccer team played its fifth game today. **(acting as a unit)**
Learn 16 The vice squad took their positions in the square. **(acting individually)**
Apply 17 The jury will render (its, their) verdict at 1:30 today.
Apply 18 The Finance Committee had presented (its, their) written reports.

Language & Writing Skills 8

Activity 1:

1. Study the spelling/definitions of the words in the color block at right.
2. Key the *Learn* line, noting the proper choice of words.
3. Key the *Apply* lines, choosing the right words to complete each line correctly.
4. Check your accuracy; rekey lines containing errors in word choice.

Choose the right word

buy *(n/vb)* a bargain; to purchase; to acquire

by *(prep/adv)* close to; via; according to; close at hand; at/in another's home

some *(n/adv)* unknown or unspecified unit or thing; to a degree or extent

sum *(n/vb)* the whole amount; the total; to find a total; summary of points

Learn 1   She stopped by a new shop on the square to buy the new CD.
Apply 2   We are to go (buy, by) bus to the ski lodge to (buy, by) ski togs.
Apply 3   Did you (buy, by) the new novel (buy, by) Margaret Atwood?

Learn 4   The problem was to find the sum; but some students couldn't.
Apply 5   He said, "In (some, sum), both ideas are true to (some, sum) degree."
Apply 6   I bought (some, sum) pears and apples for the (some, sum) of $4.30.

Activity 2:

1. Key lines 1-10, supplying needed semicolons and underlines.
2. Check work with the *Teacher's Key*.
3. Note the rule number(s) at the left of each sentence in which you made a semicolon or underline error.
4. Turn to page 118 and identify those rules for review/practice.
5. Use the Read/Learn/Apply plan for each rule to be reviewed.

Proofread & correct

RULE		
1	1	Ms. Barbour is a great coach she is honest and fair.
1	2	Joe Chin won a scholastic award Bill Ott, an athletic one.
1	3	Maxine works from 4 to 7 p.m. she studies after 8:30 p.m.
3	4	The cities are as follows: Ames, IA Provo, UT and Waco, TX.
2	5	The play starts at 8 therefore, you should be ready by 7:30.
3	6	They hired 11 new workers in 1997 6, in 1998 and 8, in 1999.
1,4	7	Troy said, "You can do it" Janelle said, "You're kidding."
1,4	8	Rona sang "Colors of the Wind" Cory sang "Power of the Dream."
5	9	TV Guide ranks No. 2 according to Information Please Almanac.
6	10	"Why," she asked, "can't people use affect and effect properly?"

Activity 3:

1. Read the ¶ at the right based on a survey of people in your age group.
2. On the basis of your own experience in viewing movies and TV, compose a ¶ indicating whether you agree or disagree with the survey results, giving reasons why you agree or disagree.

Compose (think) as you key

     A mid-decade poll of young people revealed that U.S. youths thought current TV and movie fare glamorizes violence and sex without portraying the negative consequences of immoral behavior. Over sixty percent of youths surveyed said that such glamorizations on the screen influenced them to engage in such behavior.

Source: Armstrong Williams, *USA Today*, March 2, 1995.

Learn Top-Row Technique: Symbols
Lesson 33   New Keys: /, $, %, and -

Objectives:
1. **To learn reach-strokes for /, $, %, and -.**
2. **To combine /, $, %, and - smoothly with other keys.**

33A◆ 5

Conditioning Practice

each line twice SS; then a 1'
writing on line 3; find *gwam*

alphabet 1 Di will buy from me as prizes the six unique diving jackets.

figures 2 The January 17 quiz of 25 points will test pages 389 to 460.

easy 3 Both of us may do the audit of the work of a big title firm.

| 1 | 2 | 3 | 4 | 5 | 6 | 7 | 8 | 9 | 10 | 11 | 12 |

33B◆ 16

New Keys: / and $

each line twice SS (slowly, then
faster); DS between
4-line groups; if time permits,
practice the lines again

TECHNIQUE CUES:

/   Reach down to strike **/**
with right little finger.

$ Depress the right shift
key; strike **$** with left
index finger.

/ = diagonal
$ = dollar sign
Do not space between a
figure and the / or the $ sign.

Learn / (diagonal)

1 ; ; /; /; ;; // ;/; ;/; 2/3 4/5 and/or We keyed 1/2 and 3/4.
2 Space between a whole number and a fraction: 7 2/3, 18 3/4.

Learn $ (dollar sign)

3 f f $f $f ff $$ f$f f$f $4 $4 for $4 Shift for $ and key $4.
4 A period separates dollars and cents: $4.50, $6.25, $19.50.

Combine / and $

5 I must shift for $ but not for /:   Order 10 gal. at $16/gal.
6 Do not space on either side of /:   1/6, 3/10, 9 5/8, 4 7/12.
7 We sent 5 boxes of No. 6 3/4 envelopes at $11/box on June 2.
8 They can get 2 sets of disks at $49.85/set; 10 sets, $39.85.

50C ◆ 15
Skill Assessment: Straight Copy

1. Key a 1' writing on ¶ 1; find *gwam*.
2. Add 4 *gwam* for a new goal rate. (See 1/4' checkpoint table below.)
3. Key a 1' *guided* writing on the ¶, trying to reach your checkpoint each 1/4'.
4. Key ¶ 2 in the same manner.
5. Key two 2' writings on ¶s 1-2 combined; find *gwam* on each.
6. Key two 3' writings on ¶s 1-2 combined; find *gwam* and count errors on each.

 all letters used

	2'	3'
To move to the next level of word processing power, you must	6	4
now demonstrate certain abilities. First, you must show that you	13	8
can key with good technique, a modest level of speed, and a limit	19	13
on errors. Next, you must properly apply the basic rules of lan-	26	17
guage use. Finally, you must arrange basic documents properly.	32	21
If you believe you have already learned enough, think of the	38	25
future. Many jobs today require a higher degree of keying skill	45	30
than you have acquired so far. Also realize that numerous styles	51	34
of letters, reports, and tables are in common use today. As a	58	38
result, would you not benefit from another semester of training?	64	43

50D ◆ 15
Skill Transfer: Statistical Copy

1. Key three 1' writings on each ¶; find *gwam* on each writing.
2. Key two 3' writings on ¶s 1-2 combined; find *gwam* on each.
3. Compare *gwam* with the rate you attained on ¶s in 50C.
4. Key additional 3' writings on the slower ¶s to improve your skill transfer.

Quarter-Minute Checkpoints

gwam	1/4'	1/2'	3/4'	Time
20	5	10	15	20
24	6	12	18	24
28	7	14	21	28
32	8	16	24	32
36	9	18	27	36
40	10	20	30	40
44	11	22	33	44
48	12	24	36	48
52	13	26	39	52
56	14	28	42	56

 all figures used

	3'
Since its first showing in 1939, 197.5 million people in the	4 / 48
USA have attended a theater to see "Gone with the Wind." When its	9 / 53
gross sales are adjusted for inflation, its $859 million income	13 / 57
makes it the top-selling film in our history. It exceeds "Star Wars"	17 / 62
(released in 1977) by $229 million; "E.T." (1982) by $289 million.	22 / 66
In addition, "The Ten Commandments" (1958) and "The Sound of	26 / 70
Music" (1965) outsold "Jurassic Park" (1993) and "Return of the Jedi"	31 / 75
(1983) by a large margin. "Fantasia" (1940) also surpassed "The Empire	35 / 79
Strikes Back" (1980) and "The Godfather" (1972). The classic film, it	40 / 84
seems, holds its own against the modern "blockbuster" film.	44 / 88

33C◆ 16
New Keys: % and - (hyphen)

each line twice SS (slowly, then faster); DS between 4-line groups; if time permits, practice the lines again

TECHNIQUE CUES:

% Depress the right shift key; then strike **%** with left index finger.

– Reach up to strike **–** with right little finger.

Some word processing software changes -- to a single character.

% = percent sign
– = hyphen
Do not space between a figure and %, nor before or after – or – – (dash) used as punctuation.

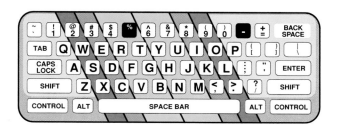

Learn % (percent sign)

1 f f %f %f ff %% f%f f%f 5% 5% Shift for the % in 5% and 15%.
2 Do not space between a number and %:   5%, 75%, 85%, and 95%.

Learn - (hyphen)

3 ; ; -; -; ;; -- ;-; ;-; 4-ply I use a 2-ply tire on my bike.
4 I gave each film a 1-star, 2-star, 3-star, or 4-star rating.

Combine % and -

5 She said that 100% of their work was done by her son-in-law.
6 Kyle, send the parcel by fourth-class mail--a saving of 50%.
7 The prime rate may reach 9%--but he has no interest in that.
8 You need 40 signatures--51% of the members--on the petition.

33D◆ 7
Skillbuilding

1. Key lines 1-8 once SS.
2. Key a 1' writing on line 7 and then on line 8; find *gwam* on each sentence.

/ and $
1 Key a series of fractions as figures: 1/4, 1/3, and 1 3/10.
2 The jacket was discounted from $172.99 to $128.99 to $98.99.

% and -
3 This outlet store gives discounts of 20%, 25%, 35%, and 50%.
4 We have 1-, 2-, and 3-bath condos--he wants a separate home.

all symbols learned
5 This 10 1/2% mortgage was rewritten at 8%--a $13,496 saving.
6 These 3-part forms--minus a 10% discount--cost $75/thousand.

easy sentences
7 Shana is to key all the forms for the city auditor by eight.
8 Six of the girls do work for me; eight do work for the city.

| 1 | 2 | 3 | 4 | 5 | 6 | 7 | 8 | 9 | 10 | 11 | 12 |

33E◆ 6
Skill Check

Key a 1' and a 2' writing on the ¶; find *gwam* on each writing.

 all letters used

	1'	2'
Just a few years ago, having the ability to operate a com-	11	6
puter was a bonus when looking for a job. Today, however, it	24	12
is an ability that is required for almost every job. Further,	36	18
you may need to key at a rapid rate and to learn the relevant	49	24
programs on the market--especially those that are needed for	61	31
your exact profession. If you can do these things, you will	73	37
be amazed at your career progress once you get the job.	84	42

| 1 | 2 | 3 | 4 | 5 | 6 |

Lesson 50 Basic Keyboarding Skills

Objectives:
1. **To improve/assess keying skill on sentences and paragraphs.**
2. **To improve skill transfer: straight copy to statistical copy.**

50A◆ 5
Conditioning Practice
1. Key each line once; then key each line again faster.
2. Key a 1' writing on line 3; find *gwam*.

alphabet 1 Jacki next placed my winning bid for the prized antique red vase.

keypad 2 717 828 939 417 528 639 707 9.9 407.96 104.39 371.3649 45205-4238

speed 3 They wish their neighbor to pay for half the land for the chapel.

| 1 | 2 | 3 | 4 | 5 | 6 | 7 | 8 | 9 | 10 | 11 | 12 | 13 |

50B◆ 15
Technique Mastery
1. Key each line once; note lines that cause you to pause or hesitate.
2. Key a 1' writing on each of lines 15, 18, and 21; find *gwam* on each writing.
3. As time permits, key again those sets of lines that caused you to pause or stop.

Technique goals
- curved, upright fingers
- quick-snap keystrokes
- no finger "flyout"
- down-and-in spacing
- eyes on copy

Keep hands/arms quiet; *reach* with the fingers.

shift keys & LOCK
1 LaCosta Spa | Halley's Comet | Palm Springs | Margate Court | Esprit Park
2 Marla Apton and Pat Cox will play Nan Epps and Larry Sparks next.
3 Sophie works in Boston for NBC; Paula works in Nantucket for CBS.

long direct reaches
4 grip hymn echo many deck must curve funny niece doubt twice brown
5 my niece | ace serve | any doubt | iced juice | sunny deck | my music echos
6 Barb decided to carve many funny faces in the mud with her thumb.

outside reaches
7 lop pox zoo spa cape pawn spot oars wasp maps span slow aqua slaw
8 old pal | low spot | all maps | alto sax | slow pace | next quiz | saw a fawn
9 Silas won a prized spot on our next squad that took a town title.

adjacent keys
10 her top saw ore buy went open coin spot skew ruin soil trot built
11 her suit | buy gas | new coin | was open | last poem | went well | very short
12 Jared was to open a coin shop in a new store built on the square.

double letters
13 mall cuff will soon meek door need seeks books sells peeks little
14 to err | for all | odd book | sell off | zoo pass | too meek | will soon need
15 Bess will take all my old cookbooks to sell at the school bazaar.

combination response
16 sign pump with fear them plum lake were make cafe name join shale
17 and you | for him | man was | pay him | they were | with care | to you or him
18 It was up to you or him to read and amend the audit form by noon.

word response
19 their sight ivory shall flame right amend eight gowns bland girls
20 six girls | ivory gown | their risk | title form | right firm | ivory tusks
21 They may make the amendment to the title form for their neighbor.

| 1 | 2 | 3 | 4 | 5 | 6 | 7 | 8 | 9 | 10 | 11 | 12 | 13 |

Lesson 34 New Keys: #, &, (, and)

Objectives:
1. To learn reach-strokes for #, &, (, and).
2. To combine #, &, (, and) smoothly with other keys.

34A ◆ 5
Conditioning Practice

each line twice SS; then a 1'
writing on line 3; find *gwam*

alphabet 1 Racquel just put back five azure gems next to my gold watch.
figures 2 Joel used a comma in 1,203 and 2,946 but not in 583 and 750.
easy 3 The auto firm owns the big signs by the downtown civic hall.

| 1 | 2 | 3 | 4 | 5 | 6 | 7 | 8 | 9 | 10 | 11 | 12 |

34B ◆ 16
New Keys: # and &

each set of lines twice SS (slowly,
then faster); DS between groups;
if time permits, practice the lines
again

TECHNIQUE CUES:
- **#** Depress the right shift
  key; then strike # with
  left middle finger.
- **&** Depress the left shift
  key; then strike & with
  right index finger.

= number/pounds
& = ampersand (and)

Do not space between #
and a figure; space once
before and after & used
to join names.

Learn # (number/pounds)
1 d d #d #d dd ## d#d d#d 3# 3# Shift for # as you enter #33d.
2 Do not space between a number and #: 3# of #633 at $9.35/#.

Learn & (ampersand)
3 j j &j &j jj && j&j j&j 7& 7& Have you written to Poe & Son?
4 Do not space before or after & in initials, e.g., CG&E, B&O.

Combine # and &
5 Shift for # and &. Recall: # stands for number and pounds.
6 Names joined by & require spaces; a # sign alone does, also.
7 Letters joined by & are keyed solid: List Stock #3 as C&NW.
8 I bought 20# of #830 grass seed from Locke & Uhl on March 4.

49C◆ 15
Skillbuilding:
Straight Copy

1. Key a 1' writing on ¶ 1; find *gwam*.
2. Add 4 *gwam* for a new goal rate. (See 1/4' checkpoint table below.)
3. Key a 1' *guided* writing on the ¶ trying to reach your checkpoint each 1/4'.
4. Key ¶ 2 in the same manner.
5. Key two 2' writings on ¶s 1-2 combined; find *gwam* on each writing.
6. Key two 3' writings on ¶s 1-2 combined; find *gwam* and count errors on each.

 all letters used   2' | 3'

Probably you have heard it said that everyone should learn   6 | 4
how to operate a computer keyboard. Although that idea stretches   13 | 8
the truth a little, no one was ever penalized for knowing how to   19 | 13
key. People in business are expected to key skillfully, but the   26 | 17
same ability is also quite useful in other areas of life.   31 | 21

Keying power is not enough, however. One must, in addition,   37 | 25
be able to apply it in the production of records in their various   44 | 29
formats. In doing so, one must also know how to use the major   50 | 33
features of a software package. Realize that a computer operator   57 | 38
must combine skill with format knowledge and software mastery.   63 | 42

| 1 | | 2 | | 3 | | 4 | | 5 | | 6 |
| 1 | | 2 | | 3 | | 4 |

49D◆ 15
Skill Transfer:
Rough Draft

1. Key three 1' writings on each ¶; find *gwam* on each writing.
2. Key two 3' writings on ¶s 1-2 combined; find *gwam* on each.
3. Compare *gwam* with the rate you attained on ¶s in 49C.
4. Key additional 3' writings on the slower ¶s to improve your skill transfer.

Quarter-Minute Checkpoints				
gwam	1/4'	1/2'	3/4'	Time
20	5	10	15	20
24	6	12	18	24
28	7	14	21	28
32	8	16	24	32
36	9	18	27	36
40	10	20	30	40
44	11	22	33	44
48	12	24	36	48
52	13	26	39	52
56	14	28	42	56

all letters used   1' | 3'

Words are the building blocks of efective writing. The   11 | 4
better we put hour ideas in words the more likely we are to   24 | 8
persuade the reader do to what we ask. If our letters ramble,   36 | 12
are not clear or exhibit poor grammer, we increse the likeli-   49 | 16
hood of having the our ideas rejected and our request denied.   60 | 20

Any week letter canbe improved by rewriting so that the   11 | 24
copy quicly conveys it's basic ideas in a clear, exact man-   24 | 28
ner. The raeder should not than need to puzle over its meaning.   38 | 33
all features of style or and content should be designed to inhance   50 | 37
its meaning instead of distract from it.   59 | 40

34C◆ 16

New Keys: (and)

each set of lines twice SS (slowly, then faster); DS between groups; if time permits, practice the lines again

TECHNIQUE CUES:

(Depress the left shift key; then strike **(** with right ring finger.

) Depress the left shift key; then strike **)** with right little finger.

SPACING CUE:

Do not space between ( ) and copy they enclose.

(= left parenthesis
) = right parenthesis

Learn (

use the letter "l"

1 l l (l (l ll ((l(l l(l 9(9(Shift for the (as you key (9.
2 As (is the shift of 9, use the l finger to key 9, (, or (9.

Learn)

3 ; ;););); ;;)));); 0) 0) Shift for the) as you key 0).
4 As) is the shift of 0, use the ; finger to key 0,), or 0).

Combine (and)

5 Hints: (1) depress shift; (2) strike key; (3) release both.
6 Tab steps: (1) clear tabs, (2) set stops, and (3) tabulate.
7 The new account (#594-7308) draws annual interest at 3 1/4%.

34D◆ 7

Skillbuilding

1. Key lines 1-8 once SS.
2. Key a 1' writing on line 7 and then on line 8; find *gwam* on each sentence.
3. Key a 1' and a 2' writing on the ¶; find *gwam* on each writing.

& and #
1 Rios & Cho will try Case #947-285 and Case #960-318 in June.
2 DP&L sent Invoice #67-5849-302 to Ito & Brown on October 19.

(and)
3 Waltz (the plaintiff) and Ross (the defendant) are in court.
4 The note for five hundred dollars ($500) pays 8.5% interest.

basic symbols
5 Twenty-four (31%) of the owners voted for a $250 assessment.
6 Only 1/4 picked Yes, 1/2 picked No, and 1/4 did not respond.

easy sentences
7 Did the girl row to the dock for the clams and six big fish?
8 They wish to make an issue of the work she did for the city.

| 1 | 2 | 3 | 4 | 5 | 6 | 7 | 8 | 9 | 10 | 11 | 12 |

34E◆ 6

Skill Check

Key a 1' and a 2' writing on the ¶; find *gwam* on each writing.

la all letters used   2'

When you key copy that contains both words and numbers,   6
it is best to key numbers using the top row. When the copy   12
consists primarily of figures, however, it may be faster to   18
use the keypad. In any event, keying figures quickly is a   24
major skill to prize. You can expect to key figures often   30
in the future, so learn to key them with very little peeking. 36

| 1 | 2 | 3 | 4 | 5 | 6 |

Lesson 49 Basic Keyboarding Skills

Objectives:
1. To improve/assess keying skill on sentences and paragraphs.
2. To improve skill transfer: straight copy to rough draft.

49A◆ 5
Conditioning Practice
1. Key each line once; then key each line again faster.
2. Key a 1' writing on line 3; find *gwam*.

alphabet 1 Frazer may have a jinx on my squad, but we kept the big gold cup.
fig/sym 2 Lizzy asked, "Wasn't R&N's check #385367-0 deposited on 1/24/99?"
speed 3 When did the field auditor sign the amendment forms for the city?

| 1 | 2 | 3 | 4 | 5 | 6 | 7 | 8 | 9 | 10 | 11 | 12 | 13 |

49B◆ 15
Technique Mastery
1. Key each line once; note lines that cause you to pause or hesitate.
2. As time permits, key again those sets of lines that caused you to pause or stop.

Technique goals
- curved, upright fingers
- quiet (steady) hands
- no finger "flyout"
- quick-snap keystrokes
- down-and-in spacing
- eyes on copy

A 1 Aldo drank a glass of orange juice and ate a large tuna sandwich.
B 2 Barb did her best to hobble back to the bike after the big blast.
C 3 Chuck could calmly pack cans with chunks of crab in creamy sauce.
D 4 Dodi avoided a blocker and dashed for the end zone at high speed.
E 5 Eugene checked the test scores posted outside the new gym office.

F 6 Fanny offered to fax the four forms to the office for her father.
G 7 Gig juggled the oranges high into the air for the giggling girls.
H 8 Hannah hopes to have the time to help coach the high school team.
I 9 Inez will initial all eight copies to mail to her insurance firm.
J 10 Jeb just jostled a jug of juice as he adjusted his jungle jacket.

K 11 Kae kept lists of work skills in a workbook on her oak desk.
L 12 Leland led all students at the rally in a few jolly school songs.
M 13 Mimi made the most of her gym time and earned a medal last month.
N 14 Neal needed some funny lines to hold the interest of the new men.
O 15 Olivia bought four opal stones and mounted some in handsome gold.

P 16 Perry prepared a piquant pepper pot soup for five hungry campers.
Q 17 Quenella quickly quoted a quaint poem to quell the squad quarrel.
R 18 Rocky rode a dark brown horse in the parade before the fireworks.
S 19 Susie sings in my school chorus and also plays in my school band.
T 20 Tommy takes a little teasing for his tendency to tell tall tales.

U 21 Uris thought it unusual for one issue to result in such a ruckus.
V 22 Viva voted to pave the levy and waive the tax for twelve vendors.
W 23 Wilf saw two women walking along the waterway when the waves hit.
X 24 Xania can fax six extra tax forms to the lax taxi firm next week.
Y 25 Yves may pay dearly for your quay property if you try to sell it.
Z 26 Zimi gave a puzzle as a prize to a dazzling dancer in the piazza.

Lesson 35 New Keys: ', ", _, and *

Objectives:

1. To learn reach-strokes for ', ", _, and *.
2. To combine ', ", _, and * smoothly with other keys.

35A◆ 5
Conditioning Practice

each line twice SS; then a 1'
writing on line 3; find *gwam*

alphabet 1 Bowman fixed prized clocks that seven judges say are unique.

figures 2 Only 1,453 of the 6,270 members were at the 1998 convention.

easy 3 She lent the field auditor a hand with the work of the firm.

| 1 | 2 | 3 | 4 | 5 | 6 | 7 | 8 | 9 | 10 | 11 | 12 |

35B◆ 16
New Keys: ' and "

1. Locate new symbol on appropriate keyboard chart; read technique statement below the chart.
2. Key twice SS the appropriate pair of lines given at right; DS between pairs.
3. Repeat Steps 1 and 2 for the other new symbol.
4. Key twice SS lines 5-8.
5. Rekey the lines with which you had difficulty.

CAPITALIZATION CUE:

Capitalize the first word and all other important words in titles of publications.

Apostrophe: ' is to the right of ; and is controlled by the right little finger.

Quotation mark: Depress left shift and strike " (shift of ') with the right little finger.

The quotation marks that you key may look the same whether at the beginning or end of a quotation. Notice in the typeset copy below, however, that the opening and closing marks are not the same.

Learn ' (apostrophe)

1 ; ; '; '; ;; " ;'; ;'; it's he's I'm I've It's hers, I see.
2 I'm not sure if it's Hal's; but if it's his, I'll return it.

Learn " (quotation mark)

3 ; ; "; "; ;; "" ;'; ;'; "Keep on," she said, but I had quit.
4 I read "Ode on a Grecian Urn," "The Last Leaf," and "Trees."

Combine ' and "

5 "If it's Jan's or Al's," she said, "I'll bring it to class."
6 "Its" is an adjective; "it's" is the contraction of "it is."
7 Miss Uhl said, "To make numbers plural, add 's: 8's, 10's."
8 O'Shea said, "Use ' (apostrophe) to shorten phrases: I'll."

Skillbuilding:
Straight Copy

1. Key a 1' writing on ¶ 1; find *gwam*.
2. Add 4 *gwam* for a new goal rate. (See 1/4' checkpoint table below.)
3. Key a 1' *guided* writing on the ¶ trying to reach your checkpoint each 1/4'.
4. Key ¶ 2 in the same manner.
5. Key two 2' writings on ¶s 1-2 combined; find *gwam* on each writing.
6. Key two 3' writings on ¶s 1-2 combined; find *gwam;* count errors on each.

> From here on, paragraph writings contain copy of average difficulty—indicated by **a.**

 all letters used

	2'	3'
If success is vital to you, you have distinct advantages over	6	4
many people who have no particular feeling one way or the other.	13	9
The desire to succeed is helpful, for it causes us to establish	19	13
goals without which our actions have little or no meaning. Suc-	26	17
cess may not necessarily mean winning the big prize, but it does	32	21
mean approaching a goal.	35	23
It is foolish, of course, to believe that we can all be what-	41	27
ever we wish to become. It is just as foolish, though, to wait	47	31
around hoping for success to overtake us. We should analyze our	53	36
aspirations, our abilities, and our limitations. We can next de-	60	40
cide from various choices what we are best equipped, with effort,	66	44
to become.	67	45

Skill Transfer:
Script

1. Key three 1' writings on each ¶; find *gwam* on each writing.
2. Key two 3' writings on ¶s 1-2 combined; find *gwam* on each.
3. Compare *gwam* with that attained on ¶s in 48C.
4. Key additional 3' writings on the slower ¶s to improve your skill transfer.

 all letters used

	1'	3'
As you build your keying power, the number of errors you	11	4
make is not very important because most of them are acciden-	23	8
tal and incidental. Realize, however, that documents are	35	12
expected to be without flaw. A letter, report, or table that	47	16
contains a flaw is not usable until it is corrected. So find	60	20
and correct all errors.	64	21
The ideal time to detect and correct your errors is while	12	25
the copy is still on a monitor or in the machine. Therefore,	24	29
just before you remove the copy from the screen or machine,	36	33
proofread it and correct every error you have made. Learn to	48	38
proofread carefully and to correct errors quickly. Improve	60	42
your production in this manner.	67	44

Quarter-Minute
Checkpoints

gwam	1/4'	1/2'	3/4'	Time
20	5	10	15	20
24	6	12	18	24
28	7	14	21	28
32	8	16	24	32
36	9	18	27	36
40	10	20	30	40
44	11	22	33	44
48	12	24	36	48
52	13	26	39	52
56	14	28	42	56

Lesson 48

35C◆ 16
New Keys: _ and *

1. Locate new symbol on appropriate keyboard chart.
2. Key twice SS the appropriate pair of lines given at right; DS between pairs.
3. Repeat Steps 1 and 2 for the other new key.
4. Key twice SS lines 5-8.

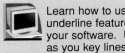
Learn how to use the underline feature on your software. Use it as you key lines 5-8 and in later activities that show underlined words, titles, etc.

Underline: Depress left shift; strike _ (shift of –) with right little finger.

Asterisk: Depress left shift; strike * (shift of 8) with right middle finger.

Learn _ (underline)

1 ; ; _; _; ;; __ ;_; ;_; I _____ go there; she _____ go also.
2 They ___ to visit _____ aunt, but _____ cousin __ at school.

Learn * (asterisk)

3 k k *k *k kk ** k*k k*k She used * for a single source note.
4 All discounted items show an *, thus: 48K*, 588*, and 618*.

Combine _ and *

5 Use an * to mark often-confused words such as <u>then</u> and <u>than</u>.
6 *Note: Book titles (like <u>Lorna Doone</u>) are often underlined.
7 I saw a review of "La Casa Verde" in <u>Latin American Fiction</u>.
8 Did you view <u>Hornblower</u>--a 12th century African sculpture?

35D◆ 13
Statistical Copy

1. Key two 1' and two 2' writings on the ¶; find *gwam* on each.
2. Key a 3' writing on the ¶; find *gwam*.

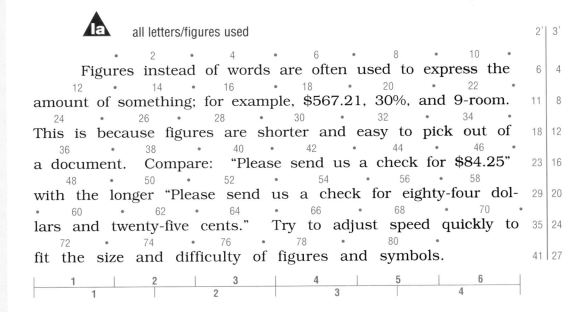

all letters/figures used

2' 3'

Figures instead of words are often used to express the 6 4
amount of something; for example, $567.21, 30%, and 9-room. 11 8
This is because figures are shorter and easy to pick out of 18 12
a document. Compare: "Please send us a check for $84.25" 23 16
with the longer "Please send us a check for eighty-four dol- 29 20
lars and twenty-five cents." Try to adjust speed quickly to 35 24
fit the size and difficulty of figures and symbols. 41 27

Lesson 48 Basic Keyboarding Skills

O b j e c t i v e s :

1. **To improve keying skill on sentences and paragraphs.**
2. **To improve skill transfer: straight copy to script.**

48A◆ 5
Conditioning Practice

1. Key each line once; then key each line again faster.
2. Key a 1' writing on line 3; find *gwam*.

alphabet 1 Dorn was quickly given a big prize for completing six high jumps.
keypad 2 7104 8285 1346 4613 7174 9396 58285 67176 1709.36 2950-46 3847.13
speed 3 Sid is to name the right goals and work for them with vigor.

| 1 | 2 | 3 | 4 | 5 | 6 | 7 | 8 | 9 | 10 | 11 | 12 | 13 |

48B◆ 15
Technique Mastery

1. Key each line once; vary speed according to word difficulty.
2. Key a 1' writing on each of lines 15, 16, and 18; find *gwam* on each writing.
3. As time permits, key again those sets of lines that caused you to pause or stop.

Technique goals

- curved, upright fingers
- no finger "flyout"
- quick-snap keystrokes
- down-and-in spacing
- eyes on copy

Keep hands/arms quiet; *reach* with the fingers.

space bar
1 a rod pan lay man for rob men jam dug may wig hay cog ham cut pay
2 to pay|is for|six men|the wig|cut hay|pay the|may rob|for the men
3 It is up to them to do their best in each try to make a new goal.

double letters
4 all off odd bee add moo see zoo fee door meek fall heed good seek
5 a book|to sell|is less|to tell|bill me|to sell|for less|the class
6 Bobby will sell them the cookbook for a little less than it cost.

adjacent-key reaches
7 has ask pod top buys hers sore cash here hope wear ruin coin were
8 we opt|as well|we hope|ask pop|buy oil|new tray|was here|her cash
9 Joi hoped for a new opal ring to wear to her next violin concert.

long direct reaches
10 my any ice fun nuts sums nice much rice must many deck myth since
11 in ice|at once|he must|so many|to curb|is glum|the brim|six cents
12 June said that I must curb at once my urge to glance at my hands.

letter response
13 as my we up red pin were join free mill case jump read noon great
14 my data|was null|few join|oil case|you read|are free|only a union
15 My war on waste at a union mill was based only upon minimum data.

combination response
16 he as is up do my she was the pup did saw for hum oak set urn mop
17 did see|for him|she saw|the mop|she was|but are|the art|a bad man
18 They may join us for tea at the inn pool if they wish to see you.

word response
19 it fur city firms shall right forks eight their fight shelf forms
20 the map|she got|for six|may dig|and pay|to work|is worn|if he did
21 Did they make the right land title forms for the eight big firms?

Language & Writing Skills 4

Activity 1:

1. Study the spelling/definitions of the words in the color block.
2. Key line 1 (the *Learn* line), noting the proper choice of words.
3. Key lines 2-3 (the *Apply* lines), choosing the right words to complete each sentence correctly.
4. Key the remaining lines in the same way.
5. Check your work; correct any errors you find.

Choose the right word

Its *(adj)* of or relating to itself as the possessor	**than** *(conj/prep)* used in comparisons to show difference between items
it's *(contr)* it is; it has	**then** *(n/adv)* that time; at that time

Learn 1 It's time for the dog to have its food.
Apply 2 Before (its, it's) time to bid, check (its, it's) number.
Apply 3 If (its, it's) not yours, return it to (its, it's) shelf.

Learn 4 If she is older than you, then I am older than you.
Apply 5 We (than, then) decided that two hours were more (than, then) enough.
Apply 6 Fewer (than, then) half the workers were (than, then) put on overtime.

Activity 2:

1. Key lines 1-10 using the correct verbs.
2. Check work with the *Teacher's Key*.
3. Note rule number(s) at left of each sentence in which you made a verb agreement error.
4. Turn to page 84 and identify those rules for review/practice.
5. Use the Read/Learn/Apply plan for each rule to be reviewed.

Proofread & correct

RULE
1   1 Sandra and Rich (is, are) running for class secretary.
1   2 They (has, have) to score high on the SAT to enter that college.
2   3 You (doesn't, don't) think keyboarding is important.
2   4 Why (doesn't, don't) she take the test for advanced placement?
3   5 Neither of the candidates (meet, meets) the leadership criteria.
3   6 One of your art students (is, are) likely to win the prize.
5   7 The number of people against the proposal (is, are) quite small.
4   8 The manager, as well as his assistant, (is, are) to attend.
6   9 Neither the teacher nor her students (is, are) here.
3 10 All the meat (is, are) spoiled, but some items (is, are) okay.

Activity 3:

1. Key items 1 and 2 as ¶ 1 of a short composition; supply the information needed to complete each sentence (in parentheses).
2. Key item 3 as ¶ 2, supplying the information noted in the parentheses.
3. Key item 4 as ¶ 3, supplying information noted in the parentheses.
4. Proofread, revise, and correct your composition. Look for mis-spelled words, improper capital-ization, inaccurate information, and weak sentence structure.

Compose (think) as you key

1 My name, **(first/last)**, is **(African/Asian/European/Oriental, etc.)** in origin.

2 My mother's ancestors originated in **(name of country)**; my father's ancestors originated in **(name of country)**.

3 I know the following facts about the country of my **(mother's/father's)** ancestors:
   1. **(enter first fact here)**
   2. **(enter second fact here)**
   3. **(enter third fact here)**

4 If I could visit a country of my choice, I would visit **(name of country)** because **(give two or three reasons)**.

47C◆ 15
Technique Mastery

1. Key each line once at an easy, steady pace.
2. Key each line again at a quicker pace.
3. Key a 1' writing on each of lines 10, 12, and 14; find *gwam* on each writing.
4. Key 1 or 2 more 1' writings on the two slower lines.

underline & CAPS LOCK	1 <u>Ballet & Modern Dance</u>; <u>The Encyclopedia of Film</u>; <u>American Theatre</u>
	2 Marilou has bought TEN OF THE BEST of the <u>Reader's Digest</u> series.
shift keys	3 The Royal Ballet; Nederlands Dans Theater; London Festival Ballet
	4 Balanchine and Kirstein founded the New York City Ballet in 1948.
apostrophe & quotes	5 Masefield's "The Dauber"; Kipling's "Gunga Din"; Bronte's "Hope";
	6 We'll read Sandburg's "Chicago" and Frost's "The Road Not Taken."
alphabet	7 hope very quit mark axle zone cord boat sign four gown such major
	8 Six able men have quietly walked off good jobs at our city plaza.
letter response	9 date upon ever only care jump sets pink fear join were milk defer
	10 As you are aware, my trade union acted upon only a few age cases.
combination response	11 fish were duty ever risk fear goal fast they safe sign hulk ivory
	12 You are to refer the big wage case to my auto union panel of six.
word response	13 then form their eight world visit title chair firms signal profit
	14 A city auditor is to sign all the work forms for the civic panel.

| 1 | 2 | 3 | 4 | 5 | 6 | 7 | 8 | 9 | 10 | 11 | 12 | 13 |

47D◆ 15
Skillbuilding: Straight Copy

1. Key a 1' writing on ¶ 1; find *gwam*.
2. Add 4 *gwam* for a new goal rate. (See 1/4' checkpoint table below.)
3. Key two 1' *guided* writings on ¶ 1 to increase speed.
4. Key ¶ 2 in the same manner.
5. Key two 3' writings on ¶s 1-2 combined; find *gwam* and count errors on each writing.

Quarter-Minute Checkpoints				
gwam	1/4'	1/2'	3/4'	Time
20	5	10	15	20
24	6	12	18	24
28	7	14	21	28
32	8	16	24	32
36	9	18	27	36
40	10	20	30	40
44	11	22	33	44
48	12	24	36	48
52	13	26	39	52
56	14	28	42	56

▲1a all letters used

		2'	3'

As you work for higher skill, remember that how well you key 6 | 4
fast is just as important as how fast you key. How well you key 13 | 8
at any speed depends in major ways upon the technique or form you 19 | 13
use. Bouncing hands and flying fingers lower the speed, while 26 | 17
quiet hands and low finger reaches increase speed. 31 | 20

Few of us ever reach what the experts believe is perfect tech- 37 | 24
nique, but all of us should try to approach it. We must realize 43 | 29
that good form is the secret to higher speed with fewer errors. 50 | 33
We can then focus our practice on the improvement of the features 56 | 37
of good form that will bring success. 60 | 40

| 1 | 2 | 3 | 4 | 5 | 6 |
| 1 | 2 | 3 | 4 |

1. Identify the rule(s) you need to review/practice.
2. **Read:** Study each rule.
3. **Learn:** Key the *Learn* line(s) beneath it, noting how the rule is applied.
4. **Apply:** Key the *Apply* line(s), choosing the correct verbs.
5. Check work with the *Teacher's Key*.

Subject/Verb agreement

RULE 1: Use a singular verb with a singular subject (noun or pronoun); use a plural verb with a plural subject and with a compound subject (two nouns or pronouns joined by *and*).

Learn 1 The speaker was delayed at the airport for over thirty minutes.
Learn 2 The players are all here, and they are getting restless.
Learn 3 You and your assistant are to join us for lunch.
Apply 4 The treasurer of the class (is, are) to introduce the speaker.
Apply 5 Dr. Cho (was, were) to give the lecture, but he (is, are) ill.
Apply 6 Mrs. Samoa and her son (is, are) to be on a local talk show.

RULE 2: Use the plural verb *do not* or *don't* with pronoun subjects *I, we, you,* and *they* as well as with plural nouns; use the singular verb *does not* or *doesn't* with pronouns *he, she,* and *it* as well as with singular nouns.

Learn 7 I do not find this report believable; you don't, either.
Learn 8 If she doesn't accept our offer, we don't have to raise it.
Apply 9 They (doesn't, don't) discount, so I (doesn't, don't) shop there.
Apply 10 Jo and he (doesn't, don't) ski; they (doesn't, don't) plan to go.

RULE 3: Use singular verbs with indefinite pronouns (*each, every, any, either, neither, one,* etc.) and with *all* and *some* used as subjects if their modifiers are singular (but use plural verbs with *all* and *some* if their modifiers are plural).

Learn 11 Each of these girls has an important role in the class play.
Learn 12 Some of the new paint is already cracking and peeling.
Learn 13 All of the workers are to be paid for the special holiday.
Apply 14 Neither of them (is, are) well enough to start the game.
Apply 15 Some of the juice (is, are) sweet; some (is, are) quite tart.
Apply 16 Every girl and boy (is, are) sure to benefit from this decision.

RULE 4: Use a singular verb with a singular subject that is separated from the verb by the phrase *as well as* or *in addition to;* use a plural verb with a plural subject so separated.

Learn 17 The letter, in addition to the report, has to be revised.
Learn 18 The shirts, as well as the dress, have to be pressed again.
Apply 19 The driver, as well as the burglar, (was, were) apprehended.
Apply 20 Two managers, in addition to the president, (is, are) to attend.

RULE 5: Use a singular verb if *number* is used as the subject and is preceded by *the;* use a plural verb if *number* is the subject and is preceded by *a.*

Learn 21 A number of them have already voted, but the number is small.
Apply 22 The number of jobs (is, are) low; a number of us (has, have) applied.

RULE 6: Use a singular verb with singular subjects linked by *or* or *nor,* but if one subject is singular and the other is plural, the verb agrees with the nearer subject.

Learn 23 Neither Ms. Moss nor Mr. Katz was invited to speak.
Learn 24 Either the manager or his assistants are to participate.
Apply 25 If neither he nor they (go, goes), either you or she (has, have) to.

Extend/Assess Basic Keyboarding Skills

Lesson 47   Basic Keyboarding Skills

Objectives:

1. **To reinforce/improve keyboard mastery.**
2. **To improve technique/speed on straight copy.**

47A◆   5

Conditioning Practice

1. Key each line once; then key each line again faster.
2. Key a 1' writing on line 3; find *gwam*.

alphabet 1 Five or six people jogged quickly along the beach in a warm haze.

fig/sym 2 This Chu & Son's May 17 check should be $45.39 instead of $62.80.

speed 3 Lana and he may cycle to the ancient city chapel by the big lake.

| 1 | 2 | 3 | 4 | 5 | 6 | 7 | 8 | 9 | 10 | 11 | 12 | 13 |

47B◆   15

Keyboard Review

1. Key each line once at an easy, steady pace.
2. Key each line again at a quicker pace.
3. If time permits, rekey lines that were awkward or difficult for you.

Technique goals

- curved, upright fingers
- no finger "flyout"
- quick-snap keystrokes
- down-and-in spacing
- eyes on copy

A/Z 1 Angela Gomez seized a banana and a frozen pizza at a bazaar.

B/Y 2 Bobby may be able to buy the very best bugle on my birthday.

C/X 3 Cecil expects to fax the next six excellent charts he fixes.

D/W 4 Waving wildly, Wanda walked down out of the dewy wilderness.

E/V 5 Everet voted to give several reviews of every evening event.

F/U 6 Fuji fussed with four fluffy furs she found at the festival.

G/T 7 Grant grabbed eight tough goats gathered at the garden gate.

H/S 8 Hans was shy so he hastily hid here in the historic shelter.

I/R 9 Iris recites ringside riddles to irritate her injured rival.

J/Q 10 Jacques quickly quit jujitsu just to join the croquet squad.

K/P 11 Parker kept putting the spunky kennel puppies in a knapsack.

L/O 12 Leona helped pull a live oriole out of the oily lagoon pool.

M/N 13 Mom demanded money for Myron's nomination on Monday morning.

figures 14 Ten boxes will go to 312 Maple, 4069 Lake, and 578 Hastings.

fig/sym 15 Item #653 will cost Brady & Son $847.29 (less 10% for cash).

Master Alphanumeric Keyboarding Technique
Lesson 36   Alphanumeric Keying Skills

O b j e c t i v e s :
1. To improve technique/speed on sentences and paragraphs.
2. To improve speed on statistical, script, and rough-draft copy.

36A◆   5

Conditioning Practice

each line twice SS; then a 1'
writing on line 3; find *gwam*

alphabet	1	Linda may have Jack rekey pages two and six of the big quiz.
6/2	2	Our house at 622 Gold Circle will be paid for June 26, 2006.
easy	3	Jena is to go to the lake towns to do the map work for them.

| 1 | 2 | 3 | 4 | 5 | 6 | 7 | 8 | 9 | 10 | 11 | 12 |

36B◆   20

Skill Transfer

1. Key two 1' writings on each ¶; find *gwam* on each.

   Note: To find *gwam* on ¶s 1-2, use the *gwam* scale below the ¶s for partial lines; on ¶s 3-4, count words in partial lines.

2. Compare rates. On which ¶ did you have highest *gwam*?

   Expected Speeds
   highest—straight copy
   next highest—script
   third highest—rough draft
   lowest—statistical copy

3. Key two 1' writings on each of the 3 slowest ¶s, trying to equal your higher *gwam* on ¶ 1; find *gwam* on each writing.

 all letters/figures used   1'

You should try now to transfer to other types of copy   11
as much of your straight-copy speed as you can.   Handwritten   23
copy and copy in which figures appear tend to slow you down.   35
You can increase speed on these, however, with extra effort.   47

An immediate goal for handwritten copy is at least 90%   11
of the straight-copy rate; for copy with figures, at least   23
75%.   Try to speed up balanced-hand figures such as 26, 84,   35
and 163.   Key harder ones such as 452 and 890 more slowly.   46

| 1 | 2 | 3 | 4 | 5 | 6 | 7 | 8 | 9 | 10 | 11 | 12 |

Copy that is written by hand is often not legible, and   11
the spelling of words may be puzzling. So give major atten-   22
tion to unclear words. Question and correct the spacing used   35
with a comma or period. You can do this even as you key.   47

Be fore you key work from rough draft study all the changes   11

tobe made. As you key, make those changes eficeintly and   23

quickly. How much of your the straight copy speed you transfer   35

is affected determined by how hard difficult the various changes were 0   46

---

1. Identify the rule(s) you need to review/practice.
2. **Read:** Study each rule.
3. **Learn:** Key the *Learn* line(s) beneath it, noting how the rule is applied.
4. **Apply:** Key the *Apply* line(s), adding commas and colons as needed.
5. Check work with the *Teacher's Key.*

Internal punctuation: Comma

| RULE 1: | Use a comma to separate the day from the year and the city from the state. |

Learn 1 Lincoln delivered the Gettysburg Address on November 19, 1863.
Learn 2 The convention will be held at Cobo Hall in Detroit, Michigan.
Apply 3 Did you find this table in the March 16 1999, <u>USA Today?</u>
Apply 4 Are you entered in the piano competition in Austin Texas?

| RULE 2: | Use a comma to separate two or more parallel adjectives (adjectives that could be separated by the word *and* instead of a comma). |

Learn 5 The big, loud bully was ejected after he pushed the coach.
Learn 6 Cynthia played a black lacquered grand piano at her concert.
Apply 7 The big powerful car zoomed past the cheering crowd.
Apply 8 A small, red fox squeezed through the fence to avoid the hounds.

| RULE 3: | Use a comma to separate (a) unrelated groups of figures that occur together and (b) whole numbers into groups of three digits each. (**Note:** Policy, year, page, room, telephone, invoice, and most serial numbers are keyed without commas.) |

Learn 9 By the year 2000, 1,100 more local students will be enrolled.
Learn 10 The supplies listed on Invoice #274068 are for Room 1953.
Apply 11 During 1999 2050 new graduates entered our job market.
Apply 12 See page 1,069 of <u>Familiar Quotations</u>, Cat. Card No. 68-15,664.

Internal punctuation: Colon

| RULE 4: | Use a colon to introduce an enumeration or a listing. |

Learn 13 These students are absent: Adam Bux, Todd Cody, and Sue Ott.
Apply 14 Add to the herb list parsley, rosemary, saffron, and thyme.
Apply 15 We must make these desserts a cake, two pies, and cookies.

| RULE 5: | Use a colon to introduce a question or a quotation. |

Learn 16 Here's the real question: Who will pay for the "free" programs?
Learn 17 Who said: "Freedom is nothing else but a chance to be better?"
Apply 18 My question stands Who are we to pass judgment on them?
Apply 19 He quoted Browning "Good, to forgive; Best, to forget."

| RULE 6: | Use a colon between hours and minutes expressed in figures. |

Learn 20 They give two performances: at 2:00 p.m. and at 8:00 p.m.
Apply 21 You have a choice of an 11 15 a.m. or a 2 30 p.m. appointment.
Apply 22 My workday begins at 8 15 a.m. and ends at 5 00 p.m.

36C◆ 12
Skillbuilding

1. Key a 1' writing on each ¶; find *gwam*.
2. Key two 2' writings on ¶s 1-2 combined; find *gwam*.
3. Key a 3' writing on ¶s 1-2 combined; find *gwam*.

		Quarter-Minute Checkpoints		
gwam	1/4'	1/2'	3/4'	Time
20	5	10	15	20
24	6	12	18	24
28	7	14	21	28
32	8	16	24	32
36	9	18	27	36
40	10	20	30	40
44	11	22	33	44
48	12	24	36	48

Ia all letters used

	2'	3'
Money is much harder to save than it is to earn. Some-	5	4
body is always willing to help you spend what you make. If	11	8
you confuse your needs and wants, you can quickly spend much	18	12
of it yourself. Often, friends and relations can become an	24	16
additional major drain if you allow them to assist you.	29	19
And, of course, many politicians at all levels think	34	23
that they can spend your money for you much better than you	40	27
can do it yourself. It is really amazing how ready some are	46	31
to spend the money of others. At times their motives may	52	35
be excellent; at other times, just selfish. So beware.	58	38

36D◆ 13
Technique Mastery

1. Key each line at a brisk, steady pace.
2. Key a 1' writing on each of lines 10, 12, and 14; find *gwam* on each writing.
3. Compare rates and key another 1' writing on the two slowest lines to boost speed.

TECHNIQUE CUES:

- curved, upright fingers
- quick-snap keystrokes
- *finger* reaches (minimum hand movement)
- low spacing motion with no finger "flyout"
- quick shifting without lifting unused fingers

alphabet 1 Shep quickly coaxed eight avid fans away from the jazz band.
fig/sym 2 Of 370 students, only 35 (9.46%) failed to type 18-20 w.a.m.

space 3 if then| so they| for them| the duty| cut corn| did wish| may hand
bar 4 She paid the duty on the old urn she got in an antique shop.

shift 5 Towne Mall| Kahn Corp.| Epps, Inc.| Jan Sperry Co.| Parker Bros.
keys 6 Spinoza Health Clinic is to open August 11 in Oakwood Plaza.

long direct 7 any much many curb sums deck myth zany neck must doubt curve
reaches 8 Erv must doubt many myths echoed by my zany aunt and nieces.

letter 9 upon ever join save only best ploy gave pink edge pump facts
response 10 You acted on a phony tax case only after a union gave facts.

word 11 visit risks their world field chair proxy throw right eighty
response 12 Mala may sign the form to pay for the giant map of the city.

combination 13 also fast sign card maps only hand were pair link paid plump
response 14 To get to be a pro, react with zest and care as the pros do.

Activity 1:

1. Study the spelling/definitions of the words in the color block at right.
2. Key line 1 (the *Learn* line), noting the proper choice of words.
3. Key lines 2-3 (the *Apply* lines), choosing the right words to complete the lines correctly.
4. Key the remaining lines in the same way.
5. Check your work; correct or rekey lines containing word choice errors.

Choose the right word

vary *(vb)* change; make different; diverge	**passed** *(vb)* past tense of *pass;* already occurred; gave an item to someone
very *(adj/adv)* real; mere; truly; to a high degree	**past** *(adv/adj/prep/n)* gone or elapsed; time gone by; moved by

Learn 1 Marquis said it is very important that we vary our attack.
Apply 2 The (vary, very) nature of skill is to (vary, very) the response.
Apply 3 As you (vary, very) input, you get (vary, very) different results.

Learn 4 In the past, we passed the zoo before we marched past the library.
Apply 5 We filed (passed, past) the desk as we (passed, past) in our tests.
Apply 6 In the (passed, past) month, I (passed, past) up two job offers.

Activity 2:

1. Key lines 1-14 supplying needed commas and colons.
2. Check work with the *Teacher's Key.*
3. Note the rule number(s) at the left of each line in which you made a comma or colon error.
4. Turn to page 108 and identify those rules for review/practice.
5. Use the Read/Learn/Apply plan for each rule to be reviewed.

Proofread & correct

RULES

1, 3   1   The new century begins on January 1 2001--not 2,000.
1   2   We played in the Hoosier Dome in Indianapolis Indiana.
1   3   I cited an article in the May 8 1999, <u>Wall Street Journal.</u>
2   4   Carl sent Diana a dozen bright red, long-stem roses.
2   5   He buys most of his clothes at a store for big tall men.
3   6   Our enrollment for 1998, 1,884; for 1999 2040.
3   7   Where is the request for books and supplies for Room 1,004?
1, 3   8   Policy #HP294,873 took effect on September 20 1999.
3   9   Della and Eldon Simms paid $129000 for their new condo.
4   10   Dry cleaning list 1 suit; 2 jackets; 3 pants; 2 sweaters.
5   11   Golden Rule Do unto others as you would have them do unto you.
5   12   I quote Jean Racine "Innocence has nothing to dread."
6   13   Glynda asked me to meet her 2 15 p.m. flight at JFK Airport.
6   14   Ten o'clock in the morning is the same as 10 00 a.m.

Activity 3:

1. Study the quotations, considering the relationship between honesty and truth.
2. Compose/key a ¶ to show your understanding of honesty and truth. Describe an incident in which honesty and truth should prevail but often don't in real life.

Compose (think) as you key

Honesty's the best policy.
--Cervantes

To be honest . . . here is a task for all that a man has of fortitude.
--Robert Louis Stevenson

Piety requires us to honor truth above our friends.
--Aristotle

The dignity of truth is lost with much protesting.
--Ben Jonson

Lesson 37 Alphanumeric Keying Skills

Objectives:
1. **To refine technique on individual letters and letter combinations.**
2. **To improve technique/speed on sentences and paragraphs.**

37A◆ 5
Conditioning Practice

each line twice SS; then a
1' writing on line 3; find *gwam*

alphabet 1 Jacques could win a prize for eight more dives by next week.
figures   2 In 1995, we had only 240 computers; as of 1998 we owned 376.
easy   3 The girls paid for the eight antique urns with their profit.

| 1 | 2 | 3 | 4 | 5 | 6 | 7 | 8 | 9 | 10 | 11 | 12 |

37B◆ 20
Keyboard Mastery

1. Key line 1 at a brisk pace. Note words that were awkward for you.
2. Key each of these words three times at increasing speeds.
3. Key line 2 at a steady, fluent rate.
4. Key each of the other pairs of lines in the same way.
5. If time permits, key again the lines in which you hesitated or stopped.

A/N
1 an and pan nap any nag ant man aunt land plan hand want sand
2 Ann and her aunt want to buy any land they can near the inn.

B/O
3 bow lob bog rob boy mob gob fob bob body robe boat born glob
4 Bobby bobbed in the bow of the boat as the boys came aboard.

C/P
5 cup cop cap pack copy cape cope pick pecks clips camps claps
6 Cap can clip a copy of the poem to his cape to read at camp.

D/Q
7 did quo quid ride quit road quiz paid aqua dude squid squads
8 The dude in an aqua shirt did quit the squad after the quiz.

E/R
9 or re ore per are her red peer here rent fore leer sore very
10 Vera read her book report to three of her friends at school.

F/S
11 if is fish fuss soft furs self fast fans sift surf fist fees
12 Floss said first to sell the fish on this shelf at half off.

G/T
13 get got tag togs grit gilt gust tang right guilt fight ghost
14 Garth had the grit to go eight rounds in that fight tonight.

H/U
15 hue hut hub hurt shut shun huge hush brush truth shrug thugs
16 Hugh said four burly thugs hurled the man off the huge dock.

I/V
17 vie vim give view five vein dive vial vice vigor voice alive
18 Vivian made her five great dives with visible vim and vigor.

J/W
19 jay wow jet own jab town just will jest when joke what judge
20 Jewel jokes with your town judge about what and who is just.

K/X
21 oak fix kid fox know flax walk flex silk oxen park axle work
22 Knox fixed an oak axle on a flax cart for a kid in the park.

L/Y
23 lay sly try ply all pry lei ally only rely reply truly fully
24 Dolly truly felt that she could rely fully on only one ally.

M/Z
25 may zoo man zap zone make fuzz mama jazz maid jams game zoom
26 Zoe may make her mark in a jazz band jam session at the zoo.

46C ◆ 20
Skillbuilding

1. Key a 1' writing on each ¶; find *gwam* on each writing.
2. Key two 2' writings on ¶s 1-2 combined; find *gwam* on each writing.
3. Key two 3' writings on ¶s 1-3 combined; find *gwam* and circle errors on each writing.

  all letters used

	2'	3'
There is a value in work, value to the worker as well as	6	4
to the employer for whom one works. In spite of the stress	12	8
or pressure under which many people work, gainful work pro-	18	12
vides workers with a feeling of security and self-esteem.	23	16
Some people do not want to work unless they have a job	29	19
of prestige; that is, a job that others admire or envy. To	35	23
obtain such a position, one must be prepared to perform the	41	27
tasks the job requires. Realize this now; prepare yourself.	47	31
School and college courses are designed to help you to	52	35
excel in the basic knowledge and skills the better jobs de-	58	39
mand. Beyond all of this, special training or work experi-	64	43
ence may be needed for you to move up in your chosen career.	70	47

46D ◆ 10
Skill Transfer: Rough Draft

1. Key a 2' writing on ¶s 1-2 combined; find *gwam*.
2. Key a 3' writing on ¶s 1-2 combined; find *gwam*.
3. Key another 3' writing on ¶s 1-2 to improve speed.

	2'	3'
It is very important to use exceeding care in addressing	6	4
envelopes. By doing so, you will make it easier for the mail	12	8
to be sorted quickly. Because of the automation employed	18	12
with mail today, various requirements have to be met to assure	25	16
quick processing.	27	18
The correct format and placement of the letter address	32	21
and destination address on the envelope are quite important.	38	25
Just as crucial as the correct placement and format of the	44	29
addresses is the ZIP code. If it is not shown, all your mail	50	34
won't be delivered as rapidly.	54	36

37C◆ 12
Skillbuilding

1. Key a 1' writing on each ¶; find *gwam*.
2. Key two 2' writings on ¶s 1-2 combined; find *gwam*.
3. Key a 3' writing on ¶s 1-2 combined; find *gwam*.

	Quarter-Minute Checkpoints			
gwam	1/4'	1/2'	3/4'	Time
20	5	10	15	20
24	6	12	18	24
28	7	14	21	28
32	8	16	24	32
36	9	18	27	36
40	10	20	30	40
44	11	22	33	44
48	12	24	36	48

Ia   all letters used

		2'	3'
It is okay to try and try again if your first efforts do		6	4
not bring the correct results. If you try but fail again and		12	8
again, however, it is foolish to plug along in the very same		18	12
manner. Rather, experiment with another method to accomplish		24	16
the task that may bring the skills or knowledge you need.		30	20
If your first attempts do not yield success, do not quit		36	24
and merely let it go at that. Instead, begin again in a bet-		42	28
ter way to finish the work or develop more insight into your		48	32
difficulty. When you recognize why you must do more than just		54	36
try, try again, you will work with purpose to achieve success.		60	40

2' | 1 | 2 | 3 | 4 | 5 | 6 |
3' | 1 | 2 | 3 | 4 |

37D◆ 13
Technique Mastery

1. Key each line once at a steady pace.
2. Key a 1' writing on each of lines 11-14; find *gwam* on each one.
3. As time permits, key lines 1-10 again at a faster pace.

TECHNIQUE CUES:

- hands steady/wrists low
- fingers curved, upright
- thumb low over space bar
- *finger* reaches without unused finger "flyout"
- out-and-down *finger* reaches to shift keys
- eyes on copy as you key

fig/sym sentences	1 I signed a 20-year note--$67,495 (at 13.8%)--with Coe & Han.
	2 Order #29105 reads: "16 sets of Cat. #4718A at $36.25/set."
shift-key sentences	3 He and Vi crossed the English Channel from Hove to Le Havre.
	4 J. W. Posner has left Madrid for Turin for some Alps skiing.
long-reach sentences	5 My uncle and my brother must have run many great races here.
	6 Mervyn must not make any decisions until Brad has his lunch.
adjacent-key sentences	7 Bert said we can stop there to buy gas and oil before going.
	8 Esther Polk sang several hymns before we lads talked to her.
alphabetic sentences	9 Bob realized very quickly that jumping was excellent for us.
	10 My wife helped fix a frozen lock on Jacque's vegetable bins.
space-bar sentences	11 Eight of the men may be sent to the dock for the heavy work.
	12 Nan will try to get as many of the women to play as she can.
easy sentences	13 Blame me for their penchant for the antique chair and panel.
	14 Did he signal the authentic robot to do a turn to the right?

| 1 | 2 | 3 | 4 | 5 | 6 | 7 | 8 | 9 | 10 | 11 | 12 |

Lesson 46 Alphanumeric Keying Skills

Objectives:
1. **To improve keying technique.**
2. **To improve speed/control on straight-copy and rough-draft ¶s.**

46A◆ 5
Conditioning Practice

each line twice; then a 1' writing on line 3

alphabet 1 Jove quickly worked a puzzle for six boys to get them going.

keypad 2 2758 2661 4583 4116 3710 3615 2366 3698 2046 2977 3928 47290

easy 3 The firm may form a panel of six to work with their auditor.

| 1 | 2 | 3 | 4 | 5 | 6 | 7 | 8 | 9 | 10 | 11 | 12 |

46B◆ 15
Technique Mastery

1. Key lines 1-21 once SS; DS between 3-line groups.
2. Key a 1' writing on each of lines 22-26; find *gwam* and compare rates on the five writings.

Technique goals
- fingers deeply curved and upright
- eyes on copy
- finger-action keystrokes
- hands and arms quiet, almost motionless

word response

1 by with then worn they make corn pens them vigor their right
2 of the| for us| if she is| by the end| pay them for| work with us
3 I shall make a big name panel to hang by a door of the hall.

combination response

4 to my of him for you they were pale pink torn card goal rate
5 to him| see me| we get in| if you did| she fed them| then you got
6 My man was to fix the water pump of a small pool at the inn.

double letters

7 all ill odd ebb hall mass fizz sell cuff purr flee good need
8 is odd| lay off| too big| all men| toss the| will pay| a good putt
9 Ann will sell all her old school books at a good price, too.

adjacent keys

10 as top was open were ruin very tray coin mask soil rent port
11 ask her| we went| top post| new coin| pop art| oil well| last week
12 Jared was to open a coin shop in an old store at the square.

long direct reaches

13 my gym fun mud ice sum run any curb nice must debt hunt glum
14 hum it| had ice| hot sun| any gym| nice run| my thumb| bring a mug
15 Ceci had much fun at the gym and the ice center this summer.

outside reaches

16 apt quo now zap opt low sap was pal aqua soap flax span slow
17 as low| was lax| now all| pro quo| will faze| polo pony| slow play
18 Laska is apt to play a top game of polo if the pony is well.

figures & symbols

19 25% $483.10 #36790 PO #472-413859 Model #1600LS 2-floor plan
20 May 9| less 5%| 30 books| 2-ply forms| Invoice #81746| Orr & Chin
21 She said: "You must keep your ____ on the copy as you key."

alphabet 22 Rob may vex a top judge with his quick flips and zany dives.
fig/sym 23 Fifty dollars ($50) is due on Account #291-4836 by August 7.
combination 24 You are to visit a gas firm with my auditor if you are free.
double letters 25 Ann will see that all the books are passed out before class.
word 26 Six of the antique firms may lend us a hand with the social.

| 1 | 2 | 3 | 4 | 5 | 6 | 7 | 8 | 9 | 10 | 11 | 12 |

Lesson 38 Alphanumeric Keying Skills

O b j e c t i v e s :
1. **To refine/assess keyboarding technique.**
2. **To improve/assess performance speed on straight copy.**

38A◆ 5
Conditioning Practice
each line twice SS; then a
1' writing on line 3; find *gwam*

alphabet 1 Quig was just amazed by the next five blocks of his players.
figures 2 On October 14, 1998, the 271 members met from 5 to 6:30 p.m.
easy 3 Keith may hang the sign by the antique door of the big hall.

| 1 | 2 | 3 | 4 | 5 | 6 | 7 | 8 | 9 | 10 | 11 | 12 |

38B◆ 19
Technique Check
1. Key each line once SS; DS between 3-line groups.
2. Key a 1' writing on each of lines 15, 18, and 21; find *gwam* on each.
3. If time permits, key another 1' writing on each of the two slower lines.

figures & symbols
1 and 163 sob 295 rid 483 fog 495 hen 637 lap 910 own 926 span
2 Case 10463 may be found in Volume 27, Section 108, page 592.
3 My note for $493 at 7.5% interest will be paid May 18, 2006.

shift keys & CAPS LOCK
4 GREAT AMERICAN SPEECHES did include King's "I Have a Dream."
5 THE ARTS by Tamplin is a history of 20th-century expression.
6 Simon & Schuster's OPERA is a quite complete reference work.

double letters
7 off odd zoo lee too door leek food hall good heel foot shall
8 Lee lost his footing and fell off a tall ladder in the mall.
9 Ella keeps a book of crossword puzzles in the school office.

adjacent keys
10 ruin part mere owes coin said true port buys flew stop point
11 Merv tried to buy a few old coins in that shop on the river.
12 Fiona said that her nephew tried out for a part in an opera.

letter response
13 dad hop few pop red you far kin gas oil vet mom get pin grew
14 As my case was set up, you saw him get only a few wage data.
15 Johnny read him rate cards on wage taxes set up at my union.

combination response
16 may few men saw pan tax ham get jam rest lend hulk bush gaze
17 A few of them ate jam tarts with the tea she served at dusk.
18 By noon they are to fix the pump at the oil rig on the hill.

word response
19 ox by got tow oak zig sir lay but for fix pan with pair turn
20 Lana is to mend a map of the ancient lake town for the dorm.
21 Tish may sign a work form to aid the auditor of a soap firm.

| 1 | 2 | 3 | 4 | 5 | 6 | 7 | 8 | 9 | 10 | 11 | 12 |

1. Key a 1' writing on each ¶; find *gwam* on each writing.
2. Key two 2' writings on ¶s 1-2 combined; find *gwam* on each writing.
3. Key two 3' writings on ¶s 1-3 combined; find *gwam* and record it; circle errors on each writing.

 all letters used

A young man asked recently why he was required to take

a course in keyboarding since he was sure that there would

always be others to perform such tasks for him.   His false

belief is common among males, particularly in high school.

The work roles of men and women have changed quickly

since the computer has become the major means of processing

words and data.   As a result, all office workers are now ex-

pected to bring keying and computer skills to the job.

The old idea that in the office men think and direct

while women merely type is no longer valid.   Now, everyone

is expected to think, direct, and communicate through a key-

board.   Learn these skills now; you will prize them highly.

45D ◆ **10**
**Skill Transfer:
Statistical Copy**

1. Key a 2' writing on ¶s 1-2 combined; find *gwam*.
2. Key a 3' writing on ¶s 1-2 combined; find *gwam*.
3. Divide this rate *by* your 3' rate in 45C above. If you did not transfer *at least* 75% of your straight-copy speed, key another 3' writing on the statistical copy.

The 50 most-used words account for 46% of the total of

all words used in a study of 4,100 letters, memorandums, and

reports.   The first 100 account for 53%; the first 500, 71%;

the first 1,000, 80%; and the first 2,000, just under 88%.

Of the first 7,027 most-used words (accounting for 97%

of all word uses), 209 are balanced-hand words (26% of all

uses) and 284 are one-hand words (14% of all uses).   So you

see, practice on these words can help to increase your rate.

38C ◆ 14
Speed Check

1. Key a 1' writing on each ¶; find *gwam*.
2. Key two 2' writings on ¶s 1-2 combined; find *gwam*.
3. Key a 3' writing on ¶s 1-2 combined; find *gwam*.

Quarter-Minute Checkpoints				
gwam	1/4'	1/2'	3/4'	Time
20	5	10	15	20
24	6	12	18	24
28	7	14	21	28
32	8	16	24	32
36	9	18	27	36
40	10	20	30	40
44	11	22	33	44
48	12	24	36	48

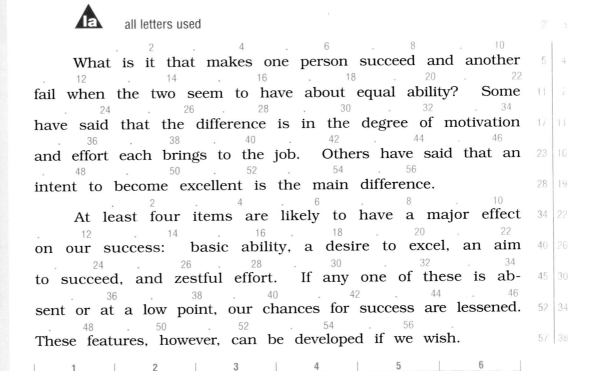

all letters used

What is it that makes one person succeed and another fail when the two seem to have about equal ability? Some have said that the difference is in the degree of motivation and effort each brings to the job. Others have said that an intent to become excellent is the main difference.

At least four items are likely to have a major effect on our success: basic ability, a desire to excel, an aim to succeed, and zestful effort. If any one of these is absent or at a low point, our chances for success are lessened. These features, however, can be developed if we wish.

38D ◆ 12
Keyboard Mastery

1. Key line 1 at an easy, steady pace, noting any words that cause you to hesitate or stop.
2. Practice each of those words 2 or 3 times to improve technique on them.
3. Key line 1 again at a quicker, smoother pace.
4. Key each of the other lines as directed in Steps 1-3.

A/Z   1   Zoe had a pizza at the plaza by the zoo on a lazy, hazy day.

B/Y   2   Abby may be too busy to buy me a book for my long boat trip.

C/X   3   Xica caught six cod to fix lunch for his six excited scouts.

D/W   4   Wilda would like to own the wild doe she found in the woods.

E/V   5   Evan will give us the van to move the five very heavy boxes.

F/U   6   All four of us bought coats with faux fur collars and cuffs.

G/T   7   Eight guys tugged the big boat into deep water to get going.

H/S   8   Marsh wishes to show us how to make charts on the computer.

I/R   9   Ira will rise above his ire to rid the firm of this problem.

J/Q   10   Quen just quietly quit the squad after a major joint injury.

K/P   11   Kip packed a backpack and put it on an oak box on the porch.

L/O   12   Lola is to wear the royal blue skirt and a gold wool blouse.

M/N   13   Many of the men met in the main hall to see the new manager.

figures   14   I worked from 8:30 to 5 at 1964 Lake Blvd. from May 7 to 26.

fig/sym   15   I quote, "ISBN #0-651-24876-3 was assigned to them in 1998."

Lesson 45 Alphanumeric Keying Skills

Objectives:
1. **To improve keyboard mastery.**
2. **To improve speed/control on straight-copy and statistical ¶s.**

45A◆ 5
Conditioning Practice

each line twice; then a 1' writing on line 3

alphabet 1 Spiro was amazed at just how quickly you fixed the big vans.

fig/sym 2 Of 26,374 citizens, 13,187 (50%) voted in the 1998 election.

easy 3 Jane may make the girl a vivid gown for the big town social.

| 1 | 2 | 3 | 4 | 5 | 6 | 7 | 8 | 9 | 10 | 11 | 12 |

45B◆ 15
Keyboard Mastery

1. Key each line once SS; DS between 5-line groups.
2. Key each line again at increased speed.
3. If time permits, rekey lines that caused you to hesitate or stop.

A 1 Andy may carry a flag of orange and black in the big parade.

B 2 Bobbie lobbed the ball to the big boy for a baseline basket.

C 3 Chuck wrote a check to cover the cost of two cruise tickets.

D 4 Dondra made a mad dash from the deli for her third delivery.

E 5 Eduardo needs to relax and let his fingers make the reaches.

F 6 Flo will take off just after four for her first solo flight.

G 7 Gig ought to get as high a grade in algebra as in geography.

H 8 Heidi hopes she can help her brother with his math homework.

I 9 Irwin is to play a violin as well as a piano in the quintet.

J 10 Judy is a just judge who seeks justice from each major jury.

K 11 Keith checks skis and quickly marks each ski by worker name.

L 12 Lolly will lead the platoon in daily field drills this week.

M 13 Matt may be the top swimmer at my new swim club this summer.

N 14 Nadia has won many gymnastic events in this city and county.

O 15 Olaf hopes to work for a good company as an account manager.

P 16 Phyllis hopes to plan a peppy party for all the top players.

Q 17 Quig quietly quit the squad and quickly quelled the quarrel.

R 18 Roxanne is ready to write a report on her recent train trip.

S 19 Stan wants a seafood salad and a single glass of spiced tea.

T 20 Tess sent a letter to her state senator to protest his vote.

U 21 Utah urged our squad to unite to upset our ubiquitous rival.

V 22 Viva visited the old village for a vivid view of the valley.

W 23 Wes was weary of waiting on the windy wharf with the welder.

X 24 Xena, fax all six x-rays if he fixes the fax machine by six.

Y 25 Yorba says that day by day his keying ability must increase.

Z 26 Zazu dazzled us and puzzled the judges with zigzag footwork.

Language & Writing Skills 5

Activity 1:

1. Study the spelling/definitions of the words in the color block at right.
2. Key line 1 (the *Learn* line), noting the proper choice of words.
3. Key lines 2-3 (the *Apply* lines), choosing the right words to complete the lines correctly.
4. Key the remaining lines in the same way.
5. Check your work; correct or rekey lines containing word choice errors.

Choose the right word

your *(adj)* of or relating to you or yourself as possessor	**for** *(prep/conj)* used to indicate purpose; on behalf of; because; because of
you're *(contr)* you are	**four** *(n)* the fourth in a set or series

Learn 1 When you receive your blue book, you're to write your name on it.
Apply 2 (Your, You're) to write the letter using (your, you're) best English.
Apply 3 When (your, you're) computer is warmed up, (your, you're) to begin work.

Learn 4 All four workers asked for an appointment with the manager.
Apply 5 At (for, four) o'clock the lights went off (for, four) an hour.
Apply 6 The (for, four) boys turned back, (for, four) they feared the lightning.

Activity 2:

1. Key the ¶, supplying needed punctuation.
2. Check work with the *Teacher's Key*.
3. Note the rule number(s) at the left of each line in which you made a punctuation error.
4. Turn to page 92 and identify those rules for review/practice.
5. Use the Read/Learn/Apply plan for each rule to be reviewed.

Proofread & correct

RULES

5   "Jump" the fireman shouted to the young boy frozen with

1   fear on the window ledge of the burning building "Will you

3   catch me" the young boy cried to the men and women holding a

1,5,1   safety net forty feet below "Into the net" they yelled

       Mustering his courage, the boy jumped safely into the net and

1   then into his mother's outstretched arms

Activity 3:

1. Read carefully the two creeds (mottos) given at the right.
2. Choose one as a topic for a short composition, and make notes of what it means to you.
3. Compose/key a ¶ or two indicating what it means to you and why you believe it would be (or would not be) a good motto for your own behavior.

Compose (think) as you key

The following creeds were written by Edward Everett Hale:

Harry Wadsworth Club

I am only one,
But still I am one.
I cannot do everything,
But still I can do something;
And because I cannot do everything,
I will not refuse to do the something
    that I can do.

Lend-a-Hand Society

To look up and not down,
To look forward and not back,
To look out and not in, and
To lend a hand.

44C◆ 17
Skillbuilding

1. Key a 1' writing on each ¶; find *gwam*.
2. Using the better *gwam* as a base, add 4 words for a new goal rate.
3. Key two 1' *guided* writings on each ¶ to reach the new goal.
4. Key two 2' writings on ¶s 1-2 combined; find *gwam* on each writing.
5. Key a 3' writing on ¶s 1-2 combined; find *gwam* and record it; count errors.

Quarter-Minute Checkpoints			
gwam	1/4'	1/2'	3/4'	Time
16	4	8	12	16
20	5	10	15	20
24	6	12	18	24
28	7	14	21	28
32	8	16	24	32
36	9	18	27	36
40	10	20	30	40
44	11	22	33	44

 all letters used

	2'	3'
Have you read any good books lately? When you analyze	6	4
why some people quickly move up in their chosen professions	12	8
while others do not, one factor stands out: Those who read	18	12
widely are most likely to be among the people at the top of	24	16
their selected career. Do you know why this might be true?	29	20
People who read well-written material often extend the	35	23
ability to communicate: to speak, to write, and to listen.	41	27
These are major skills that are required for growth in most	47	31
jobs. Reading also offers the chance to get good ideas and	53	35
to learn how best to put the new concepts to work.	58	39

44D◆ 10
Skill Transfer: Script

1. Key a 2' writing on ¶s 1-2 combined; find *gwam*.
2. Key a 3' writing on ¶s 1-2 combined; find *gwam* and count errors.
3. Divide your 3' rate in Step 5 of 44C above *into* your 3' rate on these ¶s. If you did not transfer *at least* 90% of your straight-copy speed to the script ¶s, key the script ¶s again to increase the speed.

all letters used

	2'	3'
Those who have pencils but no erasers can never make a	6	4
mistake. They must never, of course, try anything of great	12	8
importance either. Don't be ashamed of making an error	17	12
now and then, but try not to make the same one again and	24	16
again. Follow this excellent rule to become a careful worker.	29	19
As you try to develop your typing power, you will make	35	23
quite a few errors when you try out new or improved methods	41	27
of stroking. Just as in other skills, though, many of your	47	31
errors will fall away as you further your ability. Realize,	53	35
also, that even the best workers often need erasers.	58	39

Terminal punctuation: Period

RULE 1:	Use a period at the end of a declarative sentence (a sentence that is not regarded as a question or exclamation).

Learn 1 I wonder why <u>Phantom of the Opera</u> has always been so popular.
Apply 2 Fran and I saw <u>Cats</u> in London We also saw <u>Sunset Boulevard</u>

RULE 2:	Use a period at the end of a polite request stated in the form of a question but not intended as one.

Learn 3 Matt, will you please collect the papers at the end of each row.
Apply 4 Will you please call me at 555-8792 to set up an appointment

Terminal punctuation: Question mark

RULE 3:	Use a question mark at the end of a sentence intended as a question.

Learn 5 Did you go to the annual flower show in Ault Park this year?
Apply 6 How many medals did the U.S.A. win in the 1996 Summer Games

RULE 4:	For emphasis, a question mark may be used after each item in a series of interrogative expressions.

Learn 7 Can we count on wins in gymnastics? in diving? in soccer?
Apply 8 What grade did you get for technique for speed for accuracy

Terminal punctuation: Exclamation point

RULE 5:	Use an exclamation point after emphatic (forceful) exclamations and after phrases and sentences that are clearly exclamatory.

Learn   9 The lady screamed, "Stop that man!"
Learn 10 "Bravo!" many yelled at the end of the Skate America program.
Apply 11 "Yes" her gym coach exclaimed when Kerri stuck the landing.
Apply 12 The burglar stopped when he saw the sign, "Beware, vicious dog"

---

1. Identify the rule(s) you need to review/practice.
2. **Read:** Study each rule.
3. **Learn:** Key the *Learn* line(s) beneath it, noting how the rule is applied.
4. **Apply:** Key the *Apply* line(s), adding correct terminal punctuation.
5. Check work with the *Teacher's Key*.

Master Keyboarding Skills
Lesson 44   Alphanumeric Keying Skills

O b j e c t i v e s :
1. **To improve keying technique.**
2. **To improve speed/control on straight-copy and script ¶s.**

44A◆   5

Conditioning Practice

each line twice; then a 1' writing on line 3

alphabet 1 Bev quickly waxed pint jars of grape jelly for her zany mom.

keypad 2 456 789 123 471 582 693 404 987 654 321 174 285 396 490 6704

easy 3 The girls may rush the vivid signs to the town hall by auto.

| 1 | 2 | 3 | 4 | 5 | 6 | 7 | 8 | 9 | 10 | 11 | 12 |

44B◆   18

Technique Mastery

1. Key each line twice SS; DS between 4-line groups.
2. Select lines that were awkward or caused you to slow down; key each of those lines twice more.

Note: In lines 7-8, underline the words, using the Underline (word processing) feature (do not use italic).

spacing
1 us by of an to am go in is on do my elm pay she may and they
2 Kay is to pay the man for any of the film you buy from them.

shifting
3 Shep and Mark|Jane or Ella|J. Powell & Sons|Apple & Kane Co.
4 Dottie and Roby Park sang in the "Voice of Harmony" concert.

CAPS LOCK
5 UPS or USPS|CNN and TNT|NBC or CBS|ZIP Codes|SAN ANTONIO, TX
6 I can use ALL CAPS for book titles; e.g., CAST OF THOUSANDS.

underline
7 <u>its</u>, not <u>it's</u>|<u>than</u>, not <u>then</u>|<u>four</u>, not <u>fore</u>|<u>their</u>, not <u>there</u>
8 He underlines magazine titles: <u>People</u> and <u>Education Digest</u>.

apostrophe & quotation
9 you don't|he doesn't|it's his|I keyed "chose," not "choose."
10 "To succeed," he said, "you must do your best at all times."

hyphen
11 co-op plan|two-ply tire|32-cent stamp|self-esteem|up-to-date
12 Jay's just-in-time three-pointer gave us the half-time lead.

letter response
13 saw him|you are|pop art|join up|gas pump|milk cart|best hump
14 A union steward gets you a wage rate card after you join up.

word response
15 six forms|the title|for their|and shall|did amend|work audit
16 An audit of the work forms may end a fight for an amendment.

combination response
17 is up|to be|for joy|the oil|with milk|they were|the best man
18 It is up to the union man to set a rate for the rest of you.

| 1 | 2 | 3 | 4 | 5 | 6 | 7 | 8 | 9 | 10 | 11 | 12 |

Learn Numeric Keypad Operation
Lesson 39   New Keys: 4/5/6/0

Objectives:

1. **To learn reach-strokes for 4, 5, 6, and 0.**
2. **To key these home-key numbers with speed and ease.**

39A◆   5
Numeric Keypad Arrangement

Figure keys 1-9 are in standard locations on numeric keypads.

The zero (0) key location may vary slightly from one keyboard to another.

The illustrations at the right show the location of the numeric keypad on selected computer keyboards.

Macintosh LCII numeric keypad

IBM PC numeric keypad

39B◆   5
Operating Position

1. Position yourself in front of the keyboard—body erect, both feet on floor for balance.
2. Place this book, resting on easel, for easy reading—at right of keyboard or directly behind it.
3. Curve the fingers of the right hand and place on the keypad:
   - index finger on 4
   - middle finger on 5
   - ring finger on 6
   - thumb on 0

> To use the keypad, the Num (number) Lock must be turned on.

Book at right of keyboard

Proper position at keyboard

1. Identify the rule(s) you need to review/practice.
2. **Read:** Study each rule.
3. **Learn:** Key the *Learn* line(s) beneath it, noting how the rule is applied.
4. **Apply:** Key the *Apply* line(s), adding commas as needed.
5. Check work with the *Teacher's Key*.

Internal punctuation: Comma

RULE 1:	Use a comma after (a) introductory phrases or clauses and (b) words in a series.

Learn   1   When you finish keying the report, please give it to Mr. Kent.
Learn   2   We will play the Mets, Expos, and Cubs in our next home stand.
Apply   3   If you attend the play take Mary Jack and Tim with you.
Apply   4   The last exam covered memos simple tables and unbound reports.

RULE 2:	Do not use a comma to separate two items treated as a single unit within a series.

Learn   5   Her favorite breakfast was bacon and eggs, muffins, and juice.
Apply   6   My choices are peaches and cream brownies or ice cream.
Apply   7   Mary ordered ham and eggs toast and milk.

RULE 3:	Use a comma before short direct quotations.

Learn   8   The man asked, "When does Flight 787 depart?"
Apply   9   Mrs. Ramirez replied "No, the report is not finished."
Apply 10   Dr. Feit said "Please make an appointment for next week."

RULE 4:	Use a comma before and after a word or words in apposition (words that come together and refer to the same person or thing).

Learn 11   Coleta, the assistant manager, will chair the next meeting.
Apply 12   Greg Mathews a pitcher for the Braves will sign autographs.
Apply 13   The personnel director Marge Wilson will be the presenter.

RULE 5:	Use a comma to set off words of direct address (the name of a person spoken to).

Learn 14   I believe, Tom, that you should fly to San Francisco.
Apply 15   Finish this assignment Mary before you start on the next one.
Apply 16   Please call me Erika if I can be of further assistance.

RULE 6:	Use a comma to set off nonrestrictive clauses (not necessary to the meaning of the sentence); however, do not use commas to set off restrictive clauses (necessary to the meaning of the sentence).

Learn 17   The manuscript, which I prepared, needs to be revised.
Learn 18   The manuscript that presents banking alternatives is complete.
Apply 19   The movie which won top awards dealt with human rights.
Apply 20   The student who scores highest on the exam will win the award.

39C◆ 40
New Keys: 4/5/6/0 (Home Keys)

Complete the drills as directed below. If you are using word processing software (instead of the Numeric Keypad section of *Applied MicroType Pro),* enter the numbers in one continuous column. The screen will fill quickly because numbers are listed vertically. Therefore, clear the screen after each drill.

1. Curve the fingers of your right hand; place them upright on the home keys:
   - index finger on 4
   - middle finger on 5
   - ring finger on 6
   - thumb on 0
2. Using the special Enter key (at right of keypad), enter data in Drill 1A as follows:
   - 4 Enter
   - 4 Enter
   - 4 Enter
   - Strike Enter
3. Enter Columns 1B-1F in the same way.
4. Using the special Enter key, enter data in Drill 2A as follows:
   - 44 Enter
   - 44 Enter
   - 44 Enter
   - Strike Enter
5. Continue Drill 2 and complete Drills 3-5 in a similar way. In Drills 4 and 5, strike 0 with side of right thumb.

When you can operate the keypad by touch—all drills completed through p. 98—determine if a calculator accessory is available. If so, key Drill 1A at the right, striking the + key between numbers. Clear the calculator screen (click **C**); then rekey Drill 1A. Key each remaining drill twice. If the two totals of a single drill are not the same, key the drill a third time at a slower pace.

Strike each key with a quick, sharp stroke with the *tip* of the finger; release the key quickly. Keep the fingers curved and upright; the wrist low, relaxed, and steady.

Drill 1

A	B	C	D	E	F
4	5	6	4	5	6
4	5	6	4	5	6
4	5	6	4	5	6

Drill 2

A	B	C	D	E	F
44	55	66	44	55	66
44	55	66	44	55	66
44	55	66	44	55	66

Drill 3

A	B	C	D	E	F
44	45	54	44	55	66
55	56	46	45	54	65
66	64	65	46	56	64

Drill 4

A	B	C	D	E	F
40	50	60	400	500	600
40	50	60	400	500	600
40	50	60	400	500	600

Drill 5

A	B	C	D	E	F
40	400	404	406	450	650
50	500	505	506	540	560
60	600	606	606	405	605

Language & Writing Skills 6

Activity 1:

1. Study the spelling/definitions of the words in the color block at right.
2. Key line 1 (the *Learn* line), noting the proper choice and spelling of words.
3. Key lines 2-4 (the *Apply* lines), choosing the right words to complete the lines correctly.
4. Key lines 5-8 in a similar manner.
5. Check the accuracy of your copy; rekey lines that still contain word-choice/spelling errors.

Choose the right word

their *(pron)* belonging to them	**to** *(prep/adj)* used to indicate action, relation, distance, direction
there *(adv/pron)* in or at that place; word used to introduce a sentence or clause	**too** *(adv)* besides; also; to excessive degree
they're *(contr)* a contracted form of *they are*	**two** *(pron/adj)* one plus one in number

Learn 1 They're to be there to present their plans for the new building.
Apply 2 Were you (their, there, they're) for the large fireworks display?
Apply 3 Do you believe (their, there, they're) going to elect her as mayor?
Apply 4 In (their, there, they're) opinion, the decision was quite unfair.

Learn 5 Is it too late for us to go to the two o'clock movie today?
Apply 6 I am (to, too, two) give everyone (to, too, two) bowls of beef soup.
Apply 7 We are going (to, too, two) the opera; Stan is going (to, too, two).
Apply 8 She thought that (to, too, two) workers were (to, too, two) many.

Activity 2:

1. Key lines 1-10 supplying needed commas.
2. Check work with the *Teacher's Key*.
3. Note the rule number(s) at the left of each line in which you made a comma error.
4. Turn to page 100 and identify those rules for review/practice.
5. Use the Read/Learn/Apply plan for each rule to be reviewed.

Proofread & correct

RULE

1	1	My favorite sports are college football basketball and soccer.
1	2	If you finish your report before noon please give me a call.
1,2	3	I had ham and eggs whole wheat toast and milk for breakfast.
3	4	Miss Qwan said "I was born in Taipei, Taiwan."
4	5	Mr. Sheldon the owner will speak to our managers today.
5	6	Why do you persist Kermit in moving your hands to the top row?
6	7	This report which Ted wrote is well organized and informative.
6	8	Only students who use their time wisely are likely to succeed.
3	9	Dr. Sachs said "Take two of these and call me in the morning."
6	10	Yolanda who is from Cuba intends to become a U.S. citizen.

Activity 3:

1. Read the ¶ and decide whether the student's action was right or wrong (legal, ethical, or moral). Decide if stealing for any reason can be justified.
2. Compose a ¶ stating your views and giving your reasons.
3. Revise, proofread, and correct your ¶.
4. Key the ¶ at right as ¶ 1; key your corrected ¶ as ¶ 2.

Compose (think) as you key

A student sees a designer jacket hanging over the door of a locker. No one seems to be around. The student tries it on; it looks great. He likes it and wants it. He reasons that if the owner can afford an expensive jacket, he can afford another one. So quickly the student puts it in his gym bag and walks away.

Lesson 40 New Keys: 7/8/9

O b j e c t i v e s :
1. **To learn reach-strokes for 7, 8, and 9.**
2. **To combine quickly the new keys with other keys learned.**

40A◆ 5
Home-Key Review

Enter the columns of data listed at the right as directed in Steps 1-5 on p. 94.

A	B	C	D	E	F
4	44	400	404	440	450
5	55	500	505	550	560
6	66	600	606	660	456

40B◆ 45
New Keys: 7/8/9

Learn reach to 7

1. Locate 7 (above 4) on the numeric keypad.
2. Watch your index finger move up to 7 and back to 4 a few times *without striking keys*.
3. Practice striking 74 a few times as you watch the finger.
4. With eyes on copy, enter the data in Drills 1A and 1B.

Learn reach to 8

1. Learn the middle-finger reach to 8 (above 5) as directed in Steps 1-3 above.
2. With eyes on copy, enter the data in Drills 1C and 1D.

Learn reach to 9

1. Learn the ring-finger reach to 9 (above 6) as directed above.
2. With eyes on copy, enter the data in Drills 1E and 1F.

Drills 2-4

Practice entering the columns of data in Drills 2-4 until you can do so accurately and quickly.

Drill 1

A	B	C	D	E	F
474	747	585	858	696	969
747	777	858	888	969	999
777	474	888	585	999	696

Drill 2

A	B	C	D	E	F
774	885	996	745	475	754
474	585	696	854	584	846
747	858	969	965	695	956

Drill 3

A	B	C	D	E	F
470	580	690	770	707	407
740	850	960	880	808	508
704	805	906	990	909	609

Drill 4

A	B	C	D	E	F
456	407	508	609	804	905
789	408	509	704	805	906
654	409	607	705	806	907
987	507	608	706	904	908

Enrichment

For Calculator Accessory Users

Enter single, double, and triple digits in columns as shown, left to right.

A	B	C	D	E	F
4	90	79	4	740	860
56	87	64	56	64	70
78	68	97	78	960	900
90	54	64	60	89	67
4	6	5	98	8	80

Lesson 40

Lesson 43 Review/Skillbuilding

Objectives:
1. **To improve technique and speed on figure copy.**
2. **To improve control (accuracy) of keypad operation.**

43A◆ 5
Keypad Review
Enter the columns of data listed at the right.

A	B	C	D	E	F	G
477	588	707	107	41.6	141.4	936.6
417	528	808	205	52.9	252.5	825.6
717	825	909	309	63.3	393.3	719.4
1,611	1,941	2,424	621	157.8	787.2	2,481.6

43B◆ 45
Speed/Control Building
Enter the data listed in each column of Drills 1-4.

When using the calculator accessory, enter each column of data a second time (bottom to top). If you get the same total twice, you can assume it is correct. If you get a different total the second time, re-enter the data until you get two totals that match.

Drill 1

A	B	C	D	E	F	G
5	77	114	5,808	1,936	9,300	6,936
46	89	225	3,997	2,825	8,250	3,896
3	78	336	9,408	3,796	10,475	7,140
17	85	725	5,650	8,625	7,125	4,874
28	98	825	3,714	9,436	12,740	2,515
9	69	936	2,825	8,514	12,850	8,360
10	97	704	6,796	4,174	9,674	1,794

Drill 2

A	B	C	D	E	F	G
99	795	1,581	1,881	2,642	4,573	2,185
67	657	1,691	1,991	2,772	4,683	3,274
88	234	1,339	2,202	2,992	5,477	9,396
96	359	1,221	2,432	3,743	6,409	4,585
84	762	1,101	3,303	3,853	6,886	5,872
100	485	1,144	4,650	4,714	7,936	6,903

Drill 3

A	B	C	D	E	F
1,077	3,006	5,208	7,104	1,774	7,417
1,400	3,609	5,502	8,205	2,885	8,528
1,700	3,900	5,205	9,303	3,996	9,639
2,008	4,107	6,309	7,407	4,174	3,936
2,500	4,400	6,600	8,508	5,285	5,828
2,805	1,704	6,900	9,609	6,396	4,717

Drill 4

A	B	C	D	E	F
1.4	14.00	170.40	1,714.70	7,410.95	1,147.74
2.5	17.00	170.43	2,825.80	8,520.55	2,258.88
3.6	25.00	250.90	3,936.90	9,630.65	3,369.93
7.4	28.00	288.50	4,747.17	10,585.78	7,144.74
8.5	36.00	369.63	5,878.25	11,474.85	8,255.85
9.6	39.00	390.69	6,969.39	12,696.95	9,366.63

Lesson 41 New Keys: 1/2/3

O b j e c t i v e s :

1. To learn reach-strokes for 1, 2, and 3.
2. To combine quickly the new keys with other keys learned.

41A◆ 5
Keypad Review

Enter the columns of data listed at the right as directed in Steps 1-5 on p. 94.

A	B	C	D	E	F	G
44	74	740	996	704	990	477
55	85	850	885	805	880	588
66	96	960	774	906	770	699

41B◆ 35
New Keys: 1/2/3

Learn reach to 1

1. Locate 1 (below 4) on the numeric keypad.
2. Watch your index finger move down to 1 and back to 4 a few times *without striking keys*.
3. Practice striking 14 a few times as you watch the finger.
4. Enter the data in Drills 1A and 1B.

Learn reach to 2

1. Learn the middle-finger reach to 2 (below 5) as directed in Steps 1-3 above.
2. Enter data in Drills 1C and 1D.

Learn reach to 3

1. Learn the ring-finger reach to 3 (below 6) as directed above.
2. Enter data in Drills 1E, 1F, and 1G.

Drills 2-4

Enter data in Drills 2-4 until you can do so accurately and quickly.

Drill 1

A	B	C	D	E	F	G
414	141	525	252	636	363	174
141	111	252	222	363	333	285
111	414	222	525	333	636	396

Drill 2

A	B	C	D	E	F	G
114	225	336	175	415	184	174
411	522	633	284	524	276	258
141	252	363	395	635	359	369

Drill 3

A	B	C	D	E	F	G
417	528	639	110	171	471	714
147	280	369	220	282	582	850
174	285	396	330	393	693	936

Drill 4

A	B	C	D	E	F	G
77	71	401	107	417	147	174
88	82	502	208	528	258	825
99	93	603	309	639	369	396

41C◆ 10
Decimal Numbers

Enter the data in Columns A-F, placing the decimal points as shown in the copy. Strike the decimal key with ring finger.

A	B	C	D	E	F
1.40	17.10	47.17	174.11	1,477.01	10,704.50
2.50	28.20	58.28	285.22	2,588.02	17,815.70
3.60	39.30	69.39	396.33	3,996.03	20,808.75
4.70	74.70	17.10	417.14	4,174.07	26,909.65
5.80	85.80	28.20	528.25	5,285.08	30,906.25
6.90	96.90	39.30	639.36	6,396.06	34,259.90

Lesson 42 Review/Skillbuilding

O b j e c t i v e s :

1. **To improve keying technique/speed on the keypad.**
2. **To key all-figure copy by touch (minimum of looking).**

42A◆ 5

Keypad Review

Enter the columns of data listed at the right as directed in Steps 1-5 on p. 94.

A	B	C	D	E	F	G
44	55	66	714	414	525	636
14	25	36	825	474	585	696
74	85	96	936	400	500	600
132	165	198	2,475	1,288	1,610	1,932

42B◆ 35

Speed/Control Building

Enter the data listed in each column of Drills 1-3.

If you are using the calculator accessory, remember to check your totals against the printed totals.

Drill 1

A	B	C	D	E	F	G
14	19	173	1,236	1,714	4,174	4,074
25	37	291	4,596	2,825	5,285	5,085
36	18	382	7,896	3,936	6,396	6,096
74	29	794	5,474	7,414	1,400	9,336
85	38	326	2,975	8,525	2,500	8,225
96	27	184	8,535	9,636	3,600	7,114
330	168	2,150	30,712	34,050	23,355	39,930

Drill 2

A	B	C	D	E	F	G
1	3	40	123	114	1,004	8,274
14	36	50	789	225	2,005	9,386
174	396	70	321	336	3,006	7,494
2	906	740	456	774	7,004	1,484
25	306	360	174	885	8,005	2,595
285	20	850	285	996	9,006	3,686
805	50	960	396	500	5,005	6,006
1,306	1,717	3,070	2,544	3,830	35,035	38,925

Drill 3

A	B	C	D	E	F	G
126	104	107	707	4,400	3,006	1,714
786	205	208	808	5,000	2,005	2,825
324	306	309	909	6,600	1,004	3,936
984	704	407	1,700	7,000	9,006	7,144
876	805	508	2,800	8,800	8,005	8,255
216	906	609	3,900	9,000	7,004	9,366
3,312	3,030	2,148	10,824	40,800	30,030	33,240

42C◆ 10

Decimal Numbers

Enter the data in Columns A-F, placing the decimal points as shown in the copy.

A	B	C	D	E	F
1.70	10.70	74.70	417.11	1,477.04	10,754.80
2.80	28.50	85.80	528.22	2,558.02	14,815.70
3.90	39.60	96.90	639.33	3,699.03	20,868.75
4.10	74.10	41.40	174.14	4,174.01	26,909.45
5.20	85.20	52.50	285.25	5,285.08	30,932.65
6.30	96.30	63.60	369.36	6,396.09	37,149.20
24.00	334.40	414.90	2,413.41	23,589.27	141,430.55

Lesson 42

Appendix A
Repetitive Stress Injury

Repetitive stress injury (RSI) is a result of repeated movement of a particular part of the body. A familiar example is "tennis elbow." Of more concern to keyboard users is the form of RSI called **carpal tunnel syndrome (CTS)**.

CTS is an inflammatory disease that develops gradually and affects the wrists, hands, and forearms. Blood vessels, tendons, and nerves pass into the hand through the carpal tunnel (see illustration below). If any of these structures enlarge or if the walls of the tunnel narrow, the median nerve is pinched, and CTS symptoms may result.

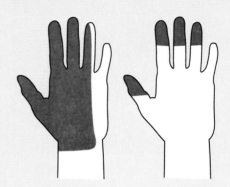

Areas affected by carpal tunnel syndrome

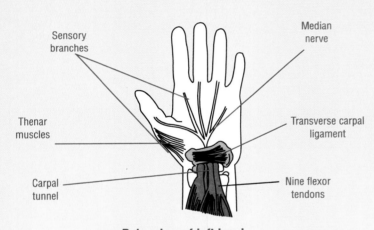

Sensory branches

Median nerve

Thenar muscles

Transverse carpal ligament

Carpal tunnel

Nine flexor tendons

Palm view of left hand

Causes of RSI/CTS

RSI/CTS often develops in workers whose physical routine is unvaried. Common occupational factors include: (1) using awkward posture, (2) using poor techniques, (3) performing tasks with wrists bent (see below), (4) using improper equipment, (5) working at a rapid pace, (6) not taking rest breaks, and (7) not doing exercises that promote graceful motion and good techniques.

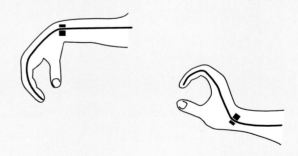

Improper wrist positions for keystroking

Symptoms of RSI/CTS

CTS symptoms include numbness in the hand; tingling or burning in the hand, wrist, or elbow; severe pain in the forearm, elbow, or shoulder; and difficulty in gripping objects. Symptoms usually appear during sleeping hours, probably because many people sleep with their wrists flexed.

If not properly treated, the pressure on the median nerve, which controls the thumb, forefinger, middle finger, and half the ring finger (see top right), causes severe pain. The pain can radiate into the forearm, elbow, or shoulder and can require surgery or result in permanent damage or paralysis.

Other factors associated with CTS include a person's genetic makeup; the aging process; hormonal influences; obesity; chronic diseases such as rheumatoid arthritis and gout; misaligned fractures; and hobbies such as gardening, knitting, and woodworking that require the same motion

over and over. CTS affects over three times more women than men, with 60 percent of the affected persons between the ages of 30 and 60.

Reducing the Risk of RSI/CTS

Carpal tunnel syndrome is frequently a health concern for workers who use a computer keyboard or mouse. The risk of developing CTS is less for computer keyboard operators who use proper furniture and equipment, keyboarding techniques, and/or muscle-stretching exercises than for those who do not.

Keyboard users can reduce the risk of developing RSI/CTS by taking these precautions:

1. Arrange the workstation correctly:
   a. Position the keyboard directly in front of the chair.
   b. Keep the front edge of the keyboard even with the edge of the desk or table so that wrist movement will not be restricted while you are keying.
   c. Position the keyboard at elbow height.
   d. Position the monitor about 18 to 24 inches from your eyes with the top edge of the display screen at eye level.
   e. Position the mouse next to and at the same height as the computer keyboard and as close to the body as possible.

2. Use a proper chair and sit correctly:
   a. Use a straight-backed chair, or adjust your chair so that it will not yield when you lean back.
   b. Use a seat that allows you to keep your feet flat on the floor while you are keying. Use a footrest if your feet cannot rest flat on the floor.
   c. Sit erect and as far back in the seat as possible.

3. Use correct arm and wrist positions and movement:
   a. Keep your forearms parallel to the floor and level with the keyboard so that your wrists will be in a flat, neutral position rather than flexed upward or downward.
   b. Keep arms near the side of your body in a relaxed position.

4. Use proper keyboarding techniques:
   a. Keep your fingers curved and upright over the home keys.
   b. Keep wrists and forearms from touching or resting on any surface while keying.
   c. Strike each key lightly using the fingertip. Do not use too much pressure or hold the keys down.

5. When using a keyboard or mouse, take short breaks. A rest of one to two minutes every hour is appropriate. Natural breaks in keyboarding action of several seconds' duration also help.

6. Exercise the neck, shoulder, arm, wrist, and fingers before beginning to key each day and often during the workday (see No. 5). Suggested exercises for keyboard users are described below. You can do all the exercises while sitting at your workstation.

Exercises for Keyboard Users

1. **Strengthen finger muscles.** (See Drill 1 on p. A3.) Open your hands, extend your fingers wide, and hold with muscles tense for two or three seconds; close the fingers into a tight fist with thumb on top, holding for two or three seconds; relax the fingers as you straighten them. Repeat 10 times. Additional finger drills are shown on p. A3.

2. **Strengthen the muscles in the carpal tunnel area.** While sitting with your arms comfortably at your side and hands in a fist, rotate your hands inward from the wrist. Repeat this motion 10 to 15 times; then rotate outward from the wrist 10 to 15 times. Extend your fingers and repeat the movements for the same number of times.

3. **Loosen forearms.** With both wrists held in a neutral position (not bent) and the upper arm hanging vertically from the shoulder, rotate both forearms in 15 clockwise circles about the elbow. Repeat, making counterclockwise circles.

4. **Stretch the arms.** Interlace the fingers of both hands; with the palms facing forward, stretch your arms in front of you and hold for ten seconds. Repeat at least once. Next, with your fingers still interlaced, stretch your arms over your head and hold for 10 seconds. Repeat at least once.

5. **Loosen elbows.** Place your hands on your shoulders with elbows facing forward; slowly move your arms in increasingly larger circles in front of you 10 to 15 times.

6. **Relieve shoulder tension.** Interlace the fingers of both hands behind your head and slowly move the elbows back, pressing the shoulder blades together; hold for 10 seconds. Repeat at least once.

Finger Gymnastics

Brief daily practice of finger gymnastics will strengthen your finger muscles and increase the ease with which you key. Begin each keying period with this conditioning exercise. Choose two or more drills for this practice.

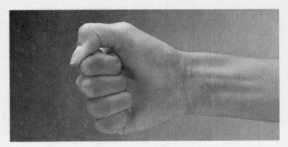

DRILL 1. Hands open, fingers wide, muscles tense. Close the fingers into a tight fist, with thumb on top. Relax the fingers as you straighten them; repeat 10 times.

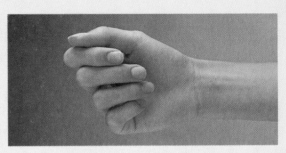

DRILL 2. Clench the fingers as shown. Hold the fingers in this position for a brief time; then extend the fingers, relaxing the muscles of fingers and hand. Repeat the movements slowly several times. Exercise both hands at the same time.

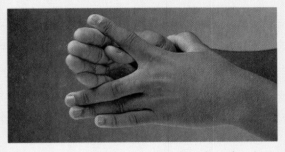

DRILL 3. Place the fingers and the thumb of one hand between two fingers of the other hand, and spread the fingers as much as possible. Spread all fingers of both hands.

DRILL 4. Interlace the fingers of the two hands and wring the hands, rubbing the heel of the palms vigorously.

DRILL 5. Spread the fingers as much as possible, holding the position for a moment or two; then relax the fingers and lightly fold them into the palm of the hand. Repeat the movements slowly several times. Exercise both hands at the same time.

DRILL 7. Hold both hands in front of you, fingers together. Hold the last three fingers still and move the first finger as far to the side as possible. Return the first finger; then move the first and second fingers together; finally move the little finger as far to the side as possible.

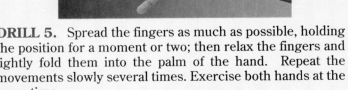

DRILL 6. Rub the hands vigorously. Let the thumb rub the palm of the hand. Rub the fingers, the back of the hand, and the wrist.

A p p e n d i x B
A Symbols Supplement

B 1 ◆
New Keys: @ and +

1. Locate the appropriate symbol on the keyboard chart.
2. Key each line twice SS; DS between 2-line pairs.
3. If time permits, rekey lines 5-7.

TECHNIQUE CUE:
@ Depress the right shift key; strike **@** with the left ring finger.
+ Depress the left shift key; strike **+** with the right little finger.

@ = "at" sign
+ = "plus" sign

The **@** is a common character in e-mail addresses and in prices of items for sale.

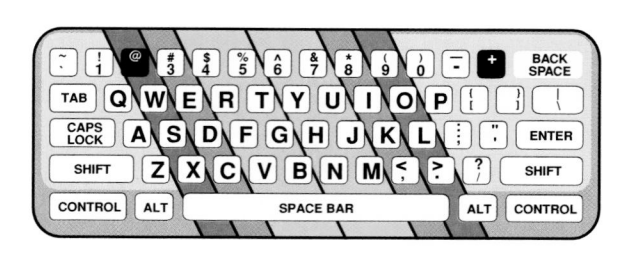

Learn @

1 s s s@ s@ s@ @sw @sxw @sxw; 32 @ .45; 65 @ .99; sold 2 @ .10
2 Buy 44 @ .98; sell 64 @ .52; hold 337 @ .19; ship 120 @ .22.

Learn +

3 + ;+ ;+ +;+ +;+; 5 + 5 or 4 + 4; A+, B+, or C+; 9 + 9; 2 + 2
4 Kim got an A+ after adding 99 + 106 + 100 + 97 + 103 points.

Combine @ and +

5 E-mail Ty at lbeckett@waco.com; Lilly at lilbertz@capso.net.
6 Buy 5 bonds @ 22.91 + 3 stocks @ 32.11 + 10 T-bills @ 45.31.
7 Add Order Nos. 6 + 9 + 81; send an invoice to cruis@mgt.com.

| 1 | 2 | 3 | 4 | 5 | 6 | 7 | 8 | 9 | 10 | 11 | 12 |

B 2 ◆
New Keys: ! and \

1. Locate the appropriate symbol on the keyboard chart.
2. Key each line twice; DS between 2-line pairs.
3. If time permits, rekey lines 5-7.

TECHNIQUE CUE:
! Depress the right shift key; strike **!** with the left little finger.
\ Reach up or down to strike **** with the right little finger (depending on its location on your keyboard).

! = Exclamation point
\ = Backslash

The location of the backslash may vary from one keyboard to another.

Learn !

1 !a !a!qa Ha! No! Watch out! Get set! Get ready! Go now!
2 Too bad! Not now! Listen to the siren! I won the contest!

**Learn **

3 \; \; \;' \;'; '\' '\'; \\\'\ \\\'\; cd\c; cd\b; cd\d; b*.*
4 Change to d:\window\psfonts to copy fonts to e:\psfonts\new.

**Combine ! and **

5 Don't erase c:\arts.doc! Save it to e:\docs before closing!
6 Back up c:\fonts now! The directory, c:\fonts, has changed!
7 Rush e:\gam\5.eps and f:\pho\9.eps to johnarns@caps.net now!

| 1 | 2 | 3 | 4 | 5 | 6 | 7 | 8 | 9 | 10 | 11 | 12 |

B3 ◆

New Keys: = and [ ]

1. Locate the appropriate symbol on the keyboard chart.
2. Key each line twice SS; DS between 2-line pairs.
3. If time permits, rekey lines 5-7.

TECHNIQUE CUE:

= Strike = with the right little finger.

[ ] Strike either [or] with the right little finger.

Two uses of brackets are
- To enclose explanations in quoted copy.
- To show—along with parentheses—units within larger units in mathematical formulas. Brackets are not used in place of parentheses.

= = "equal" sign
[ ] = brackets

Learn =

1   = =; = =; = = =; = = =; ='='='='='='; if $3x = 15$, then $x = 5$
2   Change your answer to $12x = 16$; if $8x = 24$, does $x = 2$ or 3?

Learn [ ]

3   [;[;]']' ['[']']']'[' [sic] [loco] (we [Al and I] left)
4   "They [those arriving last] knew this [the pin] was stolen."

Combine = and [ ]

5   "If $2 + 2 = 2$," she [Ana] said, "we are in serious trouble."
6   Work a problem: $z = [2(x + y)] + [4(x + 6y)]$; $x = 3$; $y = 5$.
7   If $x = 11$ and $y = 5$, what does $9[(8x + 2y - 4x) + 2y]$ equal?

| 1 | 2 | 3 | 4 | 5 | 6 | 7 | 8 | 9 | 10 | 11 | 12 |

B4 ◆

New Keys: > and <

1. Locate the appropriate symbol on the keyboard chart.
2. Key each line twice SS; DS between 2-line pairs.
3. If time permits, rekey lines 5-7.

TECHNIQUE CUE:

> Depress the left shift key; strike > with the right ring finger.

< Depress the left shift key; strike < with the right middle finger.

The > and < often appear in lines of computer code.

> = "greater than" sign
< = "less than" sign

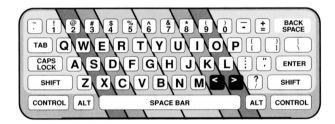

Learn >

1   >. >. >>.> >>.>; $19 > 23$; $161 > 150$; $576 > 245$; $2022 > 2020$.
2   If $a < b$, then $a + c < b + c$ and $c + a < c + b$; and $ac < bc$.

Learn <

3   <, <, <<,< <<,<; $18 < 19$; $222 < 229$; $402 < 433$; $5003 < 5010$.
4   These are mathematical sentences: $5 + 1 < 8$; $a < 9$; $2b < c$.

Combine > and <

5   Please solve these problems: $x + 8 > 9$; $1 < y < 6$; $5x > 10$.
6   X's objectives > Y's but < C's.   A's scores > B's but < D's.
7   If $2a > 3b$ and $3b > 4y$, is $y >$ or $< a$?   Can you prove $x > y$?

| 1 | 2 | 3 | 4 | 5 | 6 | 7 | 8 | 9 | 10 | 11 | 12 |

Appendix C
Keyboard Mastery

each line twice SS; then a 1'
writing on line 3; find *gwam*

To maintain your basic keying skills throughout Part 2, spend about five minutes at the beginning of each class period on one of these Keyboard Mastery exercises. Each three-line drill is designed to give you a review of all alphabet and figure keys and several common symbols. In addition, each exercise contains a sentence designed for speed. Follow directions at the left.

A

see directions above

alphabet Jake led a big blitz which saved the next play for my squad.
fig/sym Beth has ordered 26 5/8 yards of #304 linen at $7.19 a yard.
speed Good form is the key if all of us wish to make the big goal.

| 1 | 2 | 3 | 4 | 5 | 6 | 7 | 8 | 9 | 10 | 11 | 12 |

B

see directions above

alphabet Jim wondered if I gave the amazing sax player a quick break.
fig/sym Our 1998 profit was $57,604 (up 23% from the previous year).
speed Roddy may sign the six forms and work with the city auditor.

| 1 | 2 | 3 | 4 | 5 | 6 | 7 | 8 | 9 | 10 | 11 | 12 |

C

see directions above

alphabet Oz vied for a gold cup but was quickly jinxed from the fall.
fig/sym Of $3,482.70 taxes paid, $956.10 went to the city and state.
speed Vivian is to key the forms they wish to rush to the auditor.

| 1 | 2 | 3 | 4 | 5 | 6 | 7 | 8 | 9 | 10 | 11 | 12 |

D

see directions above

alphabet Florenz quickly amazed six whalers by jumping over the edge.
fig/sym Their 463 shares sold @ $59--a 10.82% profit and $27,317.00.
speed Diana may make a vivid sign to hang by the door of the hall.

| 1 | 2 | 3 | 4 | 5 | 6 | 7 | 8 | 9 | 10 | 11 | 12 |

E

see directions above

alphabet Five kids quickly mixed the prizes, baffling one wise judge.
fig/sym Joe asked, "Is the ZIP Code 45209-2748 or is it 45208-3614?"
speed The firms may make a profit if they handle their work right.

| 1 | 2 | 3 | 4 | 5 | 6 | 7 | 8 | 9 | 10 | 11 | 12 |

F

see directions above

alphabet Quincy worked six jigsaw puzzles given him for his birthday.
fig/sym I deposited Hahn & Ober's $937.48 check (#1956) on March 20.
speed Ellena may lend them a hand with the audit of the soap firm.

| 1 | 2 | 3 | 4 | 5 | 6 | 7 | 8 | 9 | 10 | 11 | 12 |

G

see directions above

alphabet Rex just left my quiz show and gave back a prize he had won.
fig/sym Review reaches: $40, $84, 95%, #30, 5-point, 1/6, B&O 27's.
speed Di may profit by good form and a firm wish to make the goal.

| 1 | 2 | 3 | 4 | 5 | 6 | 7 | 8 | 9 | 10 | 11 | 12 |

H

see directions above

I

see directions above

J

see directions above

K

see directions above

L

see directions above

M

see directions above

N

see directions above

O

see directions above

P

see directions above

alphabet · Zoe just may have to plan a big, unique dance for next week.
fig/sym · Tami asked, "Can't you touch key 65, 73, $840, and 19 1/2%?"
speed · Six of the big firms may bid for the right to the lake land.

| 1 | 2 | 3 | 4 | 5 | 6 | 7 | 8 | 9 | 10 | 11 | 12 |

alphabet · Wayne froze the ball, having just made the six quick points.
fig/sym · Flo moved from 583 Iris Lane to 836 - 42d Avenue on 10/7/99.
speed · Suella may row to the small island to dig for the big clams.

| 1 | 2 | 3 | 4 | 5 | 6 | 7 | 8 | 9 | 10 | 11 | 12 |

alphabet · Vicky landed quite a major star for her next big plaza show.
fig/sym · Items marked * are out of stock: #139*, #476A*, and #2058*.
speed · Dodi is to handle all the pay forms for the small lake town.

| 1 | 2 | 3 | 4 | 5 | 6 | 7 | 8 | 9 | 10 | 11 | 12 |

alphabet · Jacques worked to win the next big prize for my valiant men.
fig/sym · Rona's 1998 tax was $5,374, almost 2% ($106) less than 1997.
speed · Six of the eight girls may work for the auditor of the firm.

| 1 | 2 | 3 | 4 | 5 | 6 | 7 | 8 | 9 | 10 | 11 | 12 |

alphabet · Jarvis will take the next big prize for my old racquet club.
fig/sym · THE DIAMOND CAPER (Parker & Sons, #274638) sells for $19.50.
speed · A neighbor paid the girl to fix the turn signal of the auto.

| 1 | 2 | 3 | 4 | 5 | 6 | 7 | 8 | 9 | 10 | 11 | 12 |

alphabet · Belva had quickly won top seed for the next games in Juarez.
fig/sym · My income tax for 1998 was $4,560.62--up 3% over 1997's tax.
speed · Shana may make a bid for the antique bottle for the auditor.

| 1 | 2 | 3 | 4 | 5 | 6 | 7 | 8 | 9 | 10 | 11 | 12 |

alphabet · Griffen just amazed them when he quickly solved a vexing problem.
fig/sym · His sales this week are $28,193.50; that's an increase of 17.64%.
speed · Jan may wish to work for the auditor if the widow signs the form.

| 1 | 2 | 3 | 4 | 5 | 6 | 7 | 8 | 9 | 10 | 11 | 12 | 13 |

alphabet · Marj, looking very straight-faced, was to request six big pizzas.
fig/sym · I said check #4508 for $83 arrived 6/27 but had been mailed 5/19.
speed · The girls held to their theory and may fight for their amendment.

| 1 | 2 | 3 | 4 | 5 | 6 | 7 | 8 | 9 | 10 | 11 | 12 | 13 |

alphabet · Six boys quickly removed the juicy lamb from a sizzling stew pot.
fig/sym · Hall & Company's phone number has been changed to (382) 174-9560.
speed · Six big firms may bid for the authentic map of an ancient island.

| 1 | 2 | 3 | 4 | 5 | 6 | 7 | 8 | 9 | 10 | 11 | 12 | 13 |

Appendix D
Internet: An Introduction with Applications

The Internet is changing the way people communicate and learn. The number of people using the Internet grows every day. If you are not yet among the millions of drivers on the Information SuperHighway, or Internet, this article puts you behind the wheel. Mastering a computer keyboard will put you in high gear.

The power of the Internet ties closely with using a computer keyboard. To create and post e-mail messages and "attachments," you use a keyboard. To search the vast Internet for something specific, you key words and phrases to define the search. If someone says "visit www dot . . . on the 'Net,'" you must type **www.** and all the other address characters.

The more skilled you are, the less you have to think about what keys to tap. Instead, you can keep your mind on the Internet and the stuff it contains. Learn to operate the keyboard mostly by touch (without looking at your fingers). Continue improving your keying technique—the secret behind fast, accurate typing.

What Is the Internet?

Connections. If you use the Internet, you have connections. The Internet is a network of computer networks. It is millions of computers all over the world, each linked electronically to each other. The links make certain types of information stored on any one of those computers available to all the others.

To describe how much information is at hand on the Internet, we use words like *huge* and *immense* and *stupendous* and *vast*. What kinds of information? All kinds. You (or anyone else) probably can't name a subject that's *not* on the Internet. With millions of users around the globe and tons of information ready for them, the Internet serves untold purposes. This list gives a few examples of things you might do on the Internet:

- take a course online
- buy a T-shirt
- promote your small business
- look for a job
- get up-to-the-minute news
- discuss a project with an expert
- send your resume to an employer
- send a birthday card that plays music
- research your genealogy (family history)
- send virtual roses or order real ones
- download (transfer to your computer) a poem
- find good places to go on vacation

How Does It Work?

Is using the Internet like looking up topics in a humongous library? Not exactly. You see, the information is unorganized and dynamic (always changing). Using the Internet is fun because you never know what you will find. At the same time, you must keep track of the places you go to on the Internet if you ever hope to go there again! The Internet was made for information to go from point A (a sending computer) to point B (a receiving computer) along a path. It works like the post office: Information is put into an Internet "envelope," and the sender's computer puts an address on it. Another computer reads the address and passes the information to the next computer, and so on. Information going to many different addresses can go along the same network path, because Internet envelopes are sorted again and again—just like post office mail—by special computers along the way. The information (message or data) ends up at the computer to which it was addressed.

What Do Dots Have to Do with It?

The address is the key. Though many individuals and businesses and governments and schools use the Internet, no two users have the same address. These addresses are typical for an individual Internet user:

alice@acsworld.net   rsims@posey.com
cord@ucl.acs.edu   nicky@ecs.co.uk

The Internet user's name is to the left of the @ sign. At the right, dots separate the addresses into levels, called *domains*. In the U.S., the last domain tells the sort of organization it is (.**com** = commercial, .**edu** = education,

.gov = government, .mil = military, .net = network, .org = nonprofit organization) or what country it is in (for example, **au** = Australia, **ca** = Canada, **ch** = Switzerland, **mx** = Mexico, **uk** = United Kingdom). All parts to the right of the @ sign further identify the user's domain to send the information to him or her. Many Internet addresses have more dots—more domains—than these examples. Also, more domains and changes in Internet addressing are likely as users increase in number and diversity.

What's E-Mail?

Electronic mail, or e-mail, is the first and still most popular use of the Internet. E-mail involves posting (sending) messages (posts) in text form from one computer to another over a network. Speed is the e-mail advantage. A first-class letter takes three to five days going from one coast to the other; even "overnight" mail takes 18 to 24 hours. E-mail posted at 3:45 may arrive on the other side of the country or halfway around the world by 3:46. Delivery in less than five minutes is routine.

Besides posting to individuals, with e-mail you can join discussion (mailing) lists and announcement lists and subscribe to electronic newsletters and magazines (e-zines).

Discussion lists (and similar services: news groups, chat rooms, and forums) center around a topic. Everyone who joins the list is interested in that topic. For example, 125 Vietnam veterans belong to the VWAR-L discussion list. When one member posts a message, all other members receive it and may reply to it. Announcement lists are one-way mailing lists. You can receive messages, but you cannot reply. For example, you might join Monster Board's Job Opportunities announcement list.

Most newsletters and e-zines are text-only e-mail—no fancy type and no glitzy graphics. The low cost of electronic publications allows information to be released sooner and more often than through printed publications.

Is World Wide Web Another Name for the 'Net?

The World Wide Web (the web) is the main system for navigating (moving from place to place) on the Internet. It lets graphics, audio, and video travel the network paths along with text. Special software called a web browser allows you to view these sights and sounds and click on links that take you at once to related information in another place. Thus, you can just point and click to navigate the web.

Microsoft Internet Explorer and Netscape are the most common browsers today. A link that you click is more precisely called a *hyperlink* or *hypertext*—a word or phrase in a different color than surrounding text or underlined. A web browser opens to a *start page* that contains no information—just dozens of hyperlinks for jumping to other informative or fun places.

How Do You Navigate?

The places that you navigate to are called web sites, web pages, or home pages. (All three names mean the same.) When you click a hyperlink, you may jump—without knowing it—from a web site in Indiana to one in Indonesia. A few more clicks and you may land on a home page in Ireland. When you find a web page that you like, you can enter it in your browser and go back to it for updates of the information.

Hyperlinks are not the only way to navigate the web, though. Every web site has an address, called a URL (**U**niform **R**esource **L**ocator). A user can get to a web site by typing the URL in the browser's Location list box. A URL has domain names like an e-mail address. An example of a URL would be **http://www.bluemountain.com/index.html**. This URL points to the WWW computer at a business named Blue Mountain in the Commercial domain. The http (**H**yper**T**ext **T**ransfer **P**rotocol) refers to the computer language used to get into that computer. The html (**H**yper**T**ext **M**arkup **L**anguage) stands for the programming language used to create all web pages. (Some word processing applications have add-ons that let users create their own web pages without knowing HTML.) The browser keeps a list of the URLs used most recently. A user can return to a site another day by clicking its URL on this list instead of typing it again.

Another way to navigate the web is to use the browser's *search page*. You would use a search page to find information about a certain topic when you don't have a specific URL. On the search page you would type *keywords* to define your search (name the topics and subtopics you want) and select a *search engine* (tool that searches many web sites to look for your keywords and show you the search results). Common search engines are Alta Vista, InfoSeek, Lycos, and WebCrawler; but there are others.

Whether you jump to a useful or fun site by clicking a hyperlink, go to it directly by typing a URL, or search for it using keywords, you should keep track of it so that you can go to it easily another time. Browsers give you an easy way to do so. In Internet Explorer you add the site to a list of *Favorites*. In Netscape you attach a *Bookmark*. All you do is click to capture the site address (URL) and type a name for it. To return to the site later, click that name.

The Internet continues to change our lives, from how we go to college to how we stay close with cousins. One day you may globe-hop, keying URLs for web sites in Boise, Bogota, and Bangkok and hyperlinking to Bydogoszcz, Bulawayo, and Berlin—all before lunch. Later, you may seek the advice of a career coach by posting carefully keyed questions to a discussion list; then posting your family's latest news to a few friends from high school. As a keyboard operator with Internet connections, you have the world at your fingertips.

Going Places on the Internet

With this introduction to the Internet, let's put the information you just read to work. The following activities are for first-time Internet users. If you have experience using the Internet, your teacher may suggest ways that you can vary these basic activities. Or you may be asked to help someone in the class who is a first-timer.

Activity 1—The White House

For starters we'll go to the White House. Instead of Washington, DC, though, we'll go to a web site in the government domain.

On your web browser's Start page, click the Go button; key this address (URL) in the list box (upper left of the screen): **http: //www.whitehouse.gov.** (Do not type a period at the end.) Click OK.

When the web site opens, you may see only black lines, a white screen, and a couple of red-and-blue buttons.

1. Click the White House button to display a picture of the White House.

2. Click the Welcome button, and "Welcome to the White House" appears in fancy script.

Below this welcome message, you will see blocks of text, like paragraphs with underlined headings. The blue, underlined words are *hyperlinks* (hypertext), ready to jump to other parts of the White House web site. The words in black (not underlined) describe those other places.

3. Scroll down the page, reading some of the hypertext and descriptions: The President & Vice President, Commonly Requested Federal Services, Interactive Citizens Handbook, What's New, White House History and Tours, Site News, Virtual Library, Briefing Room, White House Help Desk, White House for Kids.

4. Scroll up to the History and Tours hyperlink and read that description again.

5. Double-click the History and Tours hypertext (the underlined words). More hyperlinks display. Scroll down the page, reading descriptions for these parts of the White House web site: A White House History, Art in the White House, Presidents of the U.S., First Ladies of the U.S., First Families at Home, White House Tours and Public Events.

6. Scroll to the Tours and Public Events hyperlink; double-click it. Another list of about six options is displayed. This time you will click a button (hyperlink) beside the topic you want, rather than clicking the text itself.

7. Click the button beside General Tour Information. Read the information on the screen to answer these questions:

a. When was this tour information updated?

b. Are any tours canceled today or in the near future? If so, what is canceled? when?

c. Do you need a ticket for the tour? If so, what is the cost for a ticket?

d. You will be in Washington, DC, for a four-day weekend at the end of next month. Which time should you plan to tour the White House? (1) Friday afternoon, (2) Saturday morning, (3) Saturday afternoon, (4) sometime Sunday.

e. Name two kinds of White House tours.

f. Which of the two kinds suits your situation better?

In the upper left of your screen, notice the two arrow buttons, pointing left and right. Once you have jumped from the home page to another part of the web site, these buttons allow you to go back (left) and forward (right). The back button displays the previous page; the forward button, the next page.

8. Click the left arrow to go *back* to the Tours and Public Events page; click the back arrow again to return to the History and Tours page.

9. Now, scroll down again to the Tours and Public Events hypertext. Did it change color? This color difference lets you know that you visited this part of the White House web site. (If someone else used your computer to visit History and Tours before you did, the color of the hyperlink was different already from the color of surrounding text.)

Whenever you click the color hypertext, the color changes permanently. Thus, if you return to this web site in the future, the red letters will remind you that you entered this page earlier, however briefly.

10. Click the back button once more to return to the White House home page.

11. Click the forward button. You're at the History and Tours page again.

12. Click forward again. You're at the Tours and Public Events page.

13. Click forward a third time. The general tour information displays again.

14. Now click forward once more. Nothing happens. Before there is a "next page" to go to, you must first jump there by means of a hyperlink.

15. Instead of moving forward, click the back button until the White House home page (first page) appears. If you wanted to come back to the White House web site someday, you could, of course, key the address again. But suppose you have a reason to visit this site

daily or every few hours. Or what if you lose the URL? Or confuse it with another of the hundreds of thousands of web sites available? (With a short, simple URL, the White House address is easy to remember and not likely to be lost "in the shuffle." But the same cannot be said of all web site addresses—for example, this is a URL for a weekly newspaper that lists job openings: http://search.yahoo.com/bin/search?p=%22Chronicle +of+Higher+Education%22&y=y&e=2747813&f=0 %3A86164%3A2747813&r=Education%02Bibliographies.)

Your web browser provides an easy way around this problem. You can keep a list of Favorites (Internet Explorer) or Bookmarks (Netscape) to which you can return quickly, without keying the site's address.

16. Add the White House web site to your list of favorite places or bookmarks. (The steps you take to include the site in your list of favorites will vary depending on the browser that you are using. Most browsers show a Favorites or Bookmarks menu [and/or a button] from which you can select an option such as Add to Favorites, or Add Bookmark.)

So far, the hyperlinks you've used have allowed you to jump from one part of a web site to another part of the same site. Now you will use a hyperlink to navigate to an entirely different site.

17. On the White House home page, double-click the <u>Commonly Requested Federal Services</u> hypertext.

18. Then click the Education button.

19. You're seeking information about money for college; double-click the <u>Student Financial Assistance Guide</u> hypertext. Just before the Student Guide displays, a "warning" appears.

The message notifies you that you are leaving the White House web site and entering the U.S. Department of Education web site. This notice is unusual. Hyperlinks often jump from one web site to another, but the Internet user is often unaware of it.

The warning screen may be on a timer so that it remains on the screen only a few seconds; then, the Student Financial Assistance Guide replaces it on the screen.

20. If the warning screen disappears, click the back button to display it again. (See the URL for the Education Department's Student Financial Aid site.)

Ignore this URL. You will add this new web site to your list of Favorites/Bookmarks. Like word processing files, web sites should be given short names that you will recognize at a glance. For example, you might name this one "Gov $$$ Aid."

21. Add the site to Favorites/Bookmarks.

Someday you can return to the site quickly, read the information it provides, and even print the information if you choose. (The File menu here contains Print options, just like in your word processing software.)

22. Navigate within this site briefly. Then disconnect from World Wide Web or go to Activity 2 below.

Activity 2—Appaloosa Horse Club

1. Key this URL in your web browser's address list box: **http://www.appaloosa.com**.

2. Click the buttons to display a graphic and a directory of hyperlinks to other parts of the web site.

3. Study the list of links (directory). Though the links are not described, you likely can guess the type of information you would find at most of the places—FAQs, for example. You will see this link often as you navigate the Net; the letters stand for *Frequently Asked Questions*.

4. Click FAQs. Creators of the web site anticipated that many people visiting the Appaloosa Horse Club (ApHC) site will want to ask how to register for club membership. Thus, a hyperlink allows site visitors to skip the questions and jump directly to a membership registration form. Of course, the form can be filled out on the computer screen and then submitted with the click of a button—IF credit card information is given on the registration form for the membership fee.

5. Scroll down the page, skimming the frequently asked questions and answers. At the bottom of the FAQ page— as on other pages of the Appaloosa site—is an e-mail hyperlink. Clicking this link opens the e-mail message box and enters the ApHC's e-mail address automatically. The visitor can then post a question or comment about information at the site.

6. Go back to the ApHC home page.

7. What do you think you'll find if you click Hot Spots? Click it. This page gives no information about an Appaloosa's spots; instead it offers a number of other web sites related to this one. And how would you go to one of the other places? Just double-click the hyperlink, of course.

8. Again, return to the ApHC home page.

9. Add the Appaloosa Horse Club site to your list of Favorites/Bookmarks. (Supply a name that you'll recognize.) If you must disconnect from the Internet now, you can complete this activity by opening the list

of Favorites/Bookmarks, selecting the site's name, and clicking the Go button on your browser's web bar.

10. Go to the General page (click General).

11. Read the description and history of the Appaloosa, jotting notes on a separate sheet to answer the questions below.

   a. Name the four distinguishing features a horse must have to be registered as an Appaloosa.
   b. Which of these features is unique to the Ap?
   c. What is the meaning of *sclera*?
   d. How did the Appaloosa get the name, and when did the name become official?
   e. What group of native Americans is credited with developing the Appaloosa breed?
   f. How many Aps are registered today?
   g. Is the Appaloosa a relatively new breed?

12. Go back to the Appaloosa Horse Club home page. Disconnect from the Internet or go on to Activity 3 below.

Activity 3—American Quarter Horse Association

1. Go to the American Quarter Horse Association (AQHA) web site, using this URL: **http://www.aqha.com.**

2. Click the button in the heading and the Welcome button.

3. Scan the list of links in this site. Do some of them look familiar?

4. Go to the America's Horse page; click the button at the middle of the screen to view a specimen, noting the color, markings, and conformation (body build) of this quarter horse.

5. Scroll down and read the description and history. Answer these questions as you read:

   a. Officially, what is the color of the quarter horse in the picture?
   b. Are all registered quarter horses this color?
   c. Where does "quarter" come from in the name of this horse?
   d. What is the average time for a quarter horse doing "the 440" (running 440 yards)?
   e. Name three or four defining characteristics of the quarter horse.

6. Return to the AQHA home page. If you wish, add this site to your list of Favorites/Bookmarks.

7. Do you recall seeing the word *dressage* at this site and the Appaloosa site? What does it mean? Click the Communication button; then, Related Links.

8. Look for a hyperlink to the U.S. Dressage Federation (USDF) web site. When you find it, double-click.

9. Navigate the USDF site until you can define/describe *dressage*. If you don't find useful information, go back to the Related Links page and look for another hyperlink that you think will give you the information you're looking for. Disconnect from the web as soon as you have a satisfactory answer, or whenever your teacher directs; or go on to Activity 4 below.

Activity 4—Time in a Bottle

After December 31, 1999, the phrase "turn of the century" takes on new meaning. Traditionally referring to the period 1890-1910, the expression can just as easily apply to 1990-2010. But this "turn of the century" isn't getting much attention. Why? Because January 1, 2000, also marks the beginning of a new *millennium*—a thousand years!

1. Go to the White House web site (Favorites/Bookmarks). Try to find White House Millennium Council (1998) among the sites linked to the White House home page. (**Note:** If January 1, 2000, is past, the Millennium Council site may have been removed from the web.)

2. Note the number of days, hours, minutes, and seconds until the "turn of the millennium." Then read the information provided (*What is a millennium?*, etc.)

Time capsules are often used to preserve artifacts of a culture, community, school, or family for future generations to ponder. Naturally, people became extremely interested in time capsules in the last year's of the second millennium. Use the following web addresses (URLs) to visit four time-capsule sites. (All four sites are in the commercial domain, indicated by *.com*.)

Once you study the information at each site, your teacher may assign a class project. The project would have students collaborating to develop a time capsule plan. The plan should outline (1) the purpose of your time capsule; (2) the date for sealing it and the date you intend for it to be opened; (3) a description of the capsule, including dimensions and the material it's made of; (4) a list of specific items to be placed in the capsule; (5) the approximate cost of the capsule, not including the contents; (6) how the items will be obtained; (7) any special preservation considerations; (8) whether the time capsule will be displayed or buried and where; and (9) if buried, how people in the future will know about it.

1. **http://lane@ustimecapsule.com** This web site outlines a plan for a time capsule buried in the mountains near Boston. Individuals and organizations can become members/reserve space in the huge capsule. Be sure to visit the U.S. map page and access the state you live in. Note also (1) the date the capsule will be sealed, and (2) how long it is to stay closed.

2. **http://burgh.com** Scroll to the bottom of the home page; open the list box (click the arrow) and select Our Kind Sponsors. Click the Go button. Scroll down to Time Capsules, Inc. Use the hyperlink to jump to the web site of this Pittsburgh business. As you browse, pay particular attention to the information about preserving paper (since your school time capsule is likely to contain lots of it). Jump to other parts of the site on these two hyperlinks: (1) deterioration and how we protect against it, (2) a few of the many different items you can enclose in a time capsule.

   Before you visit the third site, go to the first site to verify the date of the deadline for membership in U.S. time capsule. If you disconnected since visiting that site and you didn't save it as a Favorite/Bookmark, try this means of navigating: Open the list box beside the Go button (click the arrow). This list shows the sites visited recently from this computer. Scroll down; select **http://lane@ustimecapsule.com** if it's there, and click Go. When the home page appears, the color of hyperlinks will remind you which parts of the site you visited.

3. **http://www.interinc.com/timecapsule** Scroll to the bottom of the A-1 Time Capsules home page to see a price list and tips for buying a time capsule in question-and-answer format. Then click the Go button; key the URL for the fourth site.

4. **http://www.barrtek.com/index.htm** As with other sites you've visited, this one may show several buttons without labels. How do you know what will happen if you click a button? Hold the mouse pointer over the button for a few seconds: a clue appears beside the button and at the bottom of the screen (taskbar area).

   Examples at this site include: *facts* (button takes you to the part of the web site that gives facts and figures about Time Capsule 2000) and *careand* (button takes you to a section about the "care and feeding" of a capsule [selection and preservation of contents]). Be sure to see Who Buys and Typical Clients at this site. Note common reasons for schools to purchase a time capsule. Use the hyperlink to see what's in the capsule purchased by University of Texas at Arlington and any other schools, especially high schools, that may be listed.

Activity 5—Searching the Web by Topic

Sometimes you will want to use the web to find information on a topic, but you may not know the address of a specific site. In these cases, you will use the browser's Search page.

1. Click the Search button to display the Search page.

   Search pages let you type *keywords* (words that define your search) and choose a *search engine* (Internet tool that searches the web for your topic/keywords).

2. Type the keywords **martial arts** in the Search text box. The results of your search will vary depending on the search engine that you use.

3. Choose a search engine (InfoSeek, for example) and process your search request.

4. When the results of your search appear, the number of "hits" (martial arts sites found) may be shown. Scroll down to see hypertext and descriptions for a few of the sites you can jump to. Results appear in sets (pages) of 10 or 20. At the bottom of a page is a hyperlink that allows you to display the next set or page. Click this hyperlink and continue scrolling down.

   As you can see, the search results will lead you to a variety of sites on the subject of martial arts. In fact, the topics may number hundreds of thousands or even millions—far more than you can or want to deal with! You need to narrow the search by specifying more keywords.

5. Type the keywords **martial arts+uniforms** in the Search textbox. Go back to the top of the Search page if necessary. Some search engines allow you to start a new search while viewing the previous search results. Some engines will permit you to confine your next search to the martial arts sites already located. In that case, type the keyword **uniforms** in the Search textbox. (**Note:** Typos and misspelled words waste time on the web.)

6. Process your search request; and when the results appear, scroll down to see them.

   The results using several keywords often—though not always—suggest sites that are more targeted to the information you are seeking. If you still have too many sites, add another keyword to "zero in" on the sites best suited to your needs.

7. Repeat Step 5 above, using the keywords **martial arts+uniforms+children's.**

8. From the results of this search, choose the site(s) that you think will best describe child-sized uniforms for martial arts students. (Click the hyperlink and explore the site.) **Note:** When doing research for a report, skim sites on the first page or two that you think will be useful. If a site looks promising in the first 30 seconds or so, save it to your list of Favorites/Bookmarks and move on.

If you need more information than any of the resulting sites provide, you can go back to the Search page and perform the search again, using a different search engine.

Appendix **E**
Format Guides

BASIC FORMAT GUIDES	
Memo (p. 130)	**Top margin:** 2". **Side margins:** 1" or default. **Bottom margin:** At least 1". **Line spacing:** SS. **Other:** DS between lines of heading and other parts. After the heading To: tab twice to key the name; after From:, Date:, and Subject:, tab once.
Block Format Business Letter (p. 142)	**Top margin:** 2" or centered vertically. **Side margins:** 1" or default. **Bottom margin:** At least 1". **Line spacing:** SS. **Other:** All lines at left margin. QS between date and letter address; complimentary close and writer's name. DS between all other parts. Key the reference initials a DS below the writer's name.
Envelopes (p. 147)	**Top margin:** 2". **Left margin:** Small, 2.5"; large, 4". **Other:** USPS style is preferred but cap/lc is acceptable. Use standard abbreviations, 2-letter state abbreviations, and ZIP + 4. Space once between state abbreviation and ZIP Code.
Personal-Business Letter (p. 148)	**Top margin:** 2" or centered vertically. **Side margins:** 1" or default. **Bottom margin:** At least 1". **Line spacing:** SS. **Other:** Key return address above date; SS to date. Other letter spacing is the same as for Block Format Business Letter (above).
Unbound Report (p. 156)	**Top margin:** 2" (page 1); 1" (other pages). **Side margins:** 1" or default. **Bottom margin:** At least 1". **Line spacing:** DS (may be SS). **Other:** May underline or bold side heads. Suppress (hide) page number on page 1; other page numbers at top right margin. To document material, use textual citations. Key references on last page or on a separate page (2" top margin) in hanging-indent style.
Simple Tables (p. 168)	**Top margin:** 2" or centered vertically. **Side margins:** centered horizontally. **Bottom margin:** approximately 1". **Line spacing:** SS; blank line spaces may be added to increase row height. **Column widths:** Slightly wider than longest data entry in the column. **Row height:** Default or graduated from main title (deepest) to data entries (default). **Vertical alignment:** Center. **Horizontal alignment:** Left- or center-align words; right- or center-align numbers. **Gridlines:** default. **Other:** If gridlines do not print by default, underline column titles and the last amount in a column that contains a sum or difference.

Memo

2"

TO: Faculty and Staff **DS**
FROM: Lenore M. Fielding, Principal **DS**
DATE: November 15, (Current year)
SUBJECT: MEMO FORMAT **DS**

At a recent meeting, department heads recommended that memos be processed on plain paper instead of preprinted forms. The recommendation is a cost-cutting measure that requires only a little more effort on the part of the keyboard operators. **DS**

The customary margins are used: 2" (approximate) top margin; default (near 1") side margins; at least a 1" bottom margin.

1"   1"

Double spacing separates memo parts, including paragraphs, which are individually single-spaced. If someone other than the writer keys the memo, that person's initials should be keyed at the left margin a double space below the message. If an attachment or enclosure is included, Attachment or Enclosure should be keyed at the left margin a double space below the message or the keyboard operator's initials (if any).

Headings begin at the left margin. After To: tab twice to key the name; after From: tab once to key the name; after Date: tab once to insert the date; after Subject: tab once to enter the subject (may be bold/Cap and lowercase or ALL CAPS).

Please use this format for several days; then let me know if you experienced any difficulties. **DS**

tbh

Memo

Block Letter

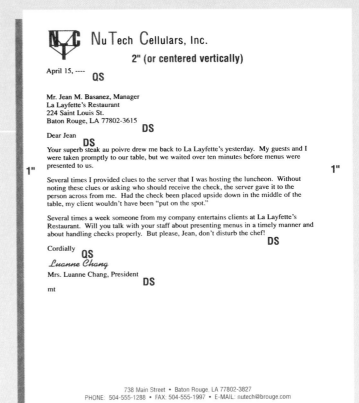

2" (or centered vertically)

April 15, ---- **QS**

Mr. Jean M. Basanez, Manager
La Layfette's Restaurant
224 Saint Louis St.
Baton Rouge, LA 77802-3615 **DS**

Dear Jean **DS**

Your superb steak au poivre drew me back to La Layfette's yesterday. My guests and I were taken promptly to our table, but we waited over ten minutes before menus were presented to us.

1"   1"

Several times I provided clues to the server that I was hosting the luncheon. Without noting these clues or asking who should receive the check, the server gave it to the person across from me. Had the check been placed upside down in the middle of the table, my client wouldn't have been "put on the spot."

Several times a week someone from my company entertains clients at La Layfette's Restaurant. Will you talk with your staff about presenting menus in a timely manner and about handling checks properly. But please, Jean, don't disturb the chef! **DS**

Cordially **QS**

Luanne Chang

Mrs. Luanne Chang, President **DS**

mt

738 Main Street • Baton Rouge, LA 77802-3827
PHONE: 504-555-1288 • FAX: 504-555-1997 • E-MAIL: nutech@brouge.com

Block Letter

Personal-Business Letter

2" (or centered vertically)

9248 Socorro Rd.
El Paso, TX 79907-2366
(Today's date) **QS**

Mrs. Susan L. Orr, Director
Graphic Arts Institute
2099 Calle Lorca
Santa Fe, NM 87505-3461 **DS**

Dear Mrs. Orr **DS**

1"   A graduate of your school, Ms. San-li Chou, has suggested that I write to you because of my interest in graphic design. **DS**   1"

To keep my choices open, I am taking a college-prep program. All my electives, though, are chosen from courses in art, design, and graphics--including photography. I do unusually well in these courses.

Can you send me a catalog that outlines the graphics programs now being offered by your school. I will appreciate it.

Cordially yours **QS**

Miguel Blanco

Miguel Blanco

Personal-Business Letter

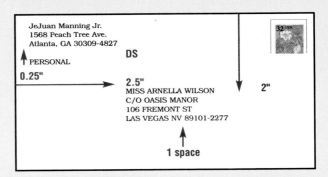

Small Envelope

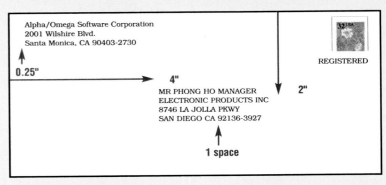

Large Envelope

Two-Column Table

2″ (or centered vertically)

NEW PERISCOPE STAFF

Editor	Krisi Stojko
Associate Editor	Brian Poole
Business Manager	Anita Solena
Photography/Layout	Malik Fredericks
Advertising/Sales	Xen Chueng
Advisor	Marcella Proust

Three-Column Table with Multiple Features

2″ (or centered vertically)

PULITZER PRIZES IN DRAMA

Since 1990

Year	Play	Playwright
1990	The Piano Lesson	August Wilson
1991	Lost in Yonkers	Neil Simon
1992	The Kentucky Cycle	Robert Schenkkan
1993	Angels in America: Millennium Approaches	Tony Kushner
1994	Three Tall Women	Edward Albee
1995	The Young Man from Atlanta	Horton Foote
1996	Rent	Jonathan Larson
1997	No Award	
1998	How I Learned to Drive	Paula Vogel

Sources: *New York Times Almanac*, 1998. The Internet: http://www.pulitzer.org/year/1998.

Unbound Report with Textual Citations

2″

COMPUTER APPLICATIONS

DS

Learning to key is of little value unless one applies it in preparing a useful document--a letter, a report, and so on. Three basic kinds of software (applications) are available to assist those with keying skill in applying that skill electronically. DS

Word Processing Software

Word processing software is specifically designed to assist in the document preparation needs of individuals or businesses. Word processing software permits the user to "create, edit, format, store, and print documents." (Fulton and Hanks, 1996, 152) This software can be used to process a wide variety of documents such as memos, letters, reports, and tables.

This software has editing and formatting features that reduce time and effort. It permits easy error detection and correction; merging of text with variables in another document or even another application (for example, database software); and graphic design of pages. These features increase efficiency while enhancing the appearance of documents. DS

Database Software

A database is any collection of related items stored in computer memory. The data in a database may be about club members, employee payroll, company sales, and so on. Database software allows the user to enter data, sort it, retrieve and change it, or select certain data (such as an address) for use in word processing documents. (Tilton, et al, 1996, 112-113)

At least 1″

Unbound Report, Page 2

DS   2

Spreadsheet Software DS

A spreadsheet is an electronic worksheet made up of columns and rows of data. Spreadsheet software allows the user to "create, calculate, edit, retrieve, modify, and print graphs, charts, reports, and spreadsheets" necessary for current business operations and in planning for the future. (Fulton and Hanks, 1996, 156)

A review of newspaper advertisements shows the skills that employers expect for most jobs: competent use of word processing and spreadsheet software and familiarity with database applications. DS

REFERENCES DS

Fulton, Patsy J., and Joanna D. Hanks. Procedures for the Office Professional. 3d ed. Cincinnati: South-Western Publishing Co., 1996.

Tilton, Rita S., et al. The Electronic Office: Procedures & Administration. 11th ed. Cincinnati: South-Western Publishing Co., 1996.

1″